FROM BENEATH THE VOLCANO

From Beneath the Volcano

*The Story of a Salvadoran Campesino
and His Family*

Michael Gorkin and Marta Evelyn Pineda

The University of Arizona Press   Tucson

The University of Arizona Press
© 2011 Michael Gorkin and Marta Evelyn Pineda

www.uapress.arizona.edu

Library of Congress Cataloging-in-Publication Data

Gorkin, Michael.
    From beneath the volcano : the story of a Salvadoran campesino and his family /
Michael Gorkin and Marta Evelyn Pineda.
        p.   cm.
    Includes bibliographical references.
    ISBN 978-0-8165-2962-9 (hard cover : alk. paper) — ISBN 978-0-8165-2963-6
(pbk. : alk. paper)   1. Families—El Salvador—Guazapa—History.   2. Oral
history—El Salvador—Guazapa.   3. Guazapa (El Salvador)—History.   4. Guazapa
(El Salvador)—Social conditions.   5. Guazapa (El Salvador)—Social life and
customs.   6. El Salvador—History—1944–1979.   7. El Salvador—History—
1979–1992.   8. El Salvador—History—1992–   I. Pineda, Marta.   II. Title.
    HQ1236.5.S2G67   2011
    306.85088'6309728423—dc23   2011016685

Publication of this book is made possible in part by the proceeds of a permanent
endowment created with the assistance of a Challenge Grant from the National
Endowment for the Humanities, a federal agency.

Manufactured in the United States of America on acid-free, archival-quality paper
and processed chlorine free.

16   15   14   13   12   11   6   5   4   3   2   1

In memory of my mother, Dorothy Gorkin, who originally nudged me in the right—that is, left—political direction.
—Michael Gorkin

For my grandchildren, Valeria and Gabriel, who are—thank God—still without a political direction.
—Marta Evelyn Pineda

CONTENTS

ACKNOWLEDGMENTS

First and foremost, we wish to express our gratitude to the family and friends of Luis Campos, all of whom appear in the book with a pseudonym. They gave us their time and their stories: they made this book possible. We can only hope that the book captures fairly and feelingly their personal remembrances and the life of their community.

Second, we thank the staff at the University of Arizona Press. They helped us do what every author hopes to do: write the best book he or she is capable of.

And finally, our warmest thanks to Marta Alicia Castro, mother and mother-in-law of the two coauthors. She not only graciously put us up during our repeated and lengthy stays in El Salvador but also, and just as graciously, put up with our repeated and unannounced interviews of some of the book's characters in her home.

FROM BENEATH THE VOLCANO

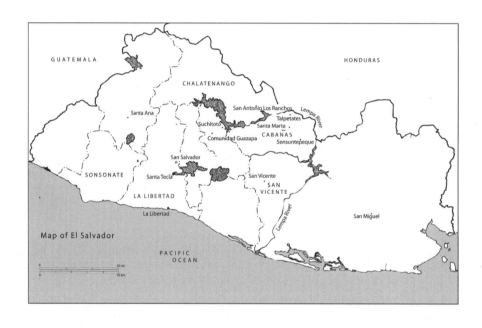

Map of El Salvador

Introduction

My first meeting—if you can call it that—with Luis Campos was hardly auspicious.[1] It happened some twelve years ago on the dirt-packed veranda of his then one-room house in Comunidad Guazapa outside Suchitoto, where he was living with his common-law wife, Julia, and their six children. My two colleagues and I had come for the second time to interview Julia as part of the book we were writing on Salvadoran women.[2] Luis apparently had just finished his morning's work in the *milpa* (a small plot of land). As we sat at the table with tape recorders running, Luis came around the corner of his house, his stained and sweat-soaked shirt hanging over his tattered work pants, a machete gripped firmly in his left hand. He seemed to be scowling. He said a curt hello to us and went off to a dilapidated chair in the corner of the veranda, near the clay oven, helping himself to a tortilla and some beans. He did not say another word to us that day. I did not know then whether Julia had informed him of the book we were doing (actually, she had not), and I wondered what his thoughts might be about such a book if and when he knew. In any case, at that moment I had no idea that eventually this tough, swarthy character would come to be quite affable and chatty and even a supporter of our book. Nor could I have imagined then—and really the idea did not enter my mind until years later, after we had come to know Luis during our annual visits to the community—that a book about this *campesino* (peasant farmer or rural dweller) and his extended family would be an interesting sequel to the Salvadoran women book.

Part of what convinced me that this might be so was the man himself. In a word, Luis is a simple man who has lived a complicated life. As the eldest son of a poor campesino, Luis might still be living a peaceful, albeit impoverished, life in the obscure hamlet of Talpetates in northern El Salvador. Generations of his family had lived in this manner, and so, very likely, would have he. However, in his early twenties, Luis, like many young campesinos, found himself drawn into the political maelstrom that was then beginning to swirl in the country. And, in short, he spent the

1

next twenty years as a political activist and then a guerrilla fighting in the Salvadoran civil war, which lasted from 1980 to 1992. After the war, Luis literally returned to his roots. He moved to a new nook in the country and continued his life as a campesino. He married a woman half his age (Julia), who had also spent years with the guerrillas, and the two of them set about building a new life. Today, at sixty-one years old, Luis lives in Comunidad Guazapa, and he remains an activist in his community. Eight of his and Julia's children live with them, and several members of their extended family live in houses adjacent to theirs. "I'm lucky to be here after what I went through," he says with a Zorba-the-Greek smile. "But thanks to God, I'm still alive and kicking."

Yet it was not only Luis's odyssey that drew me in. It was also the stories of several members of his extended family, people whom I also had gradually come to know and whose stories I found intriguing—his mother, his in-laws, and some of his children. And I became interested in the larger story of their community, which had been carved out of a former sugarcane plantation as part of the land redistribution that took place at the end of the war. Just as Luis's and his family's lives changed over the years, so had Comunidad Guazapa grown and developed at the same time. In sum, it seemed to me that with Luis as the main character and some of his family members and neighbors as additional dramatis personae, I could write an oral history that would give us one perspective on what has happened, and is still happening, in the Salvadoran *campo* today.

Of course, the perspective from Luis's family in Comunidad Guazapa is only one of many possible vantage points from which we might explore the changes that have taken place (or failed to take place) in the Salvadoran campo. No single family or community can be said to be validly "representative"—in a statistical sense—of the varied experiences of the approximately 40 percent of the Salvadoran population who continue to live in the campo. However, I do think it is true that the stories of Luis and his family that you are about to read mirror in various ways the lives of many other Salvadoran campesinos before, during, and after the civil war.

In order to better understand the narratives presented here, it is important for the reader to have in mind an awareness of Salvadoran history. Accordingly, we have appended to the book a brief chronology of the country's past, with particular emphasis on the events of the last four decades, that is, just before, during, and since the civil war.[3] Here, it might be helpful to briefly describe some of the events that influenced and altered the lives of Luis, his family, and members of his community.

For El Salvador, the most cataclysmic period in the country's nearly five hundred year history is that which began in the late 1960s and ultimately culminated in a civil war that lasted from 1980 to 1992. Like most of its neighbors, El Salvador in the late 1960s was ruled by a small economic elite (based primarily in export agriculture) and supported by a well-heeled military that wielded a hard hand against all potential threats to the status quo. The majority of the country's population were poor campesinos who subsisted by farming their small plots and, in many cases, also harvesting the coffee, sugarcane, and cotton grown in the *fincas* (farms) owned by the country's elite. In the late 1960s, this status quo began to receive a stiff challenge from a range of reformist elements—campesino leaders, urban workers, students, and some members of the clergy. While the ruling elite did make some attempts to accommodate the wage and political demands of these reformers, in the end their efforts proved to be a case of too little too late. Accordingly, the government's Fuerza Armada, together with a panoply of paramilitary organizations, sought to repress the growing number of reformist and revolutionary groups that were sprouting throughout the country. By 1980 El Salvador had entered into a lengthy and bloody civil war fought between the Fuerza Armada on one side and the joint guerrilla forces of the Frente Farabundo Martí para la Liberación Nacional (FMLN) on the other side.[4] Furthermore, the civil war took on an international dimension. Hoping to prevent a leftist victory similar to that of the Sandinistas in Nicaragua in 1979, the United States supplied the Fuerza Armada with money, armaments, and advisors.[5] And with the intention of abetting just such a leftist revolution, Nicaragua and Cuba similarly aided the FMLN guerrillas.

This brutal civil war ebbed and flowed for twelve years and was finally brought to a halt as each side realized that it was not possible to win a military victory. In the end, the United Nations, firmly and financially supported by the United States, helped the two sides negotiate a settlement in which both adversaries could claim some gains. The FMLN, in exchange for disarming and disbanding as a military force, received recognition as a legal political party, and a good deal of social legislation, including some land reform, was passed by the government.[6] But the government that represented the political right and center remained in power, and the upper and middle classes were mostly able to hold on to their considerable assets.

No matter where one stands on the political spectrum, it is clear that the costs of this civil war were enormous. Some 75,000 Salvadorans (1.5 percent of the population) died in the war, and another 9,000 disappeared. At least 400,000 people, mostly campesinos, lost their homes. And at least 500,000 Salvadorans fled the country; many, if not most, of them have yet to return. The entire country was devastated by this national cataclysm, and it is no exaggeration to state that even today, almost twenty years later, the country is still in the process of recovering from the events of those years.

However, on the positive side, the country's political foes have not chosen to renew their violent confrontation. Instead, the battle for power has resumed in the voting booths. The FMLN, despite internal wrangling, has slowly emerged as a potent force within the country. As a political party, it currently heads some 40 percent of the country's municipalities, and in the country's legislative body, the Asamblea Legislativa, it holds thirty-eight of the eighty-four seats. Most impressively from its point of view, for the first time since the end of the civil war, in March 2009 the FMLN succeeded in defeating the rightist ARENA (Alianza Republicana Nacionalista) Party for the presidency of the country—an outcome that was cheered widely and loudly throughout the campo, including, of course, the more than three hundred residents of Comunidad Guazapa. As Luis Campos proudly told us when we visited him three weeks after the victory of the FMLN's candidate, Mauricio Funes, "I've waited decades for this day. I knew it would happen sooner or later, but when we came out here seventeen years ago, who would have thought that a flag of our man, our Funes, would be flying in the corner of my yard? Sí, hombre, it's been a long time coming!"

The creation of Comunidad Guazapa is, from the FMLN's perspective, one of the many concrete and beneficial outcomes of the country's civil war. Comunidad Guazapa and several other neighboring communities are now eighteen years old, having all taken root around the base of Mount Guazapa during the closing months of the civil war. The dormant volcano had been a stronghold for guerrilla forces throughout the war, and the many tunnels dug into its ample girth had served as safe havens for FMLN combatants. Thus, as the war was sputtering to its end in late 1991, a number of these combatants descended to the mountain's foothills and began setting up de facto communities with the intention of laying claim to these properties during the ongoing peace negotiations. And, in fact, as a result of the peace accords of 1992, these new residents did succeed in gaining legal title to much of this land (see chap. 6).

When we (Marta Pineda and I) first visited Comunidad Guazapa in 1997, the community consisted of twenty or so houses tucked away on the hillside beneath the mountain. From the main road it is a twenty-minute walk to the community up a poorly maintained cobblestone road past a number of buildings painted blue and white that formerly were the main living quarters of the Morales family, the landowners who originally owned the entire spread of 100 *manzanas* (170 acres). For the past eighteen years these buildings have served principally as the community's school. From there, the road descends past a small graveyard for fallen guerrillas and then divides into half a kilometer of winding paths that pass through sugarcane fields—which still belong to the Morales family—and then finally into the community itself, where the houses and milpas sit snugly beneath the benign volcano. This walk through the lush fields and up and down the rain-carved gullies feels and looks almost exactly the same today as it did twelve years ago when we first visited Comunidad Guazapa. It is only when we begin to approach the community, passing gingerly through the cow pasture (which on Sundays serves as a well-fertilized soccer field), that we begin to sense some of the changes that have transpired here. There are more houses than before, and almost all these concrete-block structures have increased in size from one small room to two and three rooms. We see and hear more children, which is not surprising, since the community has tripled in population to about 350 persons. And we notice further that the bucolic buzz of bugs and chirp of birds has now given way to a boombox barrage of *rancheras* and hip-hop music. Moreover, among the many voices we hear as we wind up the narrow paths that run between the houses are those speaking or even yelling into their cell phones while roosters and dogs look on in disbelief—as did we when we first heard them.

The inhabitants of the community have greeted these changes happily. About seven years ago, helped by the nearby FMLN-controlled municipality of Suchitoto, all of the communities in the area were connected to the electricity grid. This was followed a year later by the installation of pipes that pumped the plentiful supply of underground springwater to the homes of the residents. One perhaps would have to be a campesino who had lived one's entire life without these conveniences to understand the full meaning of these changes (see chap. 8). Moreover, these improvements have been paralleled by a similar change in other aspects of the residents' standard of living, for example, more and better food and newer clothing. Some of this increase in the standard of living has been made possible by the steady flow of remittances to these families from members who have taken off (usually as illegal immigrants) to the United States and are now in a position to help the folks back home.[7]

Through Luis Campos and some of his family members and a couple of neighbors, it is our aim to explore some of the changes (and lack of changes, too) in the Salvadoran campo. While Luis is the main character in this saga, we have also included stories from his mother (chap. 2), his wife (chaps. 5 and 8), his father-in-law (chap. 4), his mother-in-law (chap. 9), two of his children (chaps. 10, 12, and 14), a neighbor and former comrade-in-arms (chap. 6), and a neighbor who is principal of the community's school (chap. 13). Each of these individuals offers his or her perspective on various members of the family as well as on the war, the community, and, by extension, the shifts that have occurred in the country during their lifetimes.

The reader may wonder why Luis and others agreed to reveal their stories—often in intimate detail—to outsiders. The answer, above all, lies in the fact that every person who chose to talk to us senses that he or she has lived through an extraordinary period and, as a result, has a story to tell. That they chose to tell it to us was due principally to the trust they had in Luis. He opened the doors for us to interview several of the individuals. As for Luis himself, it was the long period during which we slowly came to know him, the casual chats we had with him over the years, that likely convinced him to agree to be our main character. More than almost all of the others, Luis sees himself as a player in the panorama of recent Salvadoran history, and this, coupled with his own homegrown gifts as a storyteller, inspired him to talk to us. And even though he can barely read, he seems to have a respect and even awe for the written word. As he told us, "I've got a whole batch of memories, a whole lot of words for you, and I'd like to see them put somewhere before I leave this earth."

In gathering Luis's stories and those of others, we relied almost exclusively on tape recorders—two, to be exact, since past experience has taught me that, now and then, one tape recorder might fail precisely at the wrong moment. Occasionally, in moments before or after the interviews, one of the individuals would make a comment or tell a story for which we were unable to grab a tape recorder, and thus I wrote the story down on paper as that person talked. Most of the interviews were conducted at the homes of the interviewees. However, we discovered (and, actually, Marta and I were aware from our previous work) that to obtain frank accounts we occasionally needed to interview the person privately, away from family, friends, and the multitude of curious chickens, roosters, turkeys, goats, and dogs that often hung out on the verandas of the houses. Accordingly, we interviewed most of the individuals at least once in a restaurant near the community, or at a hotel where we sometimes stayed in Suchitoto, or at Marta's mother's home in San Salvador. Without these private talks, I doubt we would have been told many of the more personal opinions and descriptions of events.

You may be wondering at this point (and surely will wonder as you read the stories) what role the coauthors' own personal stories—our own perspectives and prejudices—may have played in influencing the unfolding of our interviewees' tales. The truest answer, unfortunately, is that we simply do not and cannot know. The fairest answer, however, is to at least acknowledge what some of our opinions and prejudices are. In particular, I think it important to state something of our political perspectives. In this matter, there was and still are some clear differences between us. Marta lived in El Salvador throughout the civil war, and during that period she was opposed to the FMLN. Subsequently, during the process of working on our book about Salvadoran women and as she came to know the people in Comunidad Guazapa, she gained a better understanding of their political preferences. As for me, I was preoccupied with other matters during the period of the Salvadoran civil war and thus had no opinions during that time. It was only in 1997, when I went to El Salvador as a Fulbright scholar, that I found myself interested in Salvadoran politics; in short, my political leanings are leftist, though I am an agnostic with regard to the FMLN as a political party. What I do feel clearly (as does Marta) is a gut sympathy for the country's poor majority, most of whom continue to live out in the campo. Precisely how these differences and similarities played out in gathering and writing the stories I am unsure. But what is certain is that our commonly shared sympathy for the country's poor—and the campesinos especially—did influence, even determine, our joint decision to undertake this project.

In my view, what has influenced the substance and shape of the stories more than our political predilections is the fact that both Marta and I are psychologists. Hence, in interviewing our subjects and subsequently choosing which areas to report, we have paid much attention to the interpersonal relationships between the various family members, both those whose stories appear in the book and those who are merely discussed in absentia. Furthermore, there is a predilection to include and subtly (we hope) emphasize some of the personal characteristics of each individual. For example, inasmuch as our focus is primarily on Luis, it is our aim that the reader emerges from the book with a complex understanding of this man and the transforming journey of his life. To a lesser extent, we hope that readers capture some of this "psychological" understanding with all of the individuals whose stories appear here. I have little doubt that, had we been historians or anthropologists, the edited material would have leaned more in the direction of the concerns and interests of those professions and (perhaps) been less revealing of the intra- and interpersonal aspects of Luis and his family.

All of this leads me to a further point, one that is contentiously debated by proponents and detractors of the burgeoning field of "oral history." Simply put, in light of the formative role that oral historians play in shaping their works, are we not to be considered as coauthors together with our subjects whose stories are reported? There are many, especially in the "postmodern" school, who would offer a definitive yes to this question.[8] Alternatively, a large number of practitioners of the oral history genre imply that the stories are fully the product of the interviewee(s) and that interviewers, as editors, are simply recording those stories for a larger, listening audience.[9] To state this debate in a more metaphorical way, the question is, Are oral historians midwives or coparents of the work? My answer is that we cannot be neatly categorized as either.

To acknowledge that we merely edit our subjects' material (which is often as far as oral historians unveil their art) is to vastly understate the role we play in shaping the final product. However, even taking into account our highly influential role, it does not appear to me that Marta and I have served as "coparents" along with Luis or any of our other subjects. Our function lies somewhere in the murky middle and, indeed, varies from subject to subject, depending on his or her personal talents and proclivity to recount his or her experiences.

In the stories below, the reader will notice that we have chosen, almost exclusively, to have the subject tell his or her story in monologue form. Some oral historians prefer to use a dialogue form, thereby emphasizing that the story is clearly the product of a give-and-take between interviewer and interviewee.[10] The decision not to use a question-and-answer format (except in the final chapter) has been influenced by two factors. First, I find that format less readable. Second, I think that the dialogue form suggests that the interviewer is doing less editing of the material than is the case in the monologue presentation. And with few exceptions (Kevin Dwyer is perhaps one of them), I doubt very much that this is so. Therefore, in consultation with Marta, I have decided to present our work in the form of monologues. In doing so, I have indicated within the text some occasions when we asked direct questions as well as various comments and asides that our subjects made during the interviewing process. The intention has been to provide the reader with a sense of overhearing a conversation rather than a speech that is being uttered, as if by megaphone, to a large, anonymous audience.

There is a good deal more that can be, and needs to be, discussed about our use of the oral history genre (e.g., matters of "subjectivity," memory, and ethical issues). Likewise, the stories that you are about to read, while intended to be interesting in and of themselves, nonetheless can be analyzed in terms of what they suggest about the changing life in the Salvadoran campo and, beyond that, in the ongoing transformation of the entire country of El Salvador. However, we have chosen to postpone our commentary in these areas until the book's epilogue. At that point, with the stories of Luis and his family in mind, we believe the discussion will take on a more meaningful resonance.

So allow us to take a step back now and let Luis and the others step forward with their tales. We hope that they will offer for you, as they did for us, an opportunity to peer into the lives of those whose words are usually not known but who are now, more than ever, claiming the right to be heard.

CHAPTER ONE

Luis

The Early Years

It is one o'clock sharp on a Sunday afternoon in January, and there he is, as agreed, waiting and swinging gently in the hammock on the concrete veranda of his house in Comunidad Guazapa. He is wearing his Sunday clothes, a pair of tan pants and a tan shirt, with a clean beige sombrero partially covering his dark, well-shaven face. By now, we—Marta and I—know him quite well, having met at least fifteen times over the past dozen years. But this time is different, and so is Luis, because he has recently agreed that he wants us to go ahead and do a book on his life and that of his family. He has even made clear why he has agreed: "These things that I have lived, I want others to hear. I want them to know me and my family and our country and why we fought and what is happening here today."

Three or four of his younger children are hanging around the dusty courtyard, curious to see what is going to happen. It is hot, maybe ninety degrees in the shade. At least ten chickens, a rooster, a turkey, and two goats are there too, oblivious to the heat but also seemingly curious. Luis's wife, Julia, whom we had interviewed many times twelve years before, is over by the *comal* (a clay dish), patting tortillas into their round pancake shape and flipping them onto the comal to be cooked. Her oldest daughter, Margarita, is there cooking with her. One of the boys is leading the family's horse over to the cistern in the corner of the courtyard for a quick drink and then helping himself to the same water.

Luis seems a bit on edge, perhaps because he has never been interviewed before—at least not by outsiders with tape recorders. But, checking his silver watch, which he wears even when he is sleeping, he says that he is ready. "How should we start?" he asks. "From the beginning," we tell him. "Let's start with your boyhood—what you remember." He nods, ponders a moment or two, since it seems he hadn't expected to start there, and then says, "Vaya pues. I remember plenty. Plenty. You don't forget things like that, do you?" And so we begin.

I was born in the hamlet of Talpetates, in the canton of Peña Blanca, in the department of Cabañas. That's where both my parents were born and raised too—a small place, maybe twenty-five families. My parents are Bonafacia and José Manuel. I am their oldest son. I am sixty years as of last June. [Julia, from the corner, shouts at us, "He's entering those 'golden years' now!" She is laughing and so is Margarita, but Luis, as if annoyed—and perhaps truly annoyed—swats the air in her direction.] Nonsense! Nobody in this house is entering any "golden years"! I'm as strong as I ever was. She knows it—right, Julia? No "golden years" for me. I'm just as strong as when I was a boy. Stronger! As a boy I would fool around. Now I'm up in the milpa seven days a week or working in the community. Hell, sometimes I wish I was a boy again—though not the way we lived then. No, no, not that way.

How was that? Hard! I mean real hard, real poor. [Luis removes his sombrero, wipes his sweating brow, and pauses for a moment.] Look, this is what it was like back then. I remember real well. You don't forget things like that. No, hombre, I don't forget a thing. [Julia, laughing and yelling in our direction, "What do you mean you don't forget? It's the 'golden years'—of course you forget. If I wasn't here to remind you—" But Luis stops her.] Quiet, quiet, over there! You've told them your story, and you can tell them more some other day. Today, I'm doing the talking—hear!

Now, what you want to know is what it was like for me as a boy up there in Talpetates, *verdad*? How we lived, what I did, no? All right. Simple. I told you, I'm the oldest son. I have one other brother, Antonio. There were two or three more, I mean, boys, but they didn't live. The rest were all girls. Me, Antonio, and nine sisters. All of us lived in our house— a usual place made of adobe. That's how all the houses in the countryside were then. And everyone was a farmer, everyone farming their few manzanas just to live, to not go hungry. My father had five manzanas that he owned, and then he sharecropped a couple more from a landowner up there. All of us—figure it, eleven kids and my parents—all living from the *maíz* and *maicillo* and *frijol* that we were growing. And a few chickens to give us eggs and a cow to give us some milk to make cheese or whatever.

There were days when we didn't hardly eat because there was nothing to eat. My mother would get up early in the morning, and she'd make tortillas with the maíz or maicillo, or if there wasn't enough of that, she'd take some dried banana skins and crush them up and mix in a little maicillo, and she'd make the tortillas out of that mix. She'd make them on a comal that she'd place on our stove—really it was just a few rocks over a fire with the comal sitting on the rocks. We'd have a tortilla and *con qué*, which was usually just salt, though some days we might have a little cheese or an egg, not a whole egg but a little dip into an egg that we all shared. That's how we lived, real hard, but the same as others living around us. Just about all of us were poor like that.

And me, since I was the oldest son, my father took me off to the milpa to work with him. No, I never spent a day in school. I never learned to read or write. Only later, much later, I figured it out a little, I taught myself. Back then, no, I couldn't tell one letter from the other. That was all right with me, though. I liked going up to the milpa with my father. I didn't want to hang around the house with my mother and all my sisters. And my father was always kind with me, relaxed. When I was real young, like five years old, he'd let me fool around and play up there. I didn't start working with him till I was seven or eight. I'd get up at dawn with him, have my tortilla and con qué with him, and then we'd head up to the fields. We must have looked like a bunch of people going to church dressed like we were in our white pants and shirts, all clean. It was simple clothing that you'd get; one colón for the pants and half a colón for the shirt. I had a sombrero and a pair of leather sandals, same as my father. Once we got up to the fields, we took off the sandals and our good white shirts and pants, and we took out of the small bags we carried a raggedy pair of pants, which is what we worked in. My mother used to wash these raggedy pants and mend them for us at night. And she'd also take care of us by bringing us something to eat at midday, nothing much, but something like some tortillas or an *atol*.

And that's how we worked during the growing season, which began around May when the winter rains came and ended after the last harvest, which was around January. My father taught me everything, and most of what I still know today I learned from him. You know, the way to burn or just chop down the old stubble and stalks first, before the rains came. And then you start planting with the first rains, punching holes in the ground with a pointed stick, making sure to keep nice, straight rows, and you put in three grains of maíz or maicillo, and that's it. You've got to keep cleaning the fields of weeds and keeping the soil loose around the stalks, and then in about three months the harvest begins. With the maíz you don't just pick it; no, you've got to fold the stalks over, wait till they get good and dry, and then you harvest the cobs. And that's it. That's what I did when I was a boy, and that's what I'm still doing today.

And I've got some of my boys helping me out these days, like I used to help my father.

Play? Sure, of course. Hell, you didn't just work all the time. No, sure, I played around, I had my fun. I didn't have brothers, not till Antonio finally came along, but I had my pals. We'd play soccer sometimes. Not with a real ball but something we'd made by rolling together a bunch of old rags. We didn't have any playing field, just an old patch of dusty ground. But it was good enough for us. Or sometimes we'd do other things, like practice shooting a bow and arrow. We made these things too. The way you do it is grab a good tough sugarcane stalk, and that becomes the bow, and you use smaller stalks for the arrow. For the point of the arrow you'd take some hard wax and shape it with your knife or machete. Yes, sure, I had my own machete, even as a kid. You needed it to work with in the milpa. Anyway, we used to just practice shooting the arrows and then cursing each other when one got lost, which was always happening, since you never knew where the damned thing was going. You couldn't hunt with it; it was useless for that. The way we hunted was different. The main thing we hunted were pigeons. We made traps out of wooden branches, and we'd bait the traps with a few grains of maicillo. The pigeon would enter, and the trap would close on him, and then we'd clean and roast him—a feast for us in those days! And sometimes we'd also have a little feast when we went crabbing, catching those little dark crabs over in the Lempa River. We'd catch them in baskets and then have us a fine meal on the spot.

Mostly, though, I would go to the Lempa with my father. It was a couple of leagues [approximately seven kilometers] from where we were living. This was when we didn't have work to do in the milpa. We'd go over in the day, fish all day, and then spend the night there and fish the next day. That was a real good time, even though sometimes we caught nothing. But sometimes we'd hit it right, and we'd come home with a batch of crayfish and twenty or more fish. And then the whole family had a little something different, a different con qué with our tortillas.

The truth is, I really loved my father the most. Naturally, as a boy you want to be with your father, right? But I loved him more because he was always kind with me, no chasing after me with a belt or cursing me out like my mother did. My father was real strong, built like a bull. But, like I say, he was relaxed with me. My mother was the one who was tough on me. Don't get me wrong. I love her, I still go see her pretty often, even though she's over in some other community. My father, he's gone. He died a few years back. He was eighty-four years old. He died from some kind of muscle disease. He was like a rag at the end. Couldn't move, couldn't see. It was terrible. My mother, she had a tough time after he went. They'd been together sixty years or so, never apart. And even though they had some problems at times, she was real tied to him. She loved him hard, yes she did.

And he did give her some problems back when I was a kid. I knew about it, but I was tied to him and I kept my mouth shut. I don't know how much to go into it. Let me just put it like this. You see, back when I was a kid working with him in the fields, sometimes things would happen. My mother was the kind that would get all jealous. And there were señoras in our hamlet that liked to talk, gossiping and all. They'd tell her that they'd seen so-and-so, you know, some girl up by my father's milpa, and she was up there for a while, and, you know, so on and so on. And my mother, she'd come sneaking up to the milpa, and she'd look around and around, and then when she saw nothing, she'd go home. Did I see? Well, yes and no. I mean, there was this girl that used to come by now and then, and on those days my father would say to me, "Boy, you've worked enough for today. Go on home."

When I'd get home my mother would start by saying, "How come so early? Why aren't you up there with your father?" I'd say, "He didn't need me anymore today." "You didn't see any girl up there, Luis?" she'd ask. "No, nothing, Mama," I'd tell her. "You're lying, boy. I know you're lying!" And next thing I knew she'd grab anything she could get her hands on, and she'd be chasing after me, and if she caught me—sometimes she did—she'd beat the hell out of me. Beat me, I tell you, till I was pissing in my own pants. And when my father came home later that day, she'd go after him too, and he, denying everything, would be slugging back at her. A real war, I'm telling you. Those days we had a real war going on in the house, and me, I got caught in the middle, and I stayed that way with my mouth shut.

Like I say, I was real tied to my father. We worked together in everything. I told you that we owned five manzanas, and we worked them together. We also sharecropped two more manzanas together—land we rented out from some rich guy up there. We had no choice, since five manzanas of poor soil and no fertilizer to improve it meant you couldn't raise enough to feed your family. And that rich guy made you pay him half your crop, and besides that, you had to give him six days a year doing whatever he wanted you to do at his finca—cutting his sugarcane, picking his cotton, or just cleaning up around his finca.

And even with those extra two manzanas you couldn't really get by, not with all those we had in the house. So, come January and the summer, my father and I would go off together to fincas around Santa Tecla or Santa Ana. Almost all the men from up where we lived were doing the same. You had to in order to survive. I started when I was fifteen years old. I was real naive then. You see, I was actually looking forward to going to these places to pick coffee or cotton or cut sugarcane. These were huge fincas, places owned by those "fourteen families"—you know, the richest of the rich in our country. I was figuring, well, at least I'm going to have a chance to eat real good now, meat or something like that. Not just work hard and make some cash for the family but also eat some good food regularly. Hell, was I wrong! Soon as we got to this finca—this was my first time—I found out quick how things stood. You weren't given any room or place to sleep; you were told you could sleep under some roof, right on the ground. And to eat, what you got was only a tortilla or two and some beans, usually with animal hairs, like rat hairs, in it. Breakfast, lunch, and dinner—always the same. It made me sick just to look at it. The first three days, I couldn't even swallow the stuff. My father told me, "Boy, you've got to eat something, or you're going to starve to death." So I forced myself, I put that filthy food in my mouth, and I ate it. Some folks who couldn't stand it went to the store they had there. They bought supplies on credit and made some food for themselves. But you know what happened with them? Came the end of the month, and when they went to get their pay, they were told they had used up all their money at the store and that *they* owed the store money. Imagine that!

We at least went home with some money. Not much, but enough to help get us through the year. Back then you made only a few colones a day. Like, if you were picking coffee, you'd get seventy-five centavos for an arroba, and if you worked your butt off, you might pick four or five arrobas a day. It wasn't much, but we needed every centavo we got. And so, even though you felt you were being taken advantage of, I mean, real exploited, you went each summer—me and my father both—and we worked in these fincas. I did it for several years. I had no choice.

And that's also how I began to see how things stood in this country. Before I went to these rich people's fincas, I hadn't any political ideas or any knowledge about things. Working those summers, getting exploited like hell, I began to see what was going on. What helped open my eyes was one summer when we were there, this was in the mid-1970s, a group of organizers came along and started talking to us laborers. "Talking" isn't the right word, not for what took place that day. They were political people, and they came with masks on, and they told us that we were to go on strike. I mean, *told* us! I can't say I understood right then who they were. Only later, I realized they were from an organization that was educating us campesinos to fight for our rights. But that day, they told us that to get our rights we had to listen to them; we had to refuse to work immediately and let the *mandador* know that we would be on strike until we got our pay raised and our hours reduced and until we were given better food to eat. And they told us—they were dead serious—if we didn't do that, the whole bunch of us, we workers and the owners too, we'd all be shot. So, of course, we went along. And you know what, the owners gave in, they caved in immediately, because they had to get the crop harvested. Next summer, though, those same landowners and many others fled the country, and we weren't brought back to do any harvesting.

By the next summer, though, I already had a good idea what was going on. It was happening in various places around the country. Groups of organizers—some were students and some were church people and some were campesinos like us—they had begun to hold these secret meetings, trying to educate the people that we had to fight for our rights. They weren't talking about war, not right then. They were talking about educating the people, making them aware how things stood in our country. It was all hidden because the right wing—the rich people and their army and militias—were going after anyone who was giving these talks or even attending them. They were killing folks, cutting off their heads and leaving them in the streets. You had to be careful. My father knew I was going, and I discussed it all with him, and he understood. But he was already getting old, and he didn't join me in this. He went on farming and also looking after my wife and daughter—yes, I'd gotten married by then, and we already had a kid. And me, when I wasn't at home, I'd be off at these meetings. And that's how I really began understanding things. Like I remember—imagine, till today I remember it—a passage that we discussed at one of these first meetings. It was a passage from the Bible, from Isaiah, passage 59, I think it was: "Throw off the yoke and free the oppressed!" We talked about slavery, what the rich in El Salvador were doing to the poor, and that our only alternative was to organize and bring about change in our country. I saw that they were right, and the more I went to these meetings, the more I knew I was going to be part of this change. I had to do it! So I kept going whenever I could get away. I went all over the country, to San Miguel or San Vicente, wherever things were beginning to stir up. I'd have to go with a note, and you'd present your note to someone before you were let into the meeting. By then, everyone was using a pseudonym. It was real dangerous. There were government informers, and if you got fingered, well, that was it for you. Pretty soon, I joined a group of organizers in the FPL [Fuerzas Populares de Liberación], and I headed one group and reported to someone who was my chief. I was hardly at home anymore, because by then I was going all over, preparing for the war that, by then, we knew was going to come.

No, my wife was none too happy about this. She didn't understand the situation, even when I tried to explain it to her. She wanted me at home. And me, too, I wanted to be with her and my daughter, but I felt I had to be out organizing. It caused lots of problems between us. She knew

I loved her, sure she did. I was crazy about her, and she was crazy about me. It was a good love that we had between us. Right from the beginning. By the time I'd become involved with the movement, we'd been married three or four years. And before that we'd been engaged for almost two years, from the time I was twenty years old and she was twenty-two. She was a little older than me, not much, just a couple of years. Actually, we're distant relatives. We're from the same area in Cabañas. Our families knew each other, so that's how we met. It was at some family occasion, I don't remember exactly what. We were sitting at the dinner table, she on one side and me on the other. I was tossing looks her way, and she played a little innocent, but I could see she was liking it. And so that's how it began. I don't think she trusted me at first, you know, because there's men that just are looking to mess around with a girl. But I really liked her, and I wanted to know her. So finally I went to her parents and asked for permission to speak to her. And they said, "And what are your intentions?" And I said, "I want to marry her. I mean, first to be engaged and then marry her." And her parents said, "All right, if that's your intention, you can visit with her. But if you've got other ideas, don't bother." And so we started to meet, me and Flora. Meeting whenever we could, usually on Sundays. Nineteen months it went on like that—months that seemed like years to me! Then my parents sent a letter to her parents—that's how it was done in those days—asking for permission for us to get married, and her parents, crying and crying, said, "Yes, we accept that they marry." And that was it: first a civil marriage at the mayor's office, and then a month later at the church with a priest. Me and Flora, finally together! And you know the way it is with the church, once you've married, that's the end. No divorces. I'm still married to her, according to the church, though we haven't been together for twenty years, maybe more.

In the beginning it was very good between us. She moved into my parents' house with me, and she worked along with the women in the house. Me, I stayed working with my father. Then, about two years later, I built a simple house right near my parents' house. Flora and me and our new daughter, we lived alone. Those were good years. Wonderful! And who knows, maybe we'd still be together if it wasn't for the war and what happened then. Like I was telling you, she didn't agree with what I was doing. Her family was not rich, but they had some money, not like mine, who were real poor. I don't think she understood how important it was for us campesinos to do something about our situation. She saw the danger, and she didn't want me to be killed or who knows what. Me, I was involved up to my neck—even more than she knew. There was no way I could stop.

I was with the FPL. In the beginning, our group wasn't involved with any military actions. We were educating people. Our group was made up of campesinos and others—students and church people and some city workers too. We'd have demonstrations, strikes, that kind of thing. But the more we got active, the more the rightists started to come down on us. So we knew that we had to get organized to fight. With weapons, I mean. But where to get these weapons? We had no supply chain then the way we did later—weapons coming into us from Cuba and Nicaragua, where the Sandinistas had made their revolution. No, hombre, we had nothing in the beginning. I'm talking about the late 1970s. We had machetes and sticks, that's all. You know what my first rifle was? A wooden gun! That's right, we made rifles out of wood and painted them, and we used these fake guns to practice maneuvers. I was head of a platoon by then, twenty-five or thirty men. We knew we had to get weapons, so what we did was go into villages where we knew there were soldiers living, guys who were with the Fuerza Armada. We'd go at night, and house by house we'd strip them of their weapons—usually old stuff, like M-14s, AG-3s—but they were arms we could use. And we also got some of our first weapons in other ways. Like this: we'd see some members of the Guardia, those bastards that were out policing in the campo and killing people for nothing; we'd see these guys get on a bus, maybe two or three of them, and then a few of our men would board the same bus. Our men weren't wearing uniforms, of course not. They were dressed like poor campesinos, with torn-up clothing and carrying a water gourd and their machetes. Nothing suspicious about them, you see. Then, when the Guardia guys got off the bus, our men got off too, and then whaaack! One shot to the back of the neck of each of them, and then we'd strip them of everything—their helmets, boots, uniforms, and their weapons. That's how we did it in the beginning. Little by little, we began arming ourselves.

Not just my group but in many places around the country. There were a number of different organizations, verdad? Each of us was gearing up for the war. And the rightists, they too were cracking down hard on anyone who they thought was a leader or just a member. By 1980, you can say, the war was in full swing. After they killed Monseñor Romero. Remember that? He was the top Catholic in the country, the archbishop in San Salvador. He was giving a talk at church in one of the neighborhoods of the capital. March 24, 1980, I remember it exactly. They shot him down. Why? Because he was a guerrilla? A terrorist? No! He was just speaking out about the injustices to his people. And a day or so later, when people gathered to demonstrate at his funeral, they were gunned down too. People with no weapons, just demonstrating their respect for the monseñor, and they were shot down in the street. That's the way it was. You remember how it was, verdad?

Most of the time those days, before the monseñor was killed, I was away from my wife and family. I'd go home for a few days, and then I'd have to take off again. Up where we lived in Cabañas things were heating up in those years. And some of my family started to get involved in it. Not as part of our militias, not fighting like I was. But my father and mother and some of my sisters had gotten involved. My father was a kind of courier and a guard, you could say. He tipped off our people, our militias in his area, where the Guardia was or the Fuerza Armada. And my mother and sisters were cooking for the groups; not traveling with them, but doing things like cleaning their clothes and bringing them tortillas and whatever to eat. It was dangerous for them. Real dangerous. But they wanted to help out. They understood what we were fighting for. And then it happened: three of my sisters got caught bringing food to some units. They were all young, teenagers. Some soldiers spotted them, and they captured them. I don't have it real clear in my head what happened. I only know a little from Marina. She told me about it later. These days, she won't talk about it anymore. She's got five or six kids, she's married to a guy who was in my platoon, and she's doing all right. She doesn't want to remember those days. I understand her. I only wish I knew who the bastards were who did it to her. I'd go after them today, I would. What those bastards did is capture all three of my sisters. Two of them, Rosa and Celina, we never heard from again. They disappeared. And Marina, the youngest— she was only fourteen years old then—they took her away and for two months they raped her night after night. Sticking it in her mouth, everything. I tell you, I just wish I knew who those bastards were. And the only way she survived is that some international group was going around visiting where prisoners were held, and they arranged for her to be released. Otherwise she would have been murdered too, like my other sisters.

Well, it was shortly after that when my whole family had to take off. The Fuerza Armada decided on a scorched-earth policy, you know, chase everyone the hell out of the area where they were living and burn down whatever was there. They came in one day, told everyone to get the hell out, and they set fire to our houses, our crops, even to our animals. They killed off everything. My family had no place to go. Where do you go when you've got nowhere to be? You spend a week here, a week there, trying to figure out what to do. Sleeping out in the open, trying to get something to eat. I went to be with them, to do what I could. And there wasn't much you could do. The sons of bitches in the army were killing off our people wherever we went.

What saved us was that we heard about some refugee camps that were being started up across the border in Honduras. United Nations people were setting these camps up to help the situation. We were told that we should try to make it up there. It wasn't our country. None of us had ever been anywhere else except El Salvador. But it was clear as hell that you were going to get shot up sooner or later, so you had to leave the country.

Not me, I wasn't planning to leave. But I wanted to get my family to some safe place, so I said, "Let's go there, it's the only way." I didn't know if it would be safe trying to get there, but I figured we had no choice. I had to get them over to Honduras. My mother and father and other sisters, and my wife and daughter with them. We decided to try to make it across the Lempa River. That was the only way to go. None of us could swim. There were hundreds of others who were heading there with us. It was the only way we could survive, we figured.

CHAPTER TWO

Niña Bonafacia

Luis's Mother

Some seven kilometers from Comunidad Guazapa, Papaturro lies deep into the countryside—another of the many repopulated communities in the area. Luis visits every few months to see his eighty-two-year-old mother as well as two sisters and his brother. They have been living there ever since the final weeks of the civil war in 1991. On a couple of occasions we went along with him unannounced (as is Luis's custom) and, above all, with the intention of interviewing his mother. Both times we found her seated on the packed-dirt veranda of her smallish concrete-block house as chickens and their chicks seemed to gather around her. "I don't move so much these days," she told us. "The arthritis. But my two daughters just nearby or my son, they're looking after me."

Similar to Luis, she is thin and has sharp facial features—high cheekbones, pointed nose—and also has a quick, alert manner and an evident taste for talk. Once in a while, during our lengthy interviews, she rose from her plastic chair and went to tend to the beans on the makeshift stone stove in the corner of the veranda or to stoke the fire under the comal. But for the most part, she sat quietly and unperturbed by the two tape recorders, her knobbed hands folded on her apron. Just above her and hanging on the concrete wall was a poster of the newly elected FMLN president, Mauricio Funes, along with a faded drawing of blue and yellow flowers made by one of her grandchildren and a calendar from the previous year.

On one occasion the metal door to the house (which also had a poster of Mauricio Funes) was closed tight. However, on the other occasion it was open, and one could see into the windowless room, where the sole furniture was two string beds, one with a pillow on it and the other adjacent to it but unused ever since her husband, Luis's father, had died seven years before. "I been by myself since my husband passed," she told us with tears in her eyes. "About fifty or sixty years we spent together, maybe more. Met him when I was sixteen and wasn't apart until he went awhile back. God's will. Took José Manuel and left me still. We had a long life together, here and there. Luis must have told you some of it, but I reckon there's a piece or two I can fill you in on if you want to know. Vaya pues."

I'm from Cabañas, was born there, raised there, got married there, and had my kids there. A little village, you could say, where everyone knew the other. A place called Talpetates. I had a mama and papa, but I grew up with my mama and grandpa. My papa lived nearby. No, he never married my mama, he just went on living with his parents. He was even poorer than us, and even though he and my mama had four kids, he never gave us nothing, hardly nothing. Just fed his own mama and papa. So, the way it was, me and my brothers and sister, we didn't have much closeness to him. The one who we looked at as our father really was my grandpa, my mama's father. He's the one who raised us like a father, and he's the one we listened to.

What did I do as a kid? Same as any other girl in Talpetates. Look, it wasn't like today. Kids go to school today; they got their time to play around. In my time there wasn't school for hardly anyone. My grandpa told me I was to be helping my mama. No learning my letters or any of that. "We eat maíz and frijol," he told me. "We don't eat paper with writing on it." And he didn't care much for me playing around either, though when he wasn't around I did play with some dolls I'd made out of rags, or I'd pretend—this was when I was real small—I'd play at making tortillas out of mud, then set them out to dry in the sun and then pretend I was selling them to others. That was my way of entertaining myself, but that was about all I did in that fooling around way. Rest of the time I was put to work, depending on what one could manage—sweeping up, getting rid of garbage, washing clothes. Helping my mama, that was my job.

Until I got married, that's how it was: me in my mama's house with my grandpa and my brothers and sister. All that changed afterward when José Manuel—I called him Chepe—when me and Chepe got married. That was when I was eighteen. By then I knew him, my husband, real well. He was maybe seven years older than me. A neighbor. He lived alone with his mama and uncle. I used to chat with him now and then, you know, when he was passing by. We'd tease each other. I called him "suffocator," because when nobody was looking he'd suddenly give me a quick hug. It was a game, sort of. Yes, sure, I liked him. He was a poor fellow. There were other fellows who wanted to start with me, talk,

talk, talk, but I distrusted them. They came from families that had some money, some land. I didn't want to be with anyone from a rich family, because the way I reckoned, they'd take off on me real quick. I preferred someone poor like me. And Chepe was from a poor family.

Chepe wanted to be my *novio* and then for us to get married. So he came and talked to my grandpa. It wasn't a big deal. They agreed quickly. Chepe didn't send a letter the way it was usually done. You know, the man's mother would have a letter sent to the girl's house, and in a week or so the girl's mother would send her reply, saying whether she liked the idea or not. But my mama said, "Who needs letters? Better a real commitment from him!" You see, my mama and grandpa both liked him. They knew he was a good, hard worker, working his small milpa and growing food for his family. So there was no problem. They agreed to us getting married.

We got married in the church and civil both. You could do it just by registering with the mayor's office, but I wanted to be married in the church too. The man was more likely to stay with one that way, that's how I looked at it. And I didn't want to be one of those women whose husbands took off on them, and then you had to go back to your mama's house. No, no! What a shame that is! So better have the marriage in the church. Chepe went along with me. And that's the way we did it. For the church ceremony, my mama and grandpa and me walked there; it was a distance from where we lived. So we stayed the night with our godparents over there. Then at dawn we had the ceremony. Yes, yes, I was dressed in white, a simple cotton dress that a señora had made for me. And afterward we had a small lunch, nothing fancy. A roast chicken with trimmings. Chepe's people and my people, just a few of us. Then we all walked back to Talpetates. I went to my house, took some things with me, and went over to my husband's house, where I would be living from then on.

How did that first night go? *Bueno*, it went fine. [Niña Bonafacia laughs deeply.] Sometimes it doesn't go so fine for a woman because she's, well, she's had experiences with others before. A man doesn't like that, and there's problems. But me, no. I took care of myself. Chepe was the only man I ever knew—all my life. So things went fine. [She laughs again, this time shyly.] Yes, it was wonderful! It felt very good to be with my Chepe, yes it did.

Within a year or so, I had my first baby. Lupe—my daughter who lives just nearby. She's the oldest. After her, a year and a half later, I had Luis. He was my first son. Sure, sure, I remember how it went. When you are young—what was I, maybe twenty or twenty-one when I brought Luis?—at that age it's easy. It hurts, sure. But afterward, you don't think about the hurt. Just the baby lying there with you, that's all you think about. I was living with my mother-in-law, but thank goodness she wasn't around when I brought Luis. She was always scared of the noise, though me, I never made noise. Only my son when he came out with his head—that's the hard part, right?—and then he started crying till I gave him something to suck on. It all happened quick. One minute I was making tortillas, and the next I had those pains running in my back and my son pushing his way out. I lay down on the floor, then wrapped some rags around my backside so that when the baby came out he'd not just flop on the floor. My husband went running off to get the *partera*. She was living a ways off, like from this house to the main road—a few kilometers. But Chepe had long legs and got her back pretty soon to help me out. By then my son was already out, but she helped cut the cord and cleaned him up like the way they do and wrap him up. It was real helpful. You pay them afterward, maybe a colón or two. It depends. In those days you paid them a little more if you had a son. That's just the way it went. I don't know how it is today. I couldn't tell you. That's how it was in my time. And I had quite a number of *bichos*, as you may know. Nine, I think. Wait a minute—no, more. Twelve, I reckon. I lost two just after they were born. They got sick and they died. Because back in those days you couldn't get to any clinic, it was a long way off from where we were living, and if your baby got sick, then they could die on you. And I lost another one, a boy, when he was eleven years old; some kind of throat infection hit him, and soon he was gone. So I had nine who lived, and I lost three when they were small. I lost two more later, but that was in the war. They were already grown by then.

With all the bichos I had, and us being poor like we were, it was tough sometimes just having food for everyone. Often, all we had was tortillas and salt. But back then people weren't like they are now. Today, people are all greedy. If they've got cheese, then they want eggs, and if they got eggs, then they want chicken and meat. Back then, you had what you had, and if a day went by and you didn't have anything, then you waited for the next day. And for clothes, you didn't have back then what you've got today. Only simple things made of plain cloth. I'd sew some of the clothing for the kids, and I'd buy some cheap things for Chepe or for Luis, clothing they'd wear up in the milpa.

At times, when I had a few hours, I'd go up to the milpa too. Regularly, I would be going that way—it must have been a couple of kilometers off from our house—to gather firewood for the stove. And I'd bring them food for their lunch up there, and sometimes I'd even do a little work up there. Me, I liked being there. Taking a machete and helping them clean the milpa, or really just being up there, the good air, the maicillo and maíz growing fine, I liked it. Though most of the time I couldn't spend much time there, since I had the bichos in the house, and I had to go take care of them with my mother-in-law.

We had a good life back then in Talpetates. Me, Chepe, and the kids. Living poor, yes, but a good life. Chepe was a good man. He didn't drink much like some others did. Maybe once in a while he'd get drunk, get all content for the day, never nasty drunk if you know what I mean. And he wasn't smacking me the way some men did. He was fine. Only thing was, well, you know how it is with some women. They put their eye on a man, and never mind that he's married, they go hanging about him if they have a chance. Now and then, some women in our village would tell me that so-and-so was up there near our milpa, carrying some firewood, and she was going by and eyeing Chepe. I don't know what was going on. I confronted him about it, but he always told me that he had nothing to do with any of that. *Nada, nada.* I told him that he better not get involved with any of that, because if he did I was going back to my mama's house. Really, though, I never would have left. I wouldn't have had the guts to leave. And Chepe was telling me, "Stop with all that, woman! Stop bothering me with that, or you'll see who will leave." So I left it alone, especially since he was telling me that he had nothing to do with any other woman.

So what was Luis like as a kid? I can answer that easy. Mischievous! That was him, right from the beginning. Very mischievous! Always up to one thing or the other. Throwing stones at other boys or biting them while they were playing some game. Or he'd have his little machete—he liked going around with it—and if he got into a fight, he'd threaten the other boy, might even cut the other kid a little bit. I had to keep my eye on him all the time. When I was around he'd behave himself. He knew I wasn't going to put up with his stuff. He knew if I caught him doing bad things, I'd haul out the leather strap and I'd give it to him real good. No, no, I wasn't going to have any bad kids. I made sure Luis and all the others behave right, that they talk with respect. I wouldn't let my kids call me or their father *vos*; they had to call me *usted*. And believe me, they listened to me—even Luis. And I'll say this: Luis never fought with any of his sisters. His father would have stopped that. I can remember Chepe telling Luis, "You treat your sisters right, boy! Later they will love you and be good to you." Luis listened to his father, and to this day his sisters do love him a lot.

Though back when he was a small boy Luis didn't play with his sisters. He didn't care for being in the house. He wanted to be outside with the other boys in the area, or, even more, he wanted to go along with his father to the milpa. Right from the time he was five or six years old he'd follow Chepe up there, and my husband liked having the boy up there with him. Even when Luis was too young to be anything useful, Chepe would let him go along with him. "Boy, you just have yourself some fun,"

Chepe would tell him. "Make little stone houses or whatever you want, you don't need to work with me yet." And Luis would do just what he wanted, taking his slingshot and go off shooting birds or something like that. I told Chepe to leave Luis with me in the morning so that the boy could bring up his lunch, and then I wouldn't have to do it. But Luis was clever. He heard me discussing this once with his Chepe, and so he'd wake real early and follow his father up to the milpa and get out of carrying up the pot of food for his father. Sneaky and mischievous, I'm telling you. And there wasn't much I could do about it, since my husband wanted his boy up there with him. Especially a little later, when Luis was seven or so. That's when he started working. And he was a good, hard worker right from the beginning. He'd work alongside his father, or he'd go into the woods with his machete and cut up some firewood and bring it back to me. *That* he didn't mind doing, as long as he didn't have to stay down with me and his sisters in the house.

When he was a kid, Luis was angry with me that I had so many daughters. Each time I'd finish giving birth, he'd come over and say, "What did you have this time, Mama?" And when I told him, "A girl"—which is mostly what I had—he'd say to me, "Oh no, all you're having is girls!" Luis wanted brothers to fool around with, to go off to the hills with him. I wouldn't let the girls go up there, but when I finally had his brother, Antonio, he was so happy. And soon as he could, Luis started dragging Antonio up to the hills to play with him. Antonio was scared at first, and he didn't want to go. But Luis made him a little pair of sandals and put Antonio on his shoulders and hauled him up there to play with him. He loved being up in the hills, building a little house from sticks and dried grass, and they made that their hut up there. I'm not sure if Antonio loved it the way Luis did, but no matter, Luis kept hauling him off to be with him. That's the way he was, my son Luis. He'd have his mind fixed on something, and one way or the other he'd go about doing it.

He and Antonio were both good workers. Both helped Chepe in the milpa. But when he got to be fifteen years old, around then I remember, Luis also began having other ideas. Girls! He made no secret of it. "That one there, I like her, Mama, I want to get together with her." I told him, "You're still a boy, Son. How are you going to get together with her and support her?" I tried to talk sense to him, but there was no talking to him right then. He saw a girl he liked, and already he wanted to *acompañarse*. I wasn't about to allow anything like that, and Luis got real angry with me. Next thing I knew, he just plain took off. Went way down to San Vicente, hours from where we were living. And he stayed there living with a relative of ours down there, helping her out and all that. And of course, chasing girls down there. This one or that one. I don't really know. I know he didn't acompañarse, or at least I don't think so, because about half a year later he showed up back in Talpetates alone, and he went back to work with his father and brother in the milpa. But still chasing girls, girls!

It went on for a while like that, and finally he stopped all his messing around because he found one he liked enough to marry. Flora. She was a woman from right around here, and Luis took a real liking to her, and she the same—she took to him. Me and Chepe, we both liked her. She came from good people, and she was herself a soft and affectionate young woman. A couple of years older than Luis, maybe. We were glad when they got married. By the church, yes. And then they moved in with us, and then later when they had their first child, they put up a house nearby, Luis still working in the milpa with Chepe and Antonio. And in the summer, when you couldn't work in the milpa, they'd go off to cut sugarcane or pick coffee on one of those rich people's fincas. No, I never went with them. I just heard from them that it was rotten conditions, bad treatment, and all that. More than that, you'll have to ask Luis.

It was only a little while after Luis and Flora had their first daughter that Luis started getting involved with those meetings. You know what I mean, right? He wasn't with the guerrillas then, he hadn't got incorporated, but he was going to meetings all the time. He never discussed any of that with me. I knew about it, though. Once in a while, he'd organize a meeting right in our house. People from all over, ones you didn't know or maybe a few you did know, they came by. I heard them talking about how they had to organize themselves, how they couldn't go on accepting things the way they were. It was serious, you could see that. And it was dangerous, since there might be some *orejas* coming to these meetings. And these orejas might go off and report you to the soldiers. Then you'd have some trouble on your hands. I can't say I know much of what Luis was doing in those times, just that he was busy with it. He got me and my daughters helping out too. Like I say, they weren't fighting in the guerrillas then, nobody going to the *monte*. They were just organizing into groups, hiding out and avoiding the soldiers, and they needed folks to help them out with some food and money. Chepe was too old then to be involved with them. He acted as a kind of watchman, tipping them off where the soldiers were coming from or going to. And me and my daughters were cooking for the groups, tortillas, frijol, whatever. Sometimes we'd make up a whole batch of tamales, and we'd sell them, and then we'd pass the money on to the groups. Sure, it was dangerous, but we reckoned to do our part along with the men.

That's how my daughters got killed. Two of them. They were just teenagers. What happened is that they were bringing food for the groups, the militias that we were forming, and some soldiers, maybe the Fuerza Armada or maybe the Guardia, they stopped them. I know this because actually three of my daughters were stopped, including Marina, who is living now over in Comunidad Guazapa where Luis is. All three got arrested, and then—according to how Marina told me—the soldiers, whoever they were, put them in a plane and flew them to some spot, and then they started abusing them. And later they were taken from one spot to another, being abused by this bunch of soldiers or another bunch. Marina managed to escape after a few months, but my other two— [Niña Bonafacia pauses, weeping softly to herself.] My other two, I never did hear anything about them again. Marina reckons they were killed. She never saw it happen, but they disappeared, and we haven't ever seen them again. That's how I lost them. When they were just teenagers, just young girls. Gone.

My husband and me, pretty soon after that, we had to take off from Cabañas. The soldiers were coming to our area, rounding up people and burning down houses. We found out later that our house had got burned down too. We had already taken the few things we could, and with the children we took off—my daughters, Chepe and me, along with Luis and his family. We all headed up to Honduras to a refugee camp there. Luis and Antonio came with us, but they didn't stay. I knew they weren't going to stay, since the both of them were incorporated with the guerrillas by then. I was scared, real scared, that I was going to lose both of them too. But what could you do? My sons went off to the monte, and the rest of us remained in the refugee camp.

And that's how it was for us the next five years, maybe even more. We were in the camp, and Luis and Antonio were off somewhere in the monte. We'd see them now and then. Sometimes Luis would come up for a few days to visit with his wife and children—by then he'd had another one or two—and Antonio would come visit his woman. Somehow they managed to sneak into the camp, and just a few days later they'd sneak out. I didn't know much about what they were doing in the monte. I knew anything could happen, and there wasn't much I or anyone else could do about it. And then one day, Antonio came to the camp with the news. He, Antonio, was wounded—not too bad that time, but a little shot up. He told us that his group and Luis's group were caught in an ambush. He had managed to get away not harmed too bad, but Luis was all messed up. He'd got shot in the back and the arm, and last he saw him, Luis was lying in a gully with his back all bloodied up and his arm hanging off of him. But, according to how Antonio explained it, Luis might make it out, since some *compas* were coming to fetch him—least that's what he understood—and there was a chance that Luis might survive it. Me, I didn't know what to think. And the days went by, the weeks, and we heard nothing more. I kept wondering where my boy was. What had happened to him?

Then there he was one day. They brought him to the refugee camp.
Alive. He was messed up a bit, his arm hanging strange from him but the
rest of him whole and all right. What a joy for me! I hadn't lost my boy
like I thought I might have done. He was all right. Weak, sort of. And
his compas had brought him back to us to get himself strong again, to
recuperate a while. And that's what Luis did. He stayed in the camp for
several months getting his strength back, and then, just like you could
have expected, he told us—me, Chepe, his wife—that he was going back
to the monte. The war was still going on, and his place, he said, was in
the monte. What could you do? Luis always was like that. He said he was
going somewhere, and then he went. There was no sense trying to talk
him out of it.

The rest of us stayed up in the camp a couple of years more. No, not
till the war was over. Before that was when we left. We found out that
we could go back to our own country. Not to our house, because that
was gone. We could go to a place called Santa Marta, near the border
of Honduras, and we'd be safe there. So that's what we did. We went
there—all of us except for Luis and Antonio, who were still in the monte.
We were up there a while. Awful place. Crowded and wasted, no wood to
cook with, nothing up there. But we had no other place to go. Then, as I
recall it, some bishop up there told us that they had been arranging for a
group of us to leave Santa Marta and go over to repopulate the area near
Mount Guazapa. No, not Comunidad Guazapa and those other communities over where Luis is. Another place called Papaturro. Near Mount
Guazapa, but a little distance away from it. Chepe and me, and Antonio
and his family, and a couple more daughters and their families—bueno,
we all jumped at the chance. Luis, no. He was fixing to go somewhere
else with another group of people. Over where he is now. He and Flora
were no longer together. Luis was with some other woman, someone
named Meches. I can't say I was happy about that. I liked Flora. To me,
she's the best woman Luis has ever been with. But things had got messed
up between them during the war. You know, a man is in the monte, and
some woman catches his eye, and next thing you know, even if he doesn't
care much for her, they get together for a while. And a woman is up there
alone in the refugee camp, and she gets together with some man, even if
she doesn't care so much for him. The war did that to people. And good
as his woman was, that Flora, Luis wound up with another, and he went
off with her and some bichos they had, and my grandson Chico—they
went off to live in Comunidad Guazapa. Marina, my daughter who'd been
abused and violated, she went over there too along with her family. The
rest of us came to Papaturro. And we been here ever since.

I like it here. I'm real comfortable here now. In the beginning, well, I can't say it was so good. When we first got here, there was nothing. Lots of trees like you see in my yard in front, and no land to farm. You had to clear it all out. Each of us got a manzana—no, wait, two and a half manzanas, including the land where you put up your house. Chepe was getting old then, so he and me worked it together. Once we got it planted, we did all right. Thing is, it took some months before you had your first maíz, maicillo, and frijol. Till then, you had nothing to eat except what some organizations were willing to give to us. And like you see, we're way out here in the campo, maybe three kilometers or so from the main road. When we got here we had no road out to the community, and worst thing was, the Fuerza Armada didn't want us here, and so they were blocking any supplies from getting through. Trying to force us out, they were doing. But somehow we managed it. And we got through that first year, and ever since we've been doing fine enough.

Except for me, the last seven years without Chepe, it hasn't been the same. He had some disease, and then he was all lame for a while. Couldn't do anything but just sit there. And then he went. Since then, it's just me here in the house. I've got my daughters that help me out, bring me some maíz and frijol and a little cheese that they get from their cow. And they give me a little cash when I need it. Luis, too. Whenever he comes he brings me some things or some cash. He's a good son, but he's got that whole brood of his over there in Comunidad Guazapa keeping him busy, and he's hardly got time to get over here. Now and then, that's all. I know some of his children, they're respectful and all, but I don't see them much. The one I know is his oldest boy, Chico—the one he had with Flora. He's the one who's a lawyer. Very good kid. He lived over here with me and Chepe back when he was in high school, back when Luis decided to get together with that Julia who he's with now. Julia, and Meches, neither of them wanted to take care of Chico, so he came over here and lived with us for maybe a year or so. Good kid. Worked hard in the milpa with us, hauled me firewood, and did his studies at the school here. Then he got some kind of sickness in his chest, and Luis came and picked him up and brought him back to Comunidad Guazapa. The boy was real tied to Luis, and he stayed there after that, and I understand that Chico is getting along with Julia these days. She's changed some, I suppose. I don't really know. I don't see her much. Can't get over there to where they're living. Haven't been there but twice. Last time was maybe ten years ago, something like that. And nowadays I can't hardly walk over to my daughter's house next door with this arthritis I got. I wish my boy Luis was around, but truth is, I couldn't manage much over there in Comunidad Guazapa with all those bichos he's now got running around. Too much noise and commotion. I'm better off here. Daughters take better care of you; they're more sweet with one, looking after one in a way that sons don't bother as much. So it's good for me to be here, even though I can't move hardly. Have to do a lot of sitting, and just get up now and then to make me some tortillas and frijol or to feed this whole new bunch of chicks and their mama and the rooster I got right here with me. That's how I spend my time. That and chatting with my daughters or son when they look in on me. Taking one day at a time. That's all you can do, take one day at a time long as you're here, right?

CHAPTER THREE

Luis

The War Years

On the right side of the main road from the capital of San Salvador to the town of Suchitoto and some five kilometers from the entrance to Comunidad Guazapa, there is a small, inconspicuous restaurant with the apt name of Guazapa Café. It's a place Luis likes to visit every so often, not for its food or even its pleasant tables out in the tree-shaded garden but rather for its display of war paraphernalia that is scattered near the restaurant's entrance. Uniforms, canteens, bomb fragments, empty cartridges from M-16 or AK-47 rifles, parts of the rifles themselves, radios and battery cases, dozens of mortar and rocket casings, and even a helicopter engine—all lie there caked in the dust of years. And the owner, a comrade of Luis, proudly smiles at his display as we enter in order to interview Luis in the privacy of the garden. "All that equipment, I know it better than you can imagine," Luis tells us in a tone that is at once proud and slightly nostalgic. "I lived with this stuff for years, I know every piece here intimately. Yes, every piece. Anyway, let's go have a beer or something."

And thus, in a corner of the garden, out of listening distance from the other patrons, Luis continues his story, focusing this time on the brutal period from 1980 to 1992, when he was in the monte as a guerrilla. He talks for an hour and a half nonstop, except for a regular chugging of his beers and a hungry downing of a full platter of chicken wings. His voice pitches up and down, and at moments he seems almost to be reliving some of the experiences. As we get up to leave, he tells us, "You've got to get all that in there, as much as you can, into that book. People these days don't remember what it was like, the hell we went through." And with a final chug of his beer, he announces, "But it was worth it. Hell, yes, it was worth it!"

Here, then, is a version, albeit abridged, of Luis's war years.

It is only with God's help that I'm sitting here, still alive, talking to you today. I suppose my mother told you some of what I went through, what we all went through. But she doesn't know, really. I never went into it with her. She had it hard enough. Why bother her, verdad? She had to hear about my sisters, about Marina. That's enough for anyone—even a strong person like she is. And what she went through herself in those early days of the war, it was plenty hard. She's lucky to be alive, too.

Remember, I told you how we got chased out of El Salvador, how we had to flee to a refugee camp in Honduras. Well, all of us were lucky to have made it there, none of us getting killed the way so many others did that night we crossed over the Lempa River. It was a massacre! We hadn't expected anything like it. We were caught by surprise. Ambushed. By the Fuerza Armada and then the Honduran soldiers who were cooperating with them on the other side. Pure hell! Hundreds of us, maybe even a thousand people, had come to the Lempa River with the few belongings we still had. It was night, and we constructed rafts out of poles in order to get us across. Hardly any of us could swim. We all stripped down to our underwear; the whole bank of the river was scattered with clothing and parcels and God knows what. We got on the rafts at various places on the river. Those rafts were big enough to hold twelve people sitting down. The few that could swim dragged the rafts with them across the river, one swimmer pulling from the front and another pushing from the back. If anyone fell off, that was it. You drowned. But the worst of it was the rockets and mortars that the Fuerza Armada were firing at us from a distance. The river was lit up like it was the middle of the day. And then when you got to the other side, you had some Honduran soldiers taking potshots at you. I'm telling you, it was a massacre. Many dead. Many never made it to the refugee camps. My family, yes. We were lucky. Not a one of us was killed. We all made it up there—yes, still in our underwear—but we made it.

Once you got up there—really, on the way because the United Nations people escorted you to the camps in their trucks—bueno, they took care of you. They had shelters for you, and they gave you clothing and food, everything. And they protected you. The camps were fenced off, and the Honduran soldiers couldn't touch you as long as you were inside the refugee camps. Step outside, that was something else. Those bastards would shoot you if they had a chance. My wife, she wanted me to stay there in the camp with her and our daughter. Me, I had no intention to stay. I talked with her, talked and talked, explaining why we had to fight, and finally one day she said, "All right, I'll go along." I convinced her to leave our daughter with my parents, and she snuck out of the camp with me and went back to El Salvador, to the monte, with me. Not with my unit, no. There was a rule that no man and his woman could be together in the same unit. So she was in another unit, working as a *molendera*. Then what happened—the way I heard it later—her unit got caught in a battle, and my wife fainted on the spot. She must have been in the guerrillas for a few months by then. That was enough for her. She couldn't stand it anymore. She asked to leave, and she was taken back to the refugee camp. We had guides who knew the way, and she went with them. I wasn't surprised. She had never really understood what I was doing, what we were doing. It wasn't for her, that's all. The only way I could see her from then on was to go back to the camp. And I did. Not often. You only got a few days off every year. But I did go back to see her when I could. Her and my daughter. And then also my new sons. That's right, I had two more sons with her over the next five or six years. I'd go back and see them all, and the rest of my family who were also up there in the same camp. I tried to keep it going with my wife the best I could, even though my mother was telling me, "Son, your marriage is getting messed up." I knew she was right, but what the hell could I do?

I was up to my ass with work in the guerrillas, busy all the time. Our group, the FPL, and four others were united by then as one group—the FMLN. That was in 1980. We were busy figuring out how to get the weapons and armaments we needed to fight the war. And we were going around recruiting people. We needed *combatientes*, and you had to train them in everything. Raise their consciousness and teach them how to use weapons and all that. Not so easy, believe me. Because you had to get these young guys toughened up so they could take whatever came our way. We didn't force anyone to join our side the way the Fuerza Armada did. They'd threaten them and force them to join up, and they'd pay them a few colones to fight with them. We didn't pay anyone to fight with us. Hell, we had no money to pay anyone! Besides, we knew we were in for a long struggle, and we needed people who were committed to the cause, people who would stick it out. No point in recruiting people who would only turn on you later.

The way we did it was that after we recruited someone and they went through basic training, we made each one take an oath. That's right, every one of us who joined as a combatiente took an oath that you were ready to fight until you won or you died. You swore that you were ready to fight for your people and that if you were captured you wouldn't reveal anything about your comrades. You see, we combatientes had our weapons with us and our ammunition, verdad? But right here, you also carried one extra cartridge in a small pouch, right over your heart. This cartridge was called *el de uno*. If you ran out of ammunition and were surrounded and about to be captured, then you took el de uno, and you killed yourself. Because, look, if they captured you and began torturing you, then you might wind up telling who your commander is, or the names of your comrades, or where your armaments were stored. So better to end your own life rather than to risk ratting on others when they were torturing you.

And believe me, they tortured real bad when they caught you and they figured you knew things. A fellow from another unit over in Sensuntepeque—this was back in the beginning of 1980 when things were heating up—he got caught with a can of paint as he was planning to write revolutionary messages on the walls of some houses. The Fuerza Armada spotted him. We were told about this by people who witnessed what they did to him, how they tore out his fingernails, burned his eyeballs with cigarettes, made him drink the paint, and then shot him and dumped him in a garbage bin. He didn't reveal anything to them, not a thing. Or that's what I was told by others. But I saw with my own eyes what happened to a guy in a unit close to mine when they nabbed him. This poor kid, they dragged him to a tree and strung him up with hammock cords. A few from my unit were nearby. We managed to get away, and we were listening from a gully. We could hear him screaming terribly. They had put a fire under him and burned him slowly to death. And him screaming, and yes, giving them information—names and everything. We were lucky he didn't know we were in hiding, but we were close enough and heard the whole thing. This kid had no weapons, no el de uno. But he would have been better off if he had had one. And that's why we made it part of the oath that you use the el de uno if you ever got caught like that.

Did our side ever torture? Look, I'm not going to lie to you. We did too. And we kidnapped people sometimes. It's no secret. Me, personally, I was never part of that. I never tortured anybody. But, look, this was a dirty war. Both sides did things that were terrible. The way I see it, the Fuerza Armada was much more involved in torturing, much more brutal. But sí, hombre, we did some torturing too. I knew people from the FMLN who were doing these things. I'm just glad I didn't get involved in that. And I wasn't caught and tortured myself, though I did have a few close calls.

But as you can see, I never had to use my el de uno. For me, the way it went is that I spent almost the whole war up in the monte. Twelve years. In Cabañas, Chalatenango, and San Vicente, going from one place to the other, attacking here, retreating there. You know, guerrilla warfare. In the beginning, I'd say, it was the toughest. We weren't well organized then. At times you didn't even have anything to eat. You'd go days with nothing, just some tree leaves or roots, or maybe you'd come across an avocado tree or banana tree or a mango tree. Later, by 1982, we had a supply chain worked out, and we got food from the villages and towns in areas where we were in control, from the churches or people living there who supported us.

And in the beginning, we didn't have enough weapons. The enemy, the Fuerza Armada, were real well equipped. And well trained, too. The United States was supplying them with all their weapons, with advisors, and with aircraft too. But they weren't used to fighting a guerrilla war. I mean, fighting up in the monte. To protect ourselves we dug tunnels deep into the mountains. It took months, working day and night. You couldn't just dump the earth nearby. At night—that was the best time to do it—you'd have to carry the earth far away or dump it in the river. These tunnels were our protection. And we used some techniques like we were told they had used in Vietnam. We'd dig deep holes along the mountain pathways, and we'd place sharpened bamboo stakes in these holes. You'd put a little onion or garlic on the points of the stakes, and then you'd carefully cover up and disguise that hole. When the soldiers came up those paths looking for us, some of them would fall into the holes, and they'd get stuck there, with the onion and garlic acting like a poison in their wounds.

We learned these things from others. From who? Cubans and Nicaraguans and others who gave us some advice. That's right, the enemy had the United States, and we had other outsiders helping us out. The Cubans and Nicaraguans supplied us with some high-quality weapons: rifles, machine guns and ammunition, and later on even some antiaircraft guns. And they provided us with advisors. These advisors taught us how to make some of our own weapons. Some things we learned here, and some things we learned by going out of the country and taking a course. Yes, I was one of those who went. To Nicaragua. Others went to Cuba. When we came back we set up workshops to make our own grenades and mines. We made grenades with pieces of lead and nails inside, things like that, and for explosive we used the ashes of a certain leaf or even burnt cow dung. Yes, really. It worked. We tossed them on the soldiers and killed them with our grenades. Me, I wasn't involved in making grenades. I took a course in making mines, the kind you used to blow up trucks. What we did is fill a metal box with pieces of lead and fragments from the bombs their airplanes were dropping on us, and for an explosive we used some stuff that we got from elsewhere, I think from Cuba. I learned how to make these mines and then also how to dismantle them. The dismantling part was more dangerous. You couldn't make any mistakes doing that. Once, and that was it for you!

I never had any problems from those mines, no mishaps, no wounds. But, yes, I did get wounded. [Looking about the restaurant to make sure nobody was watching, Luis lifts his shirt slightly, revealing an inch-long scar on each side of his back, and then rolls up his right shirtsleeve to expose a badly scarred elbow.] These are my mementos from the war. Like I was telling you, God alone knows how I am still here today. Because I thought one time that it was over for me. I figured I was finished. Dead. To this day I'm surprised I made it. In 1986. December '86 is when it happened. I was leading a group of men to go get some provisions, some armaments. The Fuerza Armada had set up an ambush for us. My brother was in another platoon near mine following after us. But it was my group that got hit. All my men began to scatter. They were new recruits, and they scattered like hell. Some got killed on the spot. And me, I ran like hell looking for a place to hide when, zaaaaap! I get hit right in my knapsack by machine-gun fire, everything spilling out and no time to grab a thing, and me diving into a trench. Soon I could see that they were closing in on me, and I look for my rifle and my el de uno, but it's all gone. No armament and no personal bullet. Shit! Better to make a run for it, I'm thinking, and I get up and start running, and then I get hit again, this time in my back right here below my kidneys. The bullet passed through one side and came out the other; this I found out way later. And another bullet hit me in the elbow, and my arm is hanging free. I'm not looking at my wounds, and right then all I know is that I'm bleeding bad. I keep running, and they are coming after me firing away, and I get to this deep gully, and I know my only chance is to take a jump and hope I survive it. That's what I did. And the soldiers came upon the gully, and no way they were going to jump down there, so for a while all they did was fire into it. I was hidden and didn't get hit down there. And later, when the soldiers had taken off, along comes my brother. He manages to come down into the gully. I tell him, there's no way I can climb out of there, that I am going to die there. We don't say much. He just takes my watch, my Seiko, and leaves me with something to drink and some sugar, and he digs a small trench for me and covers it over with branches. He didn't want any soldiers to see me down there. And he leaves then, thinking that I've had it, it's finished for me. Well, it was a good thing he hid me like that, because soon after the soldiers came, and they began looking to see if anyone was down there. I hear one say to the other, "Nobody's down there, man." And the other says, "There's got to be someone in there. The bastards came this way." "Man, I say nobody's down there, forget it." And with that they take off, but not before taking some more shots down in the gully.

I was down there in that gully four days and four nights. I had water down there—there was water at the bottom—and I had sugar, but I was growing weak. I was half out of my mind. I no longer knew exactly who I was, that I had a family, that I had children, that there was a God and a Devil. Real fucked up, I was. Finally I said to myself, I'm not going to die down here like a pure coward; a *guerrillero* can't do that. Somehow I've got to pull myself out of here. And that's what I did. Somehow I managed to get my ass out of that gully. I took a lace out of one of my boots, tied my arm so that it wouldn't flop around, and I began walking on. I was weak, real weak, and soon I was thirsty as hell. I had a razor blade with me, the only thing I had left, and with that I cut some leaves that had juice in them. I must have walked for three days, eating nothing, vomiting on and off, feeling dizzy, pale as a sheet of paper, and then I came to some place that had a fruit tree and some squash and lots of water, and I drank like a drunkard and was feeling a little better. Then, finally, I come to this small village, and I stop at the house of some woman, and she says to me, "Are you a soldier or guerrilla?" I look at her and answer, "Soldier. From the Fuerza Armada, the Chalatenango post." She says, "Fine, I'll give you something to eat, and I'll go tell the colonel at the army post up a ways." And me, I'm thinking to myself, "Oh, shit! Now I'm finished." I quickly eat the tortilla—it was awful tasting, some kind of stuff I wasn't used to—and then quick as hell, quick as I could, really, I take off to another house where this guy is, and I say to him, "Tell me, soldiers are coming by here now and then?" He answers, "Yes. And guerrillas too. And what are you?" "A soldier," I say. And he says, "Ah! You must have been in that battle down a ways. Over near Zapotal, no?" "Yes," I say. "Got hit." He's looking me over, and he says, "Some guerrillas are going to be by here soon. They're going to be buying some provisions at night. Some coffee, sugar, and milk." "And the soldiers?" I ask. But now I'm feeling this great joy, thinking maybe I'll get rescued. The guy answers, "The soldiers will be coming later, I reckon." And then he says to me, "You, you're no soldier. You're pure guerrilla!" "You're not mistaking there," I tell him. "All right, all right," he says. "Look, nobody is going to come after you. I know where your compas are, and I'll fetch them for you."

You see, the guy was a collaborator, working with us. And sure enough, he soon comes back with a platoon of guerrillas and their commander. The commander was named Margarito. I knew him. But we all had pseudonyms. "It's you, Sergio," I say. "It's been a while since I last saw you." "Right. You're Rigoberto, right?" "Yes," I answered. "What has happened to you?" "Me," I say, "I've been fighting with Death." And then Margarito says to me, "We're going to get you over to the doctor."

They try loading me on a hammock, but I can't take it, and then they put me on a horse, and we take off to one of our clinics. A place, it turns out, that's got nothing much, no medicine, no anesthetic, nothing. No beds either. They laid me down on a wooden door that they were using for an operating table. Some other comrades were there, but I had a higher rank, so they began immediately looking after me. The doctor there was a gringo, Rafael they called him, and he tells me that the wound in my back is full of worms and that it looked like my arm had gangrene. He told some assistants they were going to need to hold me down. "What's this?" I say. "We've got to amputate the arm," he says. "No, hombre!" I tell him. "No way you're going to cut off my arm. Do what you want and what you can, but I won't let you cut off my arm." "All right," he says. And he then starts cleaning up my wounds with some herb stuff that grows in the mountains and some kind of disinfectant, maybe Clorox. "This will get the worms out of your wounds," he tells me. It hurt like hell, and me, I was yelling, "Son of a bitch, son of a bitch!" And then Rafael starts—really it was sort of funny—he starts telling me jokes, even some filthy jokes, and then before I know it, traaannn! a terrible pain as he grabs my arm, and I—this I find out later—I faint on the spot. And when I wake up I find that my arm that was hanging loose from the elbow is now straight again, more or less.

Bueno, from there, after a few days they take me off to a better place, a hospital where there were a number of my comrades who got caught up in the same battle. They were recuperating there. A good place, clean and with good food. And that's where I got better. I was there two months. Real relaxing. I was still weak and pale as paper, even after the two months' rest. I didn't know exactly what I was going to do next. But I knew one thing: I had to go see my family and my children. I figured they must be thinking maybe I'm finished, dead. And really, that's how it was. My brother had made it up to the refugee camp in Honduras and told my mother he had seen me in a gully all bloodied up. He told my wife—really, she was my ex-wife by then—and he told my children too. My mother had been praying for me; they had already sat the prayer period for the dead. I found this out later. I found it out because, you see, a group of comrades came to get me from the hospital in order to carry me back to Honduras. Weak as I was, still I was able to walk slowly. They wanted to put me in a hammock, but I said no, I can make it on my own. Except you know what happened? We just about get killed on the way. Imagine! Just by luck we made it. We had to go through the mountains— no safe route there, Salvadoran and Honduran soldiers ready to pounce on you. We were moving along this path, some armed comrades in front scouting the way, me in the middle, and the rest of my comrades in the rear. Our front men suddenly came back, telling us there was a whole squadron of Honduran soldiers ready for us, and surely we were about to be shot. But our men had seen them first. Actually, we *heard* them. Funny, if you think of it. One of these Honduran soldiers had suddenly let out this tremendous fart, and the guy next to him, I guess, starts telling him off, screaming at him. And that's how we were saved—by a fart!

So we quietly double back a bit, take another route that night, and then the next day we get to Honduras. Soon as I'm up there in the camp, my mother comes running to me. She throws her arms around me, crying and crying. She never figured she was going to see me again. And then, running up to me were two of my kids, Francisco and Pacita. "Papi, papi," shouts Chico—that's what I call him—"Papi, it's you!" And Pacita and he are hugging me. My third kid is there with my ex-wife, and she's standing there amazed. She had told all of them that they weren't going to be seeing me again, that I'd been killed in the monte. And there I was, thin and pale and weak as hell, but alive. It was something, really something!

Well, I stayed up there in Mesa Grande for another month or two or maybe a little more. I was still trying to get my strength back and to get my arm so I could use it again—which, you can see, I managed. I saw my kids regularly, though I wasn't staying with their mother. We had split up two years before. She had always been against me being with the guerrillas, and she told me, "You don't love me anymore. You've got some other women over there in the monte." And I told her, "Damn, it isn't like that. I'm there because I've got to fight for our country. That's why I'm not here with you." She didn't believe me. And then one time I'm up there and I hear that she's started up with someone else. You know how it is: there's hundreds of new faces in a new place, and so she started up with one of them. It wasn't out in the open; she wasn't living with the new guy. And he made himself scarce when I was there. He was afraid I might do something to him. I didn't. I saw the situation, and I said to her, "Let's come to some agreement. You take Pacita and our baby son, and I will take Chico. Not now. I might get killed, and then Chico won't have anywhere to go. But when the war is over and things have calmed down, then Chico goes with me." She agreed to that, and that's how we left it. And me, bueno, I didn't want to be alone, so I started up with someone else. Meches. She wasn't someone I loved so much, not like I had loved Flora, my ex-wife. But she was someone I could spend some time with when I was in the refugee camp.

Anyway, I was up there in the camp recuperating for a while, and then soon as I felt myself strong enough again, I went back to the monte. I was still able to be active and contribute—sometimes heading a platoon to go transport supplies and sometimes going by myself to give lectures to new recruits. They used me for that since I had had a lot of experience, and I was able to talk to the guys and educate them some, you know, explain what it was we were fighting for and how we had to go on fighting. I liked doing that, the educating stuff. Anything I could contribute, I was willing to do. The thing I refused to do was join in the "final offensive." That's how it was called. Remember? In 1989. The idea was for us guerrillas to storm the capital city, San Salvador, and win a decisive battle. I figured it was a bad idea, that we would lose that battle. We were accustomed to fighting in the monte; there we could hold our own. In the city, hell, we didn't have experience there, and the enemy was real comfortable fighting there and well equipped. People came and tried to talk me into it, but I was in a position to refuse. And I did. I told them it was going to fail. And it did. One of our leaders, the commander who was leading the entire final offensive, this guy got killed at the beginning of the battle. From then on we were in trouble. Even though we hit them hard all over the city and we showed them we could attack them where they were strongest, after three weeks the whole thing was over. We saw that there was no way of taking the capital. It didn't work. It was a bad idea, just like I figured.

But what did work, you could say, is that from then on people all over, in the United States, the United Nations people, they could see that some kind of negotiations were going to have to take place to end the war. We couldn't win it, but we couldn't be defeated either. And you began to hear about talks going on between our leaders and theirs and with international people in between. Me, I was still in the monte then, but I figured the time had come for me to go back to Mesa Grande and pick up my boy. When I got to the camp, the United Nations people told me that if I wanted, they could get me a visa to go to Canada or Australia; but, they said, I couldn't take any family with me, I had to go alone. Hell, I wanted no part of that. All I wanted was to settle again in my own country—with my family! So I told the international people no. And then, just like I had told my wife I was going to do, I went and picked up my boy. He was real attached to me and glad to see that I had come to get him. I didn't take my new woman. Just Chico. He was six years old then. I took him with me and took him around in the monte, where I was still giving lectures and helping transport supplies. Sometimes I had to leave him someplace for a while. Always I put him to stay with some trusted compas, and then when I could I'd come back and take him with me. That's how we did it for a year or so like that. I don't think he minded too much. Like I say, he was real attached to me—always has been. Maybe ask him, no? He's twenty-six years old now, a lawyer. He turned out good, real good.

It was while we were still in the monte that we heard that the negotiations had become real serious. People were saying that some kind of peace accords were around the corner. I had my doubts. We had been fighting those bastards for years. I knew they wanted to finish us off. And the truth is, militarily we had no way of beating them; they had airplanes, and we didn't. But politically their side was weak. And in the end they had to come to an agreement, like it or not. I took Chico back with me to Santa Marta. That's where all my family was. They'd left the refugee camp and come back to El Salvador, to this place in Chalatenango. My new woman, Meches, was there too, along with our two other kids. Yes, right, I didn't mention that. I had had a couple of kids with her by then. And my ex-wife and two other kids were up there too. I stayed there in that awful place for a few months with them. Nasty! Dark and crowded. I didn't want to be there. I began looking for a better place, and since I had compas over in the area of Suchitoto, I went looking there. A guy I knew, Joaquín, he was in the area of Mount Guazapa. He and I had been on missions together. A clever guy. He was busy trying to get some of our people, FMLN people, to come over to the area near Mount Guazapa and repopulate there. Nothing was clear right then, but he figured—and in the end he was right—that we had to repopulate as soon as possible to be sure that in the negotiations that land would be ours and not stay with the big landowners. I liked the spot. It was fairly empty back then. You had lots of open space and water, and the place had trees, not like in Santa Marta. So I went back to Meches and Chico and I said, "We're going there. That's where we're going to settle in."

And that's what we did. There were only a dozen or so families at first. The landowners, the Morales, still had the title to the land. The area where they had their main house had been destroyed. Bombed. The Fuerza Armada must have hit the whole area with their air force, because some of our guerrilla units had occupied it for a time. I don't know exactly, but the place was all rubble over there in the *ciudadela*, right where we've got the school these days.[1] It was a mess back then when we first got there. We stayed there for a couple of months till we were given some building materials—boards and laminated metal and plastic—and then we moved out to where we are now. For a while we didn't know if we'd be able to stay, because the negotiations were going on, and they were real tough. But the way we figured—like Joaquín had said—better to repopulate it soon, and then we'd have a good chance of staying.

And sure enough, in the end the negotiations did go our way. I mean, we were allowed to stay. It was complicated, but yes, we were given some of the land here. Sixty-five manzanas. Yet it was part of the agreement that we guerrillas had to turn over all our weapons, destroy all our armaments. We were still armed when we came to the community here, but the deal was that we had to be fully demobilized. The FMLN was recognized as a legal political party. And all of us guerrillas had to destroy our weapons, just as all the soldiers of the Fuerza Armada had to return to their bases and stop any further actions against us. That was the deal. Some people still had their doubts, but I was hopeful.

So the way it went is that all of us guerrillas here in Comunidad Guazapa and all those in the surrounding communities agreed to come over to the ciudadela and bring every weapon or piece of equipment we had. We had to empty our storehouses. Up on Mount Guazapa, deep in the tunnels, we had all kinds of weapons—mines, rockets, rifles, bullets.

We had to bring it down to the ciudadela. Even our uniforms. Everything. We had to put it in a pile and then watch a bulldozer roll over it all. Smaaash! Like they were a bag of onions. For a lot of the men, this was hard to watch. The weapons were our protection, the rifles were like your mate. And in one moment it was smashed. I'm telling you, some of the men were crying. I swear, these guys who had gone through hell, tough guys really, they stood there crying. Me? No, not then. I wanted the war over. I'd had enough.

What was hard for me was what happened later that day after we watched everything get smashed. The deal was that after the turning over of our weapons, we were all taken in a truck to a place in Suchitoto. Not just us. Men and women from all over the area, hundreds of compas. Some of these people you knew for years. Some were from my own platoon. We came to say farewell to each other, since we were from different parts of the country, and now some were going one way and some were going another way. It was a sad scene, having to say good-bye to these people. They were your family all those years, since you seldom got a leave during the war to go visit your wife and children. The rest of the time your compas were the ones who watched over you, and you watched over them. Now they were going their own way, and who knows if you'd ever see them again. No, hombre, it was not easy to watch them go off. Real sad. But I kept telling myself, well, at least the war is over. Finally over. And now we can take up life again as civilians. Go back to farming. Start again in our new community. And that's good. Real good!

CHAPTER FOUR

Jorge
Julia's Father

Literally a stone's throw from Julia and Luis's house is the similar though somewhat larger and better-furnished house of Julia's parents, Jorge and Mari. There are fewer children about the place these days than there were twelve years ago when we first met them. Almost all, like their oldest daughter, Julia, have moved out to places of their own. But Jorge seems much the same as he did when we first met him: still with hair like steel wool and a pot belly, still ill kempt and eschewing social graces, and still preferring to wear tattered pants, no shirt, and no shoes as he sits on the veranda or as he saunters about his front yard with the chickens, ducks, horse, and cow—or now, as he sits in his hammock in front of two tape recorders talking about his life.

Jorge is the same age as Luis, give or take a year. And both come from the same northern district of Cabañas. Apart from this, however, the two men could not be more different. While Luis is an extroverted political activist who wholeheartedly threw in his lot with the guerrillas, Jorge shied away from involvement and, one gathers, participated for only one year as a courier with the FMLN during the war. And while Luis is a raconteur with an undeniable taste for gossip, Jorge prefers one-sentence answers and has an equally undeniable distaste for gossip. The latter trait, of course, is admirable under some circumstances, though not to us in our role as interviewers. In sum, it took us a handful of lengthy sessions to finally hear from Jorge some of his life story—his boyhood, his marriage to Mari, his experiences during the war, and his work as a campesino.

Jorge acknowledges—and those who know him concur—that he is and always has been most content when working in his milpa. There, working first with his father and then with his sons, he has year after year proved

43

himself to be a fine farmer and today is one of the most successful farmers in the community. Year after year he has had good harvests. And that,
together with his wife's small income and with the remittances they receive
from their four sons who have gone as *mojados* to the United States, has
enabled Jorge and Mari to establish a standard of living for themselves
somewhat better than that of many others in the community.[1] But predict-
ably, Jorge hesitates to talk of such things, including mention of the small
truck that sits conspicuously in his front yard.

Thus, what follows is Jorge's story, or at least those fragments that we
were able to glean from his expurgated reminiscences.

I'm not so good at talking, you know. My wife talks better. But all right, I'll
go along with it, if you think I've got something to tell you. So what do you
want to know? The truck? No, it's nothing. I've had it for a little while. It's
useful at times, that's all. It's nothing. I don't know how to drive it. One
of my sons knows; he's the one who drives it. No, no, we had nothing like
that when I was a kid. You were lucky just to have a few animals, that's all.

These days, I'm not doing much. I've got the milpa all cleaned, I'm
ready to go. You can't do anything until the rain comes, maybe in another
two weeks. Then I'll be busy again. Sowing the maíz and frijol. You get
started around May, and then you've got your hands full for the next eight
or nine months. Me and a couple of my sons who work the milpa with
me. Meanwhile, there's not so much to do. Me and some other fellows
from the community here are working at straightening the road, clearing
out some boulders. Got some supplies from the municipality of Suchitoto, gravel and some cement. We work in the mornings, volunteer work.
That way the dirt road from here in the community to the main road will
be passable when the rains come. I don't mind it, no, not at all. Keeps me
busy until I get back to the milpa.

[Jorge suddenly jumps up from the hammock, grabs a stick, and starts
shouting at two goats that have come into the yard and are over at the
kitchen trying to grab a tortilla. "Damn goats," he mutters. "They belong to
my neighbor, and they keep coming in here looking for something to eat,
damn them!" He then sits down again in the hammock, fidgeting with
the stick and obviously far more interested in the goats than in the tape
recorders. Finally, munching on a tortilla himself, he says he is ready "to
get back to the talking stuff."]

Me, I'm from Cabañas, same as most of the people here in the community.
Same as Luis and the others. Or actually, I was born in Chalatenango,
over where my grandfather—my father's father—had his land. About ten
manzanas is what he had. Then, when I was a boy still, we got some land

over in Cabañas, and we moved over there, near the Lempa River. Yes, sure, I worked with my father. I'm the oldest. There's me, three younger brothers and a sister. No, none of us went to school. What for? There was no point to it. Some kids around there went, but what good did it do you? You couldn't eat from it. None of us brothers went. Soon as you were big enough to grab a machete you went off to work in the milpa. My brothers and me and my father or sometimes just us boys and my mother. Because, you see, my father had a certain liking for his *guaro*, and when he'd tie one on he'd be out of it for a couple of weeks, him all happy but not working, and my mama taking care of him, feeding him soup until he came out of it, and then when he'd be sober again she'd curse him out. But those times when he was drunk, which was now and then, my mama and us boys would work without him.

We worked hard, sunrise to sunset. The soil wasn't all that good up there, but you could grow your maíz and maicillo, mostly maicillo, and also sesame; frijol no, the land wasn't good for that. So the tortillas we ate were made usually from maicillo, but look, you ate what you had, no? And we had other stuff to eat. We had our chickens, and some pigs, and a cow that gave us milk to make cheese. And my father and me, sometimes we'd go fishing down in the Lempa River. We'd use a line with a hook or a net, depending on what was running that day. We'd catch us some bass and catfish, or we'd catch crayfish and crabs and sometimes a whole bunch of what we call *platiadas*, you know, those little fish that you fry up. We'd take whatever we caught and bring it back and share it with the whole family. The rivers were good to us poor people back then. Today, the rivers don't give you hardly anything; the fish are gone, maybe because of the war and all the bombs that fell in the rivers, or maybe the fertilizer has run into the rivers and killed them. No, there's no fishing in the Lempa these days like there was back when I was a kid. Anyway, besides the fishing, we also did a little iguana hunting. There were plenty where we were living, and in the winter they got real fat, and sometimes we'd catch us two or three. In the summer, say, February and March, the iguanas go lay their eggs, hiding them real well, but we might catch one that still had her eggs inside, and so we had both the eggs and the iguana to eat. Those eggs were good—different from chicken's eggs, but tasty. And with the iguanas, we'd roast them over the fire. Or my mama would make a soup out of them—a soup she made with toasted maíz that you grind up and toss into the soup together with the pieces of iguana. I used to really like eating iguana, but today not much. Maybe I stuffed myself with it too many times back then. Can't touch the stuff today, I can tell you that.

I must have been eighteen years old—I think it was around then—that I caught a look at the woman over there. [Jorge points in the direction of the kitchen where his wife, Mari, is making tortillas.] She must have been fifteen or thereabouts. She was living in the same hamlet as us, a little ways off, and I'd see her going about now and then. I put my eye on her. I don't know if she was putting her eye on me. But I figured to go talk with her parents, her father really, and he said it was fine by him, so I talked to her, and she agreed to get together with me. No, we had no wedding or any of that. She just came to our house, where I was living with my parents, and she moved in with me. I guess it was fine with my parents, I don't know. They didn't say anything one way or the other. Mari just moved in, and that was it. She helped my mama out, and I went on working like always with my father.

About a year later Mari gave birth. In June, forty years back. She gave birth to Julia, the one who lives down below. That day Mari was working with my mama, and suddenly she said the kid was about to come out. I went running to fetch the partera, who was about half an hour away. We came back fast as we could. The partera went right into the house. I can't say exactly how it went. Men stayed outside the house, just waiting to hear. And pretty soon the partera came back outside, told me everything is fine and that I had a daughter. Vaya pues, if that's what we had, then that's what we had. You accept what comes, even if it's a girl, verdad?

My mama took right to the kid. It was her more than anyone else that took to feeding the little one, holding her and cleaning her up. And so the kid, Julia, took to my mama. That's the way it is, right? The kid takes to the one who's feeding them or rocking them and all that. And pretty soon my father came to me and said, "Look here, Jorge, we're going to keep this one." My sister was the only daughter my parents had, and she had already moved out of the house. My mama figured she wanted another girl to grow up with her. You know, someone to help her out later as the kid grew up. I didn't see any problem with it, and it was all right with us. It wasn't like we gave her away and that was the end of it. She was still our daughter, but a year or so later, when Mari and me moved into another house not too far away from my parents' house, Julia stayed with my parents. And that's the way it went. She's our daughter, but she was always together with my parents. She's the only one. The rest of our kids grew up in our house.

Me and Mari's father got along well. So one day he comes to me and says, "Jorge, how about you and me starting up a liquor still?" Lots of folks out where we were living were making their own liquor. It was illegal, but folks were doing it anyway, trying to make a little money out of it and, sure, drinking a bit themselves. I wasn't too hot on the idea, but I told him, "Vaya pues, I'll go along with you." It's nothing difficult to do. Anyone can do it. You just grab a sackful of maíz, and you put the sack in a bucket of water. In twenty-four hours you pull out the sack, and already each kernel has swollen up and sprouted a small green shoot. You take that swollen maíz and toss it into a clay container together with a bunch of sugar and water, let it set there fermenting for another day, then dump the water and repeat the whole business for another day. And then you've got your *chicha*. Now if you want to make some real guaro, what we call *agua ardiente*, you've got to boil up your chicha and put a tube into the boiling container that catches the steam and drips it out into another container, and then you've got your agua ardiente.

Me and Mari's father did this for a couple of months, but I didn't like the idea. I figured all I'm going to have from this is trouble. We sold some liquor, made some money, but you had to put that money back into buying more sugarcane. It wasn't worth it, I figured. No real money from it, and there was always the threat of the Guardia coming around, and if they caught you, well, you'd be in some trouble because, like I say, it was against the law. We didn't get caught. At least not while we had our still. Only later. We got caught because of my uncle, my father's brother. He had his still, and someone must have tipped off the Guardia, because they came looking for him one day. Now this uncle of mine, Oscar, had two women, one living right near us, and one living on the other side of the Lempa. So one day the Guardia shows up, they pass in front of my house, and they ask if I know Oscar. "Yes, sure," I said. "Where does he live?" they say. "Up in the house over there," I tell them. But when they get to his house—it was early, like, six in the morning—and they knock on the door, he wasn't there. They sit there waiting awhile, and then his woman, the one he had living on our side of the river, she shows up. And they start questioning her. "You know this Oscar, no?" "Of course," she says. "He lives here with me." "And where's he right now?" they say. "I reckon," she says, "since I was just out chasing after a calf that got away down by the river, so if you ask me, I reckon he's over on the other side of the river. He's got a woman over there too."

So the Guardia decide to just hang around, and when he finally came back they were out of sight. His woman couldn't tip him off, and Oscar, he goes up to his still and has a drink or two, and right then the Guardia show up on him. He starts running off, but they catch him. And this uncle of mine, he gets taken to court and winds up spending six months in prison. And me, I get tagged with a fine. Even though I told the Guardia that I had shut down my still months before and that I was willing to show it to them, but no, they didn't want to see or hear anything. They just started beating on both me and my uncle. Real nasty. They whacked us all over our bodies, even in the face. We were purple from it. In a way I got away cheap. I got hit with a fine of 150 colones. But I didn't get tossed into jail like my uncle, who in a way got away cheap compared to what they might have done to him.

Like what happened to Mari's father just a little after what happened to us. They killed him. Shot him dead, right in the Lempa River. It never should have happened. My father-in-law and me no longer had our still, but he liked his drink, and on the day he got shot he was walking around drunk, and he was also carrying a pistol. The Guardia came looking for someone else who they knew was running a still. That guy saw them coming and ducked behind the house, while my father-in-law didn't see them till they were close by. Instead of just staying where he was, he started running off, figuring they might confiscate his pistol, I reckon. He ran to the river, tried to swim across, and the Guardia figured that he was the one with the still—even though my father-in-law was thin and the guy with the still was fat—they didn't know who looked like what, and they shot my father-in-law in the river. It was a complete mistake. But what could you do? The Guardia walked away, and Mari and her family were left without a father.

A little while after that happened, my father and the rest of my family decided to move down to San Vicente. No, it wasn't because of the Guardia or that stuff. My father had other reasons that made him want to move. Up in Cabañas where we were, it was a day's walk just to get to the nearest town. My father had been down in San Vicente, and he liked it there. There was a town called La Cruz Verde, and my father figured that by selling the land we had in Cabañas we could get a place to live, separate houses for him and my mama and for me and my kids and for my brother and his new woman too. And we could get us some land right near the town. That's the main reason we decided to move. Yes, yes, it's true there was some kind of family problem going on, though I can't say exactly what it was about. Some problem in Mari's family, as I recall. It was a problem, I think, involving some woman, but I didn't put my nose into those things, so I can't tell you exactly what it was. But it wasn't because of this thing that my father wanted to move. It was to live in a place near town. Which is what we did. We got our houses right on one of the main streets, and that way you could buy and sell things real easy. Much better, we figured, than where we were living in Cabañas.

And it worked out for us—at least for a while. Me and my father working the milpa near the town, and a couple of my kids started going to some school. Wasn't bad in the beginning. What we hadn't counted on— how could you have known, verdad?—is that soon enough you began to have political stuff happening there in San Vicente. This was sometime in, let me see, in the late seventies. It happened like this. My father and I, during the summer when we weren't working in the milpa, we'd go cut sugarcane in one of the fincas there in San Vicente. You didn't get paid much, three or five colones, depending on which finca you were working on and really depending on whatever the owner wanted to pay you. You had to earn that money in order to get through the year, because our four manzanas didn't provide us with any extra money to buy things for the house—sugar, salt, coffee, a little clothing, some sandals. So we worked cutting cane for a few colones a day. Dawn till noon, we worked. You knew you were just handing over your labor like for nothing, but you figured you had no choice. What else could you do? Bueno, then what happened—a year or two after we were there—was that one day when we were all heading over to the sugarcane fields, some folks stopped us. Organizers. I don't know who they were exactly, some campesinos like us it seemed, and they said, "Look, this coming Monday when you get to the sugarcane fields, you tell the boss you're not working unless they pay you fourteen colones. Refuse to work, you hear!" Well, we figured, why not try it. And so when we get there that day and the mandador tells us to start working, we tell him, "Not today. Not unless we get paid fourteen colones." The mandador went and got the owner—actually the owner's son, since the owner was someplace else that day. And the son tells us, "Look, my papa isn't one of these rich landowners. He can't pay you that." But the boy knew that he had to get us to work, not lose the day, so he offered us nine colones. We refused. Then, after some negotiating, we agreed on eleven colones. And that's what we got paid that day, and even when the owner came back, we went on getting our eleven colones through that harvesting time. Later, I heard that on other fincas in the area, where the owners were rich as hell, the workers did get their four-teen colones.

You see, that's how it started. Us going on strike, us getting paid a little better than before. And some of these organizers began having meet-ings, hidden meetings, which we went to. You went but you didn't tell no one you were going, since you didn't know who would open their mouth about your going. My father and me, we both went. It was there I began hearing things I'd never heard before. Things like, "La tierra es de quien la trabaja" [The land belongs to the one who works it], and how we work-ers had to get together, get organized, and we had to fight for our rights. What happened, just like we were suspecting it would, is that the Guardia and groups like El Orden came along and started looking for the organiz-ers and anyone else they figured was involved.[2] Soldiers started patrolling the streets, and you even had airplanes circling overhead on some days. One time I was at the market, the weekly market where you could sell things. I'd gone to sell a cow and two calves I had. Shortly after I get there with my animals, three trucks of soldiers arrive, firing their rifles into the air. They round up all of us there in the market, even the women selling fruit drinks, and they start checking everyone's papers, looking for some-one to haul away. Nobody got hauled away that day, but it was getting dangerous, I'm telling you. And soon after that I'm in the house at night, the middle of the night. Mari and my kids were there. We were all asleep, and suddenly I hear this hard knocking on the door, and then someone shouting, "Señor, open the door!" And I answered, "I don't know who you are, but look here, in the middle of the night I don't open the door for nobody." "It's the Guardia," one of them shouts. "We're just watching over your house. Don't worry about anything. Just open the door. We'll finish quickly, we're just registering the house. Now open up!" "All right," I say, "I'll let one person in, that's all." I'm standing there thinking these fools are about to kick in the door. I open it, one of them comes in, and he starts with questions. "Where are you from? Let me see your identity card." I show him, and then he says, "It says you're from Cabañas. How long have you been here?" "About two years now," I say. "And why did you come here?" he says. I tell him about my father's decision to move, to buy land here, to live nearer to a town instead of deep in the countryside. And he nods his head and then starts asking me about some guy, Jaime López. He doesn't tell me that they've already killed this guy, who was one of the people organizing the strikers. "You know him?" he asks. "I don't know him," I say. "Never heard of him." He asks a few more questions, and I answer that I don't know about this guy or anyone from his family. And that's it. I don't know if he believed me or not, but he handed me back my identity card and left.

This is what was happening in those days. The Guardia watching over us, and then some mornings you'd wake up, and you'd find a dead body or several dead bodies lying in the street. They weren't people I knew. I reckon they were from places near La Cruz Verde, because folks we did know from town began disappearing, and then their bodies were dumped in other places. By then, me and my father took to sleeping in the hills at night. We'd work in the days, Mari or one of the kids would bring us food, and we'd go deep into the hills to sleep. We were scared that at any moment, any night, the Guardia or some other group would show up, and we'd be hauled off, and that would be the end of it.

Hell, how could you go on living like that? My father and I figured we'd better get out of La Cruz Verde before something happened to us. We decided and we went real quick one day. My father managed to sell a small piece of land, enough to rent us a truck to take us out of there. We wanted to go back to Cabañas, where we came from, but we had heard there were problems there too by that time. So we headed for Honduras. We loaded up our truck with whatever we had—all the kids, the beds, cooking stuff, and a cow. Yes, a cow. And good thing we had the cow with us, because when we got to the border of Honduras, you know, they don't use colones. You had to have Honduras money, lempiras, and by selling the cow—real cheap, we had to let her go for—we got a few hundred lempiras from some

Honduras person, and we were able to make it into Honduras and buy us some food on the way. No, we didn't have any trouble crossing the border at that time. Others did, yes, I know. But for us it was easy, no problems. We crossed over, and when we heard about the refugee camp up there, we reckoned that was the best place for us to head for.

We were up there in Mesa Grande seven years. From '80 to '87. I suppose you've heard about the place, verdad? Lots of folks crowded together. But you didn't go starving there. The international people running the place took care of us. They had it set up real well. You had seven different camps up there, and each camp had its own directorate. No, I never got involved in any directorate stuff. I worked. Look, you didn't just sit around all day doing nothing. Kids went to school, and if you were old enough, an adult, you worked. At all kinds of things. Making furniture, or cooking utensils, or clothing or shoes or hammocks. Everyone according to what he could do. I made hammocks for a while, and I worked in the chicken coops for a short time too. Nasty, dirty work, with those chickens. I didn't care for that. I moved over to the group that was growing vegetables. That I liked. Tomatoes, onions, cabbage, radishes, lettuce—we grew all those things in the plots we had up there. The vegetables were brought to a place where they passed the stuff out to the families. You'd go once a week to this distribution place, and you'd get your weekly supply of maíz—five pounds per family. And you'd get rice and frijol and whatever vegetables we'd be growing then. And the international people brought in other things like bananas and watermelons and oranges. We ate real fine up there.

Besides working, if you wanted to, you could go to classes up there. Mari went. And I gave it a try too. I didn't know my letters then, and I learned a few, how to write my name and to read and write a little. But it doesn't come to you when you start late. Today, if you ask me, I hardly remember a thing. Mari knows a bit more. Me, no, not much. What else did I do up there? Well, we got married by the church, me and Mari. We had built a church out of adobe up in Mesa Grande, and one day a monseñor came visiting. He told the people that if they had children, then they ought to be married. Mari and me agreed. I'm a Catholic, and I reckoned the priest was right about all that. So we got married. Not just us. Maybe sixty other couples too. One big wedding for all of us. We wore our good clothes, and if I remember, Mari was wearing white. [Jorge looks off to the kitchen and yells, "Hey, Mari, you were wearing a white dress when we got married up there in—" And before he finishes the sentence, Mari booms back, "No, no! No white dress! Regular clothing, that's all."] Anyway, that's how it was, a huge bunch of us getting married. No, there were no cakes or celebrations.

You just went back to your house like any other day—except now you were married, that's all.

While we were up there, people from the FMLN—Luis and others—were coming by now and then doing recruiting for the guerrillas. They'd sneak in at night, because if the Honduras soldiers saw them, they'd have shot them. They'd stay a few days and then sneak back out with recruits. Me, no, I didn't go join the guerrillas. Nobody came asking me to join, and I figured to stay in the refugee camp. My two oldest kids, Julia and Marcos, went off and joined. Julia stayed with the guerrillas the longest. She went off when she was fourteen. Ask her what she did, because I'm not aware of all of it. My oldest boy, he went off when he was thirteen. He was with the guerrillas for a while, but he got caught by the Fuerza Armada, and he wound up fighting on their side. He tried to escape and managed it, but then he got caught by them, and they threw him into a jail cell, and they really messed him up. Later, much later, he told me what he went through, the hell they put him through. He was lucky to survive it. It took balls to get through it, he told me.

Me, I didn't get involved with the guerrillas until after we left the refugee camp and went back to El Salvador. To a place called Santa Marta. We were up there for four or five years. It was an area controlled by the FMLN, and a lot of folks from the refugee camp came back down there to live. Me and my family didn't have any land of our own. Some folks managed to get their own milpas. Not us. What I did was work in a cooperative organized by the FMLN. Many of us campesinos were working together on that large farm—growing maíz, maicillo, frijol. We took our harvests to the storehouse, and the way it worked was that each family got their weekly supply from the same storehouse. According to how many kids you had, that's how they handed it out. Pretty much the same way it had been up in the refugee camp, except you didn't have so much in the way of vegetables or fruits. But you got by, you managed.

Apart from farming, there was a year or so when I was working with the FMLN as a courier. We had our people, the guerrillas, way up in the hills. Santa Marta was a hilly place, and we had to supply our forces with all kinds of things. Food, munitions—that type of thing. I never got involved carrying munitions. Only food. Huge containers of cooked rice, bottles of cooking oil, batches of tortillas and frijol. Everything cooked. We'd go at night in groups of maybe forty men, maybe once or twice a week. This was near the end of the war that I was doing this. It was still a little dangerous, but me, I never had any problem. We had a guide who knew the paths up through the hills, and we were told that if we ran into soldiers, well, you were supposed to drop what you were carrying and take off fast as you could into the hills. Nothing like that ever happened to me.

[Jorge pauses and nods in the direction of the other side of the veranda, where Mari is lying in a hammock.] That lady over there had a problem, some kind of close call, once or twice. I don't know the details, not all of them anyway. Ask her, she'll tell you, I reckon. But me, no problems that year I was working as a courier. And after that, bueno, they were signing the peace accords, and the war was over.

After that, it was in '92, we heard about some of our people who were starting up a new community—a few of them—way over near Mount Guazapa. My brother went to see what was happening, and then my father and me went and had a look. The place was nice enough, not crowded and not so hot like up in Santa Marta. They didn't have anything over there, no houses, nothing. But my father said he liked the place, and I did too. He and my mama and Julia and her kids went down there, and I guess it must have been a month or so later that me and Mari and our kids went too. Luis was involved in organizing a lot of this since he'd gone down with his family. They sent a truck to pick us up. We took whatever we had, a few beds and some cooking utensils and a little food, and we headed over there. Over here, I mean—where we are today. What is it, something like sixteen or seventeen years that we're here now? And like you see, it's worked out real well for us. No more moving about, real steady now.

I've got my milpa up in the foothills here. It's a walk of fifteen or twenty minutes. Up there is where I am each day. The land is real good. I mean, if you treat it the way you should, fertilizing and spraying it during the growing season and cleaning it real well at the end of the harvests, then you're going to get good crops. If you're lazy the way some folks are, then you don't do so well. But I was raised not to be lazy. You want to eat, then you work. I like it. Staying busy in my milpa. You've been up there, no? The air is real good up there, something pure. And you don't have all the commotion going on like radios or TVs or just plain commotion like you've got in the house. A person who just hangs around the house, he's going to start thinking about this or that, rotten thoughts maybe. Up in the milpa, a person's got his mind on his work and isn't bothered by anything. And if you work the land well, and if you've got good luck that year, then you're going to do well. I mean, you've got to have good luck. You can do things the right way, but without luck—without God's will—then you're not going to have anything. That's the way I see it. Without God looking after you, there isn't going to be anything for you. No life even, because He's the one who gives us everything. And the way I see it, He's been good to us. We're doing pretty good these days. Sí, hombre.

CHAPTER FIVE

Julia

The Early Years

At forty years old, Julia is Jorge's oldest child. For the past sixteen years, she has been *ajuntada* with Luis. Although Julia was born only a few kilometers away from Luis's village of Talpetates, and although she also fought as a guerrilla in many of the same locales as did Luis, they did not come to know one another until each moved separately to Comunidad Guazapa. ("I had my eye on her up in the monte, but only from a distance," claims Luis. "She never looked my way.") Still trim and pretty, with bright hazel eyes, Julia has a rather soft-spoken, understated manner. And, quite the opposite from Luis, who has a flair for oratory, she prefers to speak in short, clipped phrases and in an unflappable tone that seldom changes, no matter what the subject might be.

In her manner and speaking style Julia has not changed at all since we met her twelve years ago. What has changed, however, is that Julia has become—at least with us—more open than she was when we first met her. As a result, much of what she says here (and in a subsequent chapter) is more frank and revealing than what she had told us years ago. This reflects, in part, the many visits we have continued to make to Comunidad Guazapa over the years. But perhaps no less important in enabling her to talk freely was the decision we made this time to interview her twice away from the community—in nearby Suchitoto and in the capital, San Salvador—and therefore far from the crowd of children and relatives as well as the no less vociferous roosters, turkeys, goats, and dogs that continue to be omnipresent on her veranda and in the front yard.

In this chapter Julia recalls some of her childhood experiences, her decision to join the guerrillas when she was thirteen years old, and much of what happened to her during the subsequent nine years that she spent in the monte. "I was lucky, it all worked out pretty good for me," she now says. "And looking back, it was worth it—for sure. Though for some others in my family and Luis's family it was real costly—yes, real hard on them."

Here, then, are some of Julia's recollections and reflections.

All those meetings you've had with my father, I tell you, now you know more about him than me. He's usually not the talking type. My mother, yes, she'll give you an earful if you let her. My father, no. Maybe with his friends sometimes, and maybe with my grandfather back when he was alive. They farmed together, and they had to communicate, no? But with his children, my father prefers to keep quiet. I mean, he'll yell at them, take a stick to them if he wants to, but he doesn't get into conversations. He comes back from his milpa, grabs a couple of tortillas and beans, and then he's taking a siesta in the hammock until he goes back to the milpa again. Truth is, I don't think I ever had a conversation with him in my life. Whatever I know about him I've heard from others—my mother or grandmother. With me he's never got into things.

The one who was like a real father to me was my grandfather Miguel. And my grandmother Cecilia, she was more like my mother than my own mother. How did that happen? Well, I can't say exactly how it came about, but the people who raised me were my grandparents, not my own parents. I grew up with them in their house. The way I heard it—Papito Miguel told me this—is that my mother and father were living together with them when they first got together. I don't know if they were married in the church or civil or nothing at all. I never asked. I just know that my mother was real young, like fifteen or sixteen, when she had me. And my parents were always fighting with each other, right from the beginning. My mother would then take off, carrying me with her, down to where her mother lived about a kilometer away. My grandmother Beatriz—right, my mother's mother—was living then with her own mother. And this lady was a foul-mouthed woman who was making her living by selling homemade liquor. This I saw with my own eyes later when I was older and occasionally went down there, and she would start chasing me away. I suppose she was worried I'd start talking about her liquor still. It was illegal, and, you know, kids see something and then they start talking about it. Anyway, according to my grandfather, back when I was a year old, something like that, my mother had gone down to her mother's place. She'd grabbed me with her. Papito Miguel came down a few days later to visit me, and he found me sitting there on the veranda all alone, drunks all about the place. My mother was nowhere to be found. My grandfather was real annoyed and snatched me up and took me back to his house.

A few days later my mother came back to live there too with my father, but from then on it was Papito Miguel and Mamita Cecilia who were like my real parents. And my parents moved out to a house of their own way up the hillside. That's where they raised my brothers and sisters.

I've asked my mother about the whole thing, but she doesn't like to talk about it. She'll fill you in on most things, but on that all she's ever said to me is, "It was your father's fault." I can't see how she allowed that to happen—and with her first kid! Look, I've got all these kids of mine, but there's no way I'd be giving one away. She must have been messed up in her mind at the time. All that fighting with my father. And her own father had just been shot around that time. Killed by the Guardia. They were the ones policing the countryside back then, and if they wanted to shoot you, they did. I never knew the man—he got killed when I was nine months old, they told me—but he was running a still. Making liquor just for himself, the way I heard it. Seems that someone put a finger on him, and the Guardia came to get him. He heard they were coming, and he took off. We were living close to the Lempa River, and he figured if he could swim across, then he could escape. He dived into the water with the Guardia firing at him, and him managing not to get hit while he was swimming underwater. When he came out the other side, hoping to get some air, he got hit. One shot to the head by a Guardia guy who was standing there waiting for him. Dead on the spot. From then on, my mother was without a father, and her mother, Beatriz, was raising the kids by herself in that house with drunks around and God knows what else going on. Me, I figure I was real lucky to have been snatched up by Papito Miguel and taken to live with them.

I liked Papito Miguel's and Mamita Cecilia's house. Real nice and big. My grandfather had made it with his brothers, you know, the old way, out of adobe. It had three rooms. My parents were in one of them until they moved out. And my grandparents and I were in another room. My grandmother and me slept in one bed, my grandfather in the other bed. You know, beds like you still see around these days—without mattresses but with cords strung on a wooden frame and a *petate* on top. No, we had no toilet or latrine. For that you'd go out in the fields a ways and do your business since nobody was living there. What I liked is that we had all this space around us, like two manzanas. Only one other house, my aunt's place, was nearby. And we had this huge *jocote* tree in front of the house. During the season, I'd go climbing up the tree and eat myself silly with jocotes. I loved them, and I had them all to myself.

At times, Sundays mostly, I'd go up to where my parents moved, and I'd play around with my brothers and sisters, who were coming into this world one after the other. And I'd see my parents once in awhile, like when my father might come in from fishing down in the river with Papito Miguel. Most of the time, though, I was alone with my grandmother doing things with her. She was real easy with me. She herself worked hard all day long. Cleaning up, making tortillas, doing laundry down by the river—all that housework stuff. I'd help by fetching firewood or going down to the river and getting jugs of water. In the mornings I'd let the cows out to pasture, and in the evenings I'd bring them back into our wooden corral. My grandmother was the one who milked them, since I was scared to do it, figuring one of them was going to kick me in the head. She'd take the milk and make cheese out of it, which we ate with our beans and tortillas. And she and my aunt's girl taught me how to make tortillas. "Someday you're going to have to learn this," she told me. "You might as well start now." I was about eight years old at the time. It takes awhile to learn how to make them just right. We didn't have one of these hand grinders like I've got today. Back then, you had only a stone slab and stone rolling pin. You'd take the maíz and crush it and then add water. That's the part you've got to adjust just right. Too much water, and the tortillas come out soggy, too little, and they're dried out. Then you work them around in a circle in your hand—right, you've seen me doing it all the time, no? Pat, pat, pat! Nice and circular, not too fat and not too thin. And then you've got to get the comal very hot, or else the tortillas will stick to it, and you don't want that happening. Simple enough, once you get used to it. And damn, all those tortillas I've made since then for my family and back in the monte for the platoon, I got it down real good now. I can't say I enjoy making them day after day, but my family tells me they come out just right.

School? Yes, I went a little. Not when we were living up in Cabañas out in the country. My grandmother didn't want me to go. And I was scared to go. There was some lady giving lessons in some other village, but you had to walk through the mountains to get there, and after trying it out a few times, I figured it wasn't for me. I didn't want to make that walk all by myself. So I didn't go to school until we moved to San Vicente. I was about ten years old then. I'm not real sure why we moved. I liked it just fine where we were. But one day, my father and Papito Miguel said we're going to be moving down to San Vicente. I understood that some kind of dispute was going on between either my father's family or my mother's family. I still don't know what it was about. All I know is that suddenly one day we were all off to San Vicente. My grandfather and father had bought some land down there, and my parents moved into one house with my four or five brothers and sisters, and me and my grandparents moved into a house nearby.

And that's how I got to go to school for a while. A fine school, with desks and a blackboard and nice lady for a teacher. It was right down the street from where we lived. I'd get up early in the morning, bring breakfast to my grandfather and father in their milpa, and then run off to school. I liked the learning, and I even liked playing baseball during recess. I never had done that before. I was good at it—really! I could hit real far. And I liked the learning part, reading and math and all that. I was figuring I'd learn a lot, maybe finish a number of years there. But no. This was 1979 or 1980, and the troubles were starting up then. My grandparents and parents didn't tell me what was going on. Though, of course, I knew something bad was happening and that maybe we were in some danger. Papito Miguel and my father weren't coming home at night, they were sleeping up in the hills. There was talk of people getting dragged away, beaten and even killed. And then one Sunday morning the head of our school was found in the street. Shot dead. Next day the school didn't open. It closed down. No teachers, no students, nobody.

Soon after that my family decided we better get out of there. We didn't have anyplace to go to then. We headed back north where we came from only to find that people were fleeing from there too. Seemed like there was no safe place anywhere. I guess my father and grandfather talked it over, and they decided we had to get out of El Salvador. They had heard there were refugee camps in Honduras run by some international people. Better to go up there for the time being, they reckoned. And so we were off again.

I don't think anyone was figuring at the time that they'd be spending the next six or seven years in Honduras cooped up in a refugee camp. No way. Me, I sure didn't have an idea like that. Soon as you got there you could see it wasn't going to be too good. There were several camps up there run by these international people, the United Nations people. We got put into one called Mesa Grande. Same one where Luis's family wound up, though I don't remember ever seeing him there. Not surprising, because there were a thousand or more of us living in that camp up there. It was like a jail, really. The whole place was surrounded by barbed wire, with Honduran soldiers making sure you couldn't go wandering about outside. Each family got a laminated tin house with a laminated tin roof. Hot, hot. And the whole area was packed earth, which turned real muddy whenever you got some rain. And it seemed like it rained all the time, much more than in El Salvador. You'd go sliding around in your sandals, getting stuck in that muddy mess.

Up there in the camp the international people gave you everything. They had this supply store, which you'd go to on Saturdays, wait on a long line, and they would give you your week's supplies. Maíz, frijol, eggs, cheese, sugar, salt, chicken—every family got a chicken once a week. And sometimes if they got hold of some bananas, they'd pass them out, and you'd have fried bananas in the morning. Everything, they gave you everything. Even soap to wash yourself in the showers they had up there. I can't say anything bad about how we were treated. No, not at all.

But for me, the only good part of being cooped up there is that I was able to go to school again in the afternoons. I was living with my grandparents, and in the mornings I'd help Mamita Cecilia make breakfast and then lunch. Then in the afternoons I'd go to the school we had there, a place run by teachers from El Salvador who'd fled just like us. These folks organized a school for the children who wanted to learn. I was one of them. I was, let's see, about twelve years old. I was put into third grade at first, and then I went into fourth grade. I learned math, science, language. That I really liked, and the teachers were serious, good at teaching. I even got to play baseball again, and, like I told you, I was pretty good at it. Hitting, that's what I liked. We had a team up there, and I was part of it.

But after a year or so up there, it got to be real boring for me. A kid thirteen years old can't take that so easy. It was like being in jail for me. I was looking for something more, something else to do. And what happened is that these FMLN people, guerrillas, they were up there in the camp giving lectures. The way they got there is that they put on civilian clothes, came in as refugees, and they'd spend a few days giving talks and recruiting people. Then they'd sneak out again. Me, I went to some of their talks. Up to then I can't say that I really understood why we had to flee El Salvador, I mean, nothing more than that it was dangerous. All the stuff about why there was fighting and killing going on, I didn't really know what the devil was happening, and my grandparents and parents didn't talk about it. So when I went to these talks I began to have some idea. I mean, I can't say that I understood a whole lot then. But it was obvious—like they told us—that we'd been forced out of our country and that we had a right to go back and live there. The way they put it was that we had to organize and fight; that was the only way we'd get to live in our country again. Besides, they told us we'd be free to move about, not stuck behind a barbed-wire fence. They even told us it would be fun. What did I know? I wasn't afraid, no. I don't know why. Five of my uncles, two on my father's side and three on my mother's side, were with the guerrillas. I figured, fine, I'm going to join too.

Now, if you were young like me, you weren't supposed to just take off and go back to the monte with them. The FMLN people went to your family and checked out if the parents were in agreement. Since I was living with my grandparents they went to them. To me, Mamita and Papito had been saying, "Don't go!" My grandma was worried she'd never see me again. She could see, though, that I was determined, and I guess she understood that one way or the other I was going to try to go. So when the FMLN people came my grandparents said, "Look, it's up to her. If she wants to go, let her decide." And that was it. I was set up to join.

The way the FMLN people did it is they planned your escape. You couldn't just walk out the front gate, right? The Honduran soldiers would have arrested you or shot you. The FMLN had guides who knew how to pull it off. It was a huge camp, and the guides knew when the Honduran soldiers would be out on patrol. You went at night. I went with a bunch of others. We crawled under the fence one by one, and then, keeping a good space between each one of us, we headed off into the hills. It took us several days, usually moving at night, until we got to a place called Los Naranjos. It was in El Salvador, in Chalatenango. The FMLN had a training camp there. And that's where we got inducted into the guerrillas.

I spent about a month there. You had basic training. Exercises and learning how to assemble and disassemble a rifle, M-16s, usually. Some of the young people were real good shots. Girls, too. They could hit a bull's-eye from way far out. I wasn't very good at it. I'd take aim, try to line it up just right, and I'd usually miss by a couple of hand lengths. So I wasn't made a combatiente. Instead, they assigned me to be a molendera. Me and three others were given this entire unit, maybe one hundred combatientes altogether, and we were the cooks for that bunch. I can't say I liked that work at all, but I wanted to contribute what I could.

For a year or so that's what I did, sometimes working as a molendera together with other girls and sometimes by myself with just one platoon of thirty or so combatientes. In the beginning, we didn't always have maíz to make tortillas. We hadn't got our supply chain worked out yet. How did we eat? Well, we'd steal. Mostly, at those times, we'd steal from houses when some of the compas knew that those families had men with the Fuerza Armada. We'd steal from them. You had to survive, right? Later, we had it organized, and we had regular supplies of maíz and frijol. Then we were all right. For us, the molenderas, it was nothing easy. You worked your butt off. Go try carrying pots around on your head while walking through the monte. And try starting a fire when you've just had some heavy rain. And when we were in spots where the Fuerza Armada might spot you, then you had to do your cooking in a trench. We had to make long canals from where we were cooking, cover them over, and in that way the smoke from our cooking would blow out far from us. Clever, right? But it took a lot of time and was a pain in the butt.

But it wasn't because of all that lugging pots and cooking that I decided, if I had a chance, to stop being a molendera. Fact is, I've never liked cooking. To this day I don't like it, even though my family likes the way I make tortillas. Back then I figured maybe I could contribute in some other way. Some of the girls were radistas, and I got to know real well the one in our unit. I used to talk to her, and she showed me how she worked. So one day I went to the commander of our unit and I told him, "I'm getting bored making tortillas every day. I want a change." And he said, "What do you want to do?" "I reckon I can be a radista," I told him. And he said, "What makes you think so?" I told him that his radista had been showing me how she did it. I told him that when I'd had free time I was watching and learning from her. "I like that work," I said. But then he began telling me that maybe I'd like to work as a nurse. "It's important work," he said. "Why don't you try that?"

What could I say? He was my commander, and he decided I should take a course in nursing, a short course of a week or so. Well, I went along with it, and sure, it was easy learning how to dress wounds and give injections. But it made me sick to my stomach, right to the point that it made me vomit. Others, they could fix a wound one minute and then go off and eat lunch. I couldn't. No way. So I went back to my commander and told him, "I can't do it. It's easy to learn, but it makes me vomit." "All right," he said. "You want to be a radista. I can see that. You'll have to take another course." "I don't really need a course," I told him. "Your radista has taught me everything, and I reckon I can already do it." "Oh really!" he said. "All right, I'll send you over to a small platoon that needs a radista, and we'll see how you do."

So that's how I became a radista, which is the way I worked with the guerrillas most of the time I was with them. Seven years as a radista, something like that. I liked the work. Better to be carrying the radio and a couple of sets of batteries on my back than to be lugging pots on my head and making tortillas. It was interesting work. You had to have a good memory for numbers. Somehow I did. What you did was send and receive messages by code between your unit and another unit. Say, a message like, "Remplago battalion is heading from Guarjila over to Las Flores." Every place and movement had a code. The codes were in numbers and letters. You had to memorize them from a code book. Thing is, every month or so the codes were switched. Most radistas were women. We'd meet together every month or two and discuss what we were doing, and then we'd switch the codes. Easy work as long as you had a good memory for that kind of thing.

Being a radista was a fairly safe job, it turned out. It wasn't like being a combatiente like Luis was. These days, sometimes he and I will talk about the war, and he can't imagine that I hardly ever had a close call, and I never got wounded. But that's how it was for me. Never got wounded. I was lucky. Some of those around me, they did get killed or wounded bad. As a radista, though, you are pretty well protected. You're back there with the commander of your platoon and maybe four or five armed guards with you. I didn't even have to carry a rifle. You're giving him the messages. The combatientes in your platoon, the scouts and those planting mines, they're the ones in real danger.

Only a couple of times or so, my unit had a close call. Once was right up above here, when my platoon was on the side of Mount Guazapa. Suddenly we saw that the Fuerza Armada was coming up from below, and then right above us, they had called in the air force to bomb us. Serious stuff. Those five-hundred-pound and one-thousand-pound bombs. We would have been finished off, except we had these deep, deep bunkers dug into the mountain. No way they could touch us in there. We survived with no problem.

The other time that my platoon almost got hit was when we were in the north and the Fuerza Armada had set up an ambush for us, for my platoon and another one that was with us. The way it must have happened is that there was an oreja in one of our units, and he had tipped them off. We were attacked by parachutists who had been flown in before, and they were waiting for us. My unit didn't have any casualties. The other platoon right to the side of us got hit bad. Five dead, including the commander and the radista. When the fighting was over and the parachutists were gone, we collected our dead compas. We dug a huge trench and buried them all there. We stood around for a moment of silence—that's how it was done—and then someone talked about each of the compas. You know, where each came from, a few words about their lives. That's all. Later, the families were informed. And the rest of us just went on. What else could you do?

For me, personally, one of the hardest things that happened was not anything to do with fighting or being attacked. It was getting pregnant. Yes, pregnant. Up there in the monte. It was a couple of years or so after I'd been up there. I had some kind of boyfriend. Nothing real serious, sort of a flash of light kind of thing. And the thing is, I didn't even know I was pregnant. Nobody ever told me what to expect. I was already a radista working with my unit, and then I started to feel sick. Nauseous and vomiting a lot. I remember going this one time to get something to eat, and after taking one look at it I was walking off empty-handed. An old woman there, a molendera, asked me what was wrong. When I told her, she said to me just like she knew, "Well, I reckon you've got it." I didn't catch on. And she said, "I reckon you're pregnant." I didn't pay much attention, since a few days later I was feeling better already. But then, a few months later, I could feel it inside me, something kicking me, and I remembered what the lady had told me. Well, that was real bad. Right about then, you see, our platoon was having a tough time. We were on the run every day, and sometimes we had to spend days at a time hiding out in some cave. We didn't have much to eat and hardly anything to drink during those days. And I was feeling real weak. So finally I went down to a hospital that we had in a safe town in Chalatenango. Not much of a place.

No real beds, but good doctors. And a few other girls like me, all pregnant. I didn't know what to expect. I just watched what they did, and when my turn came I did the same. Not too hard. In three hours or so the pains were over and my baby was born. Sad thing was, she was all sickly. You could see that right off. And me, I didn't have a drop of milk to feed her. Real sad. My baby wasted away day by day, and before she was two months old she was dead. Real sad. I told myself, no way I want to go through that again. Better to wait until the war was over.

That was my idea. And I did try to wait. I didn't get involved with anyone for a couple of years or so. The FMLN told us all in the beginning that it was best not to get involved with anyone. They didn't want couples getting hitched up, and then one of them might get killed, and then the other would take off and go home, quit the guerrillas. They even had a rule, seeing that people were getting hitched up anyway. They had this regulation that if you did start up with someone, then you or your partner got sent to another unit. Way off. You couldn't see each other every day, only once every few weeks if the commander gave you permission.

So how did I get started again? No, not at any party. Yes, we did go to fiestas once in awhile. Down in some safe town that the FMLN controlled they might be having a celebration of one kind or another. Truth is, I didn't care much for those things. I didn't go to the monte for fiestas. I don't like drinking liquor—no kind of liquor. But I did go sometimes to be with my friends. I never enjoyed it. What happened is that you had dancing that went on all night. I like dancing, though the way it was up there, well, there were hardly any women. You'd wind up dancing nonstop hour after hour right through the night. I felt exhausted by the end of it, and in the morning you had to walk a long way back to your platoon. Not much fun in that, not at all.

It wasn't at any fiesta that I met Carlos. It was at a meeting of various platoons where there was a presentation about something or other. Really, I didn't meet him. I just saw him, and he saw me. He was a machine-gunner with another platoon. The next thing I knew, I was getting letters from him. Quite often. He must have got permission from his commander to come pay me a visit, because one day he suddenly showed up. And that's how we started. Him visiting me, and me visiting him. You could only spend a day or two together, and you could only visit each other if nothing else was going on, no fighting, I mean. I had my own tent or lean-to, and he had the same. Your compas were good about it. They gave you privacy. We were together for a while and then it happened again. My second time—pregnant. I can't say I was happy about it. I didn't want to be having babies then. Though at least this time I knew what was happening and what to expect. I didn't discuss it with anyone. We women up there didn't go gossiping about these things. We kept it to ourselves.

Me, I didn't say anything. I just took a lot better care of myself and made sure to eat and drink enough. I kept going around the monte with my platoon, doing my work as a radista for three months or so, and then I went and told my commander. He was fine about it. He told me to go where it was safe. And by then I did have a place to go to. My parents had left the refugee camp in Honduras by then and made their way back to El Salvador, to a place called Santa Marta. It was a town controlled by our people, the FMLN. I went to my mother's house, and that's where I gave birth. Yes, in the house. A partera came, and she helped me deliver the child. Margarita. My oldest daughter, the one who just finished high school. She's nineteen years old now, going on twenty. She was born real healthy, and she's stayed that way since then. She's my first, a real good kid. Carlos never came and visited; he was in a unit way far off. I stayed with my mother about a year, since my grandparents were still up in Honduras. I figured that was it for me, no going back to my unit. I didn't want to leave my daughter.

Then I get word one day that my unit wants me back. Not as a radista, no. They need a molendera, I'm told. And they tell me, if I want, I can bring my baby with me. I thought about it real hard, and I decided, if they need me, I've got to go, especially since I was able to bring Margarita with me. I can't say I liked being a molendera this second time any more than I liked it the first time. Carlos came to visit me a few times, and we were sort of back together. That was all right with me. Then, maybe a year or so after getting back, I got pregnant again. Damn, I thought. I'm not ready for this. I'd got used to taking Margarita around with me, but no way I could be up in the monte with two kids. I knew then that for me the war was over.

As it was, by the time I gave birth to José, they were already negotiating the peace accords. I wasn't so confident that those negotiations were going to work. After nine years in the monte it was hard to imagine that the war would really be ending. But my time was over, that was for sure. I was living with my grandparents then. They had come back from Honduras, and I moved in with them in this shabby little place we had in Santa Marta. A whole lot of refugees were living there by then, everyone trying to figure how to start their lives again. We were all crowded together there in Santa Marta, one family on top of the other. So dark, you hardly ever saw the sun. Awful. And Carlos, well, he had gone elsewhere. He never came to see me or Margarita or José. To this day, he's never seen José. When I realized what was happening, that he'd gone off with someone else and was living with her, I went and told him, "Look, if you don't want to be with us, then go your way." Truth is, I didn't mind so much. "Just send me some money now and then for the children," I told him. Since then, I've never heard from him again. And he never sent me one centavo. I know where he lives up in Chalatenango. I've got a relative up there. I have no wish to see him. José, neither. Margarita went to see him a little while back for the first time. I guess she was curious. I don't know, I never discussed it with her.

As for me, I'm glad we were able to get out of Santa Marta. I couldn't see staying there much longer. A couple of years was about all I could take. Good thing that this uncle of mine came over here to Comunidad Guazapa, which, actually, had no name back then. It was just starting up. My uncle came over, took a look, and then came back and told us it looked like a good place. "Why not give it a try over there?" he said. So we all went—my grandparents, parents, some of my brothers and sisters, and me and my kids. Luis, too, as it turned out, though I didn't know him then. I was just glad to get out of Santa Marta and try my luck elsewhere. That's how I got here. Back in '92. I've been here ever since.

CHAPTER SIX

Joaquín

How the Land Was Won

Abutting the dirt-packed front yard of Luis and Julia's house and separated by a wire mesh fence to keep each other's chickens, roosters, and goats separate is the house and yard of Joaquín and his family. Joaquín is a short, barrel-chested, sixty-year-old man who looks like and evidently was one tough hombre. He and Luis were comrades in the guerrillas, and, according to Luis, they carried out a number of missions together; exactly which missions Joaquín will not say, despite occasional coaxing by his curious interviewers. What he will acknowledge—and with obvious pride—is that he was the organizer and founder of Comunidad Guazapa. It was Joaquín who prompted Luis to resettle in the community during the closing days of the civil war. And to this day Luis continues to be grateful to Joaquín for urging him to come and for all of his organizational efforts in helping Comunidad Guazapa get on its feet.

These days, Joaquín has returned to farming, and, similar to Luis, he is one of the community's political activists—a staunch supporter of the FMLN. He is also known as a well-read and contemplative man. "He's the smartest one we've got here," Luis insists. "A real intellectual. He knows about everything." Indeed, as one talks to this tough and somewhat sullen man, one notes that his style of speaking and recounting is quite different from that of others, carefully phrased analytical statements that seem to have been brewing in his mind for years. And what makes this even more remarkable is that Joaquín, like Luis and Jorge and all the other men of their age in the community, entered the guerrillas back in the late 1970s with no formal schooling and virtually illiterate. "I learned to read better

66

in the monte," he says, "and since then I devour whatever I can. That's my pastime—reading. A man can never know enough."

We interviewed Joaquín only twice, with the understanding that we would not write about his role in the guerrillas, his personal life, or his family. He agreed to tell us about his political and social views, and, most important (from our standpoint), he enthusiastically agreed to recall for us how Comunidad Guazapa was founded and his role in it. Sitting on the front porch of his veranda, dressed in sandals and short pants but shirtless, he sketched out this history in precise, even meticulous, detail. The emotional meaning of it for him only became clear at the end of the interviews when he told us, "I sit here today in wonderment. I struggled for this, believed we would win, but never thought I would see it. I am overwhelmed by what we have now. And to see what we have accomplished, one can feel in a dreamland—and sometimes I do feel that I am not quite awake with my feet on the ground. That's the truth."

Hence, a view of this "dreamland" from the founder: his hawk's-eye view of how the land of Comunidad Guazapa was won.

Luis told me you want to know how we got started, verdad? Bueno, I think I can fill you in on that. Might be that I get a detail wrong here or there, but I remember those days very well. So let's see, where to begin? The peace accords were signed on January 16, 1992, in Mexico. You know that, right? But we—I mean some of us in the FMLN—we had made a decision a couple of months before not to wait for the signing to start repopulating places like over here near Mount Guazapa. Better to get a grip on the land here, repopulate it with our people, so when the peace accords were signed, *if* they were signed, then we'd be in a better position to keep this land.

I say "if" because there were many of us, me included, who didn't really believe there was going to be peace. Why? Look, the Fuerza Armada had done whatever it could to kill us off. All those years they had been trying to destroy us, and I knew they hadn't changed their minds. It was the international community, Europe and the United States especially, that wanted the war over. The gringos had pumped a hell of a lot of money into the war, supporting the Fuerza Armada, and they realized that even with all that help the Fuerza Armada wasn't about to defeat us. So Reagan and the European leaders wanted the whole thing over, a negotiated settlement, I mean. The Salvadoran government was headed by Cristiani, a multimillionaire, and the gringos were pushing him to negotiate. But he was afraid to do it. It wasn't that he disagreed with the gringos. It's just that he knew the army wasn't fully behind him. There were many in the high command of the Fuerza Armada, generals and colonels, who had been filling their pockets for years with money coming from the United States—directing the war against us and filling their pockets at the same time. They didn't want to stop all that. And they were threatening Cristiani, telling him not to negotiate. And Cristiani, he felt he was screwed either way he went—the gringos pushing him hard one way and the top command threatening him the other way. Well, in the end he went along with the gringos. The top command of the Fuerza Armada got paid off, and, I hate to say it, some of our top people, like Villalobos, they got paid off real well too. And Cristiani went off to Mexico—without telling anyone he was going—and he signed the peace accords there on January 16.

And me, where was I? Right here in Comunidad Guazapa, though we didn't have a name for the place right then, and I was busy organizing the repopulation of this area. The FMLN had given me the job to plan out the settlement of our people in the area. They had confidence in me, since I had been in the guerrillas from the beginning—for fourteen years I'd been incorporated. In the last year or so I was with my group fighting right in this area. So I knew every inch of this terrain real well. For that reason, they figured I should do the planning of how to settle our people here.

The problem we had in the beginning—I'm talking about December '91, while the negotiations were going on—is that the government didn't want us to have this land, not here or anywhere around here. Too close to the capital. They didn't want guerrillas, or ex-guerrillas and their families, too close to San Salvador. The Fuerza Armada, seeing that we had a grip on the land here, attempted to prevent us from bringing in our families, and what they did is block the main road leading from Suchitoto to the capital. They had a rough bunch, very aggressive, detaining any trucks with civilians. But I knew this area well, and I had compas who I was in contact with all through the hills around here. So what I did was go find my family. I didn't really know where they were. Somewhere up north, probably in Chalatenango, and probably in the area of Santa Marta, I figured. I didn't really know. When you're in the war, you don't exactly know these things. So I went looking for them. It took me a few days, but I tracked them down—my wife and my five kids. I found them, and I found Luis too. We knew each other from the war, we'd been on some missions together. We got a couple of eight-ton trucks, loaded them to the brim with all our stuff—beds, tables, benches, a few chickens, and some food supplies. And my family and Luis's family headed over this way. Normally, it's a three- or four-hour trip, but it took us a hell of a lot longer because when we approached this area we had to go through narrow dirt roads in the hills, with my compas informing me where and when we could pass.

And that's how we were able to bring in other families over the next few weeks. Sure, the Fuerza Armada saw what was going on. They had planes and helicopters flying overhead to intimidate us, but they were no longer able to bomb us. And they couldn't stop the influx. To Comunidad Guazapa, we managed to bring in about fifteen families, almost all of them from Cabañas. Luis knew the people up there, and he was helping to organize and bring them over. And we brought in other folks from other places, according to who the FMLN organizers decided. And I had the job of assigning who would be going to which new community. All of the families who came and eventually formed the six communities we have here now, all of them had at least one member who had been with the guerrillas, and they had their identification papers from the FMLN. I selected the area of what became Comunidad Guazapa as the place for me and my family. Luis, too. He liked the look of this area, and he wanted to be here with me. We knew each other from the war. We had been on some of the same missions together. No, I won't go into that. Some of that information is still secret, known to only a few people. Better to keep it that way. You don't know who might be bothered if they heard the details now. Luis knows some of it, not all of it. I'm not saying we were commanders, no. We each had a small group under us at times, and that's all. And we are both people of conviction. Each of us was incorporated in the guerrillas for a long time, and we stayed loyal to our ideals. Not everyone in the guerrillas was like that. Some of them lost conviction, even some of our leaders. Luis and me, no. We both come from dirt-poor backgrounds, and we have always had our feet on the ground. We know what we fought for, and we've both stayed with it, each in his own way. Exactly what I did in the war—look, those details aren't necessary, right? In any case, they have remained secret for years, and I shall keep it that way. What I can tell you about is how we got started here. That's what you want to know, verdad?

Well, in those first weeks when we had gathered a heap of people over here, we had no houses, of course, and at that point we had no legal claim to the land. We had hundreds of people all huddled together in the area of the ruined remains of the landowner's house. It was a bombed-out area. I don't know who had destroyed it, the Fuerza Armada or us. Probably both sides during the fighting in the beginning of the war. I wasn't here then, so I don't know. What I can tell you is that the place was a mess. Fortunately, it was not the rainy season, so you could sleep out in the open or under some plastic sheet or whatever. And the Lutheran Church and some other groups donated food to us—maíz, frijol, rice. We couldn't have survived without that help, since most were like me; I didn't even have a *cinco* in my pocket. And what we did is cook and eat together. The women made the food in huge pots, and each got a portion to eat. Nobody was complaining or making problems. We were all happy just to be there, to be alive and have some hope.

Soon, just about when they were signing the peace accords, the Lutheran Church from San Salvador decided to donate building materials so we could construct our houses—laminated metal sheets for the roof, some wooden boards, and plastic sheeting. Few of us knew anything about building houses. Me, I had grown up in a house made out of adobe. I wasn't aware of how to build a house from these materials. But we all managed it with the help of a couple of fellows who did know what they were doing. We went out to the area where we have our houses now and began setting up these shacks, cutting down some trees to use as pillars and crossbeams for the roof, and then nailing the laminated metal on the roofs and the boards for walls and with the plastic to keep out the rain when it came. We did all this to stake our claim to the land, since the negotiations hadn't gone into any detail about what land was going to be redistributed to whom. And in the end, a lot of former guerrillas didn't get any land; only farmers got land. Others were given loans to set up workshops of one kind or another, and many didn't get a damn thing in the end.

But those of us who did get land, like us in Comunidad Guazapa, the way it worked was this. The Banco de Tierras was set up by the government, and each family was provided with a loan of thirty thousand colones to buy land. Representatives from the FMLN negotiated with the Banco de Tierras, and they in turn were negotiating with the landowners. This went on in various areas throughout the country. In our case, there was a family, the Morales, who owned the land where we were—about one hundred manzanas. The father had died, and the mother was holding about two-thirds, and her sons owned the other third. The sons had the best land, flat land, where you've got sugarcane growing. The mother had some of the flat land, but most was up on the hillside, where nothing was growing. There were just trees—a few mango trees among them—and a lot of wild growth like you see when nobody has been cultivating the land. The sons refused to sell their land. We never discussed this with them, not then and not since. But the mother did agree to sell her land. I can only guess that the mother must have figured that her land wasn't being used for anything, and, in any case, why try to hold on to it if you had all of us, ex-guerrillas and our families, who were establishing themselves in the area. She must have figured it was better to take the money, which was pretty damned good money for that land—nine thousand colones for each manzana, and she sold us all of her sixty-five manzanas—better to have that cash than to invite problems with us and merely try to hold on to land she wasn't using anyway. So the thirty thousand colones that were lent to each of us families by the Banco de Tierras, it went to pay her for the land. And each of our families got title to their 3.2 manzanas. And in the end—even though the Morales sons fought like hell against it—we also got title to the area where they used to have their huge house.

We needed that space to set up a school and a health clinic, and in the end the six communities in this area got the title to that space.

Once we had our land and had parceled it out to each family, we were eager to start planting. It took a while, since we had to clear all the trees and underbrush, and then we had to get hold of some tractors—a couple of them—and we plowed all the land of all the milpas. Two of us, me and another guy, were the only ones who knew how to drive tractors. I had picked it up during the few months when I was in Honduras in the refugee camp with my family. So me and my pal did the plowing. We had some basic tools—shovels, picks, machetes—that were donated to us and also some seeds that were given to us in the beginning. Everyone helped each other out. Since I was doing the tractor plowing for everyone, someone else planted my milpa for me. Mutual aid, that's what it was. A kind of pure socialism right there in the beginning. It felt real good to me.

Our biggest problem at that point was how to get enough water for all of our families. There were a few shallow wells in the area, and that was just about enough during the rainy season, though you had to walk a distance to some of these wells, and you had to do it three, sometimes five times a day. Men and women did it together, the women carrying the plastic containers on their heads and the men lugging it on their shoulders. That was the water we had for drinking and cooking. There was another well about a kilometer and a half away, and that well is where we went to wash clothing and to bathe. As I said, in the rainy season we managed all right. In the dry season, though, we had our problems. But fortunately some outsider, a guy from Spain, came to our community and helped us to dig better wells. And in that way we were able—after about a year—to manage in the dry season too, as long as we were careful not to overuse the water we had.

We began to have our first harvests, and with that money some of us started to pay back our loans. It didn't leave you with much money for anything else, but we had contracted to pay off those loans—thirty thousand colones to the Banco de Tierras and another fifteen thousand colones to a different government organization that had lent us money to buy animals in the beginning. No, I didn't mention that, right. We were stuck with these huge loans, and the ARENA government wanted us to repay them. But then some compas let us know that the money for the loans wasn't coming out of the government or taxes from Salvadorans. No! It turns out that the government had been given that money by international organizations; it had been a donation to the government that was to be passed on to us. Hell, once we got wind of that, those of us in the communities decided to go to the capital and hold demonstrations against the government, insisting that they pardon those loans. The money was meant for us! They were just planning to pocket it, use it for whatever else they wanted. It took us a couple of demonstrations, huge demonstrations, and the government realized it had to go along with pardoning the loans. I had already paid back two thousand colones—Luis did too, the way I understand it—and we never got that money back. But at least we didn't have to pay anything more.

No, no, there was no violence during those demonstrations. Not on our side and not on theirs. The United Nations troops, a whole hell of a lot of them, were all over the country, and the government wasn't about to attack us, and we weren't about to provoke any attacks. Those UN troops were real helpful in keeping the peace here those first couple of years. They separated the Fuerza Armada from us and made sure that each side—theirs and ours—went along with agreements we had signed in the peace accords. The Fuerza Armada moved back to their encampments, and as they took each step, our side turned in more and more of our armaments. In stages, that's how it went. And with the UN troops investigating and watching over the whole thing. Otherwise, who knows what might have happened?

Anyhow, by the end of our first year or so we were already well established. Not living as comfortably as we do today, but comfortably enough. In Comunidad Guazapa—and in the other communities around here— the people got themselves organized and were cooperating nicely. Each community set up its own directorate to manage the affairs of the community. Over here, I was the first president. I did it for the first two years, and then Luis took over. During my time, we got a school going and a health clinic. This we did in cooperation with the other communities. At first, it was only nursery school through first grade, then the second year we expanded up to sixth grade. We had some outside teachers coming in and two or three young people—like Lucita, who these days is principal of the school—these young people, teenagers really, were trained to teach the kids even younger than themselves. I don't remember exactly when the Ministry of Education recognized our school as a legitimate operation—not too long after we started, if I'm not mistaken. And from then on we had teachers sent out here, with the government paying their salaries. That way we were able to enlarge the school to the way it is now, nursery school through twelfth grade.

With the health clinic we also made good progress right from the beginning. A Salvadoran organization called IMU [Instituto de Mujeres] immediately helped us set up a temporary clinic, and later we were able to make it permanent like we have it today. It's not a place where you stay overnight if you're ill; for that you have to go to the hospital. But for lesser things, for consultations or for some emergency aid, we set up the clinic, and today it's open five days a week. IMU pays for a doctor to come here, daily I think it is, and the doctor has assistants from the communities here.

So, you see, right from the beginning we worked hard to establish our place here. And I think we did a damned good job. That's my opinion, anyway. But, yes, we also made some mistakes. Not big mistakes, but a few things we should have done differently. Like, we should have planned a road coming up from the main Suchitoto road to our community that was better than the one we have today. We couldn't cut through the Moraleses' sugarcane, but still we could have built a better access road than what we've got now; and it's too late to change because now there's other families living in the places where we should have put in an access road. Besides that mistake, we were a little short-sighted in forgetting to put up a recreation area for the kids, especially a decent soccer pitch. We could have done it, but our minds weren't focused on those things back then. Now we haven't got the land to do it. And maybe the other mistake we made—though we couldn't have avoided it the way we set up so quickly—is that we've got some people in the community that it would have been better if they had, well, at least in my opinion, if they'd have gone elsewhere. People, I'd say, who've got some wrong thinking and wrong ways about them. And you can't just toss them out now. They've got their title to the land, and there's no way to get rid of them. So what can I say? Most folks here are fine, and the rest we just live with them, that's all.

For me, it's not these errors that we made in the beginning that disturb me. What I wish we could have continued is the way we lived when we first came here, everyone helping out the other. Mutual aid. A true socialist spirit. That's what I would have liked us to continue. I don't mean to say that we don't help each other anymore. We still engage in collective work. Look, we just got some gravel from the municipality of Suchitoto to help us even out the road that goes around the sugarcane fields to the community. Well, the men here are doing that labor together, nobody getting paid for any of it. And I'll give you another example of how we're working collectively. We're all pitching in to patrol, or, really, to keep an eye out, so that *maras*, which you've got all over the country and in areas near here, bueno, we're making sure they don't come into our community robbing anyone or messing around with anyone here. And we keep good track of our own kids, making sure they don't take the wrong path and get involved in any of that kind of delinquency. So, in these ways, we're still very much involved with helping each other. But it's not the same as in the beginning when we were starting out here, all for one, and one for all.

Yes, of course, I'm a socialist. That's what I believe in, and that's what I fought for. I'm a realist, though. The kind of socialism I'd like to see doesn't exist anywhere in the world. No, not even in Cuba, even though I admire a lot of what they've done with their education and health systems and other things too. Unfortunately, the world we live in is run according to capitalist values. Take El Salvador, which, of course, is what I know best. The education system, the media, the church—all are supporting the capitalist system. What I mean is that the capitalist ideal is that you produce for yourself, and if you make out well, no matter how your neighbor is doing, then good for you. Socialism is just the reverse. In true socialism, everything is shared equally; everyone with equal obligations and with equal benefits. We're a long way from being a socialist country here. It'll take a lot of political changes and a lot of psychological changes in the way people see things. We're a long way from that here in El Salvador.

But we've just elected a new government, and for the first time we've got an FMLN man as president. Let's see how that goes. As I see it, we could do with a lot of changes here. Like land reform. We need a better distribution of land. There's still many wealthy families here with fincas of 250 manzanas or more. Much of that land is going unused or hardly used at all. And we've still got many campesinos who've got no land of their own. We need to change that, the way I see it. Start with those who have the big fincas and then move on to those with one hundred manzanas or so. And so on. No, no, I don't see us getting the land that belongs to the Morales sons. I don't see them selling it, and there's no way it'll be confiscated or bought from them. We could use that land to expand our community, but it's not about to happen. No time soon, anyway.

No, I've never figured to try and enter politics in any official way. A man needs to recognize his limitations. It would be foolish to wish to be what one can't be. I have a daughter who's all involved with politics. Me, I just work with the FMLN Party around here, trying to encourage people to vote for us, cooperate with the party. But I'm not all that involved. What I am now is what I was before—a farmer. I work my land like others here, like Luis, Jorge, like all of us who are working our milpas. When I get some time off, I read. I read whatever I can get my hands on. I learned how to read when I was in the monte. Before I got incorporated with the guerrillas, I was more or less illiterate. But in the monte I taught myself, and I began reading documents. Today I read some political books, history. I tried reading Marx, but you've got to have some background for that. So I stick to what I can understand. That's my passion—reading. I try to get a firm grip on what is happening in the world and what is happening in our country. So I listen to the news on TV and I read. A man can never know enough, can he?

CHAPTER SEVEN

Luis

A New Life and a New Wife

Again it is a sunny Sunday afternoon, midsummer, and we have arranged to meet Luis on the veranda of his house. But this time, uncharacteristically, when we arrive he is nowhere to be found. Nor is his wife, Julia. Only their oldest daughter, Margarita, is there, and she tells us she hasn't seen either of them for the past half hour or so. "I think they're down there in the gully among the bushes, but I don't know." So we make ourselves comfortable—or, rather, as comfortable as one can be in the heavy heat of the veranda—and are offered some tamales, which we eat under the scrutiny of the chickens and the cantankerous rooster.

A half hour goes by, and still there is no sign of Luis. Finally, Margarita heads down into the gully and then returns with the news, "They'll be here pretty soon. They said you should wait for them." And fifteen minutes or so later, there they are: Luis, Julia, and the two family dogs. Julia is carrying a pickax and shaking her head in exasperation, the two dogs are barking meekly, and Luis is wearing a broad grin on his face while carrying in his right hand a half-meter-long armadillo. He brings the limp prize over for our inspection, drops it on the veranda, and then, taking off his wet and muddied shirt, he goes over to the water cistern and dumps a couple of buckets of water over himself. "Be with you in a minute," he tells us.

Actually, we had come that day to interview Luis about his first years in Comunidad Guazapa, but at least for the moment there was no point in diving into that part of his story. Luis—and we too, for that matter—were still thinking about the armadillo, which by then had been brought over to the kitchen. Accordingly, we set the tape recorders running and began with Luis's armadillo story, or stories.

I had just finished a few chores around the house and had given the horse a drink from the cistern. I shaved and washed up—I knew you were about to come—and I lay down in the hammock to rest for a few minutes. Then I hear my dogs barking like hell, and no matter how hard I shout at them, they don't stop. I go over to them, and they start running down into the gully, still barking. Then I figured what it was. They must have spotted some animal down there, an armadillo, I figured. They lead me over to a hole in the underbrush, and, sure enough, in the hole there is the armadillo's tail barely visible. I rush up to the house, get my pickax and machete, and Julia comes back down there with me. At this point, the armadillo is out of sight, but I know he's in there. I start digging away furiously. And the more I dig, the more he's digging himself in deeper. Finally, I get him by the tail, but I tell you, with all my force I couldn't get him out. An armadillo has these sharp claws, and when he's grabbing on hard, it's tough as hell to get him to let go. Me, I'm lying there halfway into the hole pulling at him, and Julia is hanging on to me and pulling both of my legs, and one of the dogs grabs hold of her dress and is pulling on her. Imagine that! [Luis laughs and laughs, and now even Julia is laughing with him, and so are Margarita and a couple of her brothers.] So you see, just as I'm lying there pulling like that, Margarita comes down and says, "The visitors are here." Well, you'll excuse me, right? There was no way I was going to let the critter go. And finally, I manage to get him out of there, holding him by the tail. He tries to leap out of my hand, so I take my machete and whack him in the back of the neck, and that finished him off.

What am I going to do with him? Hell, eat him, of course! Later, maybe tomorrow. I've got to clean him out first. Remove the shell and take out the guts. Then with the meat inside, you put on some spices and fill it with whatever else you've got around, some onions and garlic maybe, and then you bake him like a turkey. You don't get a whole lot of meat, but it's enough for everyone to have a bit or two. Tastes like pork or chicken. Not bad. It makes for a little something different, a little different con qué for the tortillas.

Not everyone likes it, but I do. I've always had a taste for armadillo. Since I was a kid. I'd hunt them with my father. I think I was five years old when I caught my first one. We had a dog back then too, and he'd sniff them out. That first one I caught was much harder to catch than the one I got today. That one took me two days trying to dig him out; me and my father working together. We took him home, and my mama cooked him up. And me, all they gave me was the head, telling me it was an ice cream cone. It hardly had any meat on it, as I remember.

Years later, when I was up in the monte we used to catch a lot of them. The way we'd catch them was to leave around some remains of the *masa* that the women were making tortillas out of. Armadillos like that stuff.

They'd come around at night to grab some, and we'd be waiting there for them. Puuuum! One shot with an M-16 and you had yourself a meal. No, no, we didn't do this when the Fuerza Armada was around. Only when we were way in the monte or into the jungle, and they were nowhere near us. But you know how we caught a whole lot of armadillos—at least for a while? With our dog. A stray dog that somehow started tagging along with us. He was with us for half a year or so. He was white, so we painted him up black with soot from the fire, spread it all over him, so the Fuerza Armada couldn't spot him. He was a fine dog, a great companion. We never gave him a name; we'd just snap our fingers when we wanted him to come over. And he was a great hunter of armadillos. The best. He'd go after them quietly, not like the dogs I've got here. You'd never hear a peep out of him. He'd stalk them quietly, you wouldn't even know he was gone, and then he'd be there with an armadillo in his mouth as a present for you. Later on, though, as we were going through the monte there were times he'd start barking, and once the Fuerza Armada nearly caught us because of our dog. We tried to give him away to people up in the monte, but every time we gave him away somehow he always came back to us, found us somehow. We couldn't keep him. A doctor, a foreign guy who was with us at the time, injected him with something. Real sad. We all felt it. Here he had provided us with all those armadillos and been a loyal companion. Real sad. [Luis gets up from the hammock, goes over to the comal, and takes a couple of tortillas and beans, which he then eats in silence. We stop the tape recorders and visit for a few moments with Julia, who is still patting up the masa into tortillas and tossing them onto the comal in her new kitchen, which is set apart from the house. Luis had recently built it for her out of logs he hauled from the hillside. Then, as Luis finishes up his meal, he calls us back over and suggests we resume.]

So where were we? Right, I told you about us being demobilized and all that, I remember. And you talked with Joaquín like I told you, verdad? He's a smart guy and was a good compa back during the war. He was one of the founders here. Real clever how he went about it. Those were hard days when we first came here. You had to have clever people like him, otherwise God knows how it would have gone for us. Because the people who owned this land, the Morales family, they were not too easy to deal with. They didn't part with the land too easy. But, like you see, we managed it. We got the right to be here, we got our lands.

I don't know all the details like Joaquín does. What I know is that our people, the FMLN, negotiated a deal with the government. There was a redistribution of land in many places around the country. Some rich people had to give up their land so that some of us who had no land would be able to farm again. I mean, these rich landowners didn't just give it away; they were paid for it. The Banco de Tierras acted as a go-between. They negotiated with the landowners, and they paid them for whatever land they got and then gave to us. I'm not saying the landowners were happy about it. Many weren't. The Morales family that owned the land here were none too happy. But in the end they got paid well. They had about one hundred manzanas. A good-sized finca. They were growing sugarcane. Their big home—where we have the school now—was destroyed in the war, but hell, that wasn't where they were living. The father and the brothers all had their big, fine homes in the capital. They came out here on weekends and during the harvest. The Banco de Tierras negotiated it that we got about sixty-five manzanas and the bombed-out area where they had their home. The Morales family kept about a third of the land. The best land! They got most of the flat land that runs between where they had had their home up to the foothills of Mount Guazapa. The land we got was a little of the flat land, and then from the foothills up toward the mountain. They went right on growing sugarcane; they're still growing it today. You've seen some of them out here in their van, no? They come around harvesttime, December, January. They aren't good people, not at all. Just a bunch of boozers and womanizers who take their money and throw it away gambling. But these days we've got decent relations with them. Nothing much. "How are you? Hello, good-bye." That's about it. No real talking or any of that, except if a cow of ours wanders into their cane fields, then we'll let them know. No, we don't mess with their sugarcane. Some folks from another community grab some once in awhile, but the Morales know it's not us from Comunidad Guazapa. So these days things are easy with them.

In the beginning, no way! When we first got here we had our troubles with them. We built our houses out where we had our land on the hillside. Some organizations had given us all some boards and laminated metal to build these places. Nothing too sturdy, but good enough. And we cleaned up the ciudadela area—right, where the Moraleses' bombed-out home had been. There was a short walk up from the main Suchitoto road to the ciudadela. We turned that area into a school with separate classrooms. Problem is that to get from the main road and then the ciudadela out to where we are living, well, it's a hell of a long walk all around the sugarcane fields. Maybe two kilometers. The direct way is much shorter, only half a kilometer, but it means you've got to walk on the paths that cut through the sugarcane fields. Back when we first got here, the Moraleses told us we couldn't put a foot on their property. And when some of us took the paths through the sugarcane fields—yes, I did and many of us did—these Morales guys started shooting in our direction. That's right, *they* had rifles! We had destroyed ours when we demobilized, but these guys, hell, they still had some rifles with them. One of our people even got wounded.

They weren't trying to kill us, but they wanted to intimidate us, you see. What they forgot is that, unlike them, we were people who'd spent years in the monte. We were accustomed to being shot at. You can't intimidate folks like us all that easy, see? No, hombre! And after awhile, when they saw they couldn't intimidate us and that all we were doing is walking and not robbing, they stopped that bullshit. And since then it's been calm. Our kids go to school walking on the paths through the sugarcane fields, we all go that way—no problem. Like I say, we're on hello-how-are-you terms now.

In the beginning, when we were given the title to the sixty-five manzanas, we had to figure how to divide the land. All of us had been given some tools and seeds and some start-up money. The way it worked out was that every family got 3.2 manzanas, no matter how many kids you had. All of us here were people who had been with the FMLN during the war. That's the only way you could come live here. Look, Julia had a brother who was with the other side, the Fuerza Armada, and he wanted to rejoin his family. But there was no way he was going to be allowed here; besides, he wasn't a decent guy. Maybe she'll tell you about him. Me, I'll just say that he wasn't a type that fit in here.

Anyhow, the way we were advised to divide the land was to draw lots, you know, like a lottery. Each one was to get a number, and when your number was drawn, then you'd say which 3.2 manzanas would be yours. Some parts of the land were much better than others; some was flat land down near the sugarcane fields, and some was way the hell up the hillside, right to the foot of the volcano. But we, since we were all compas and knew each other from the guerrillas, we said, "No, everyone should have a piece of the better land, the flatter land, and a piece of the worse land up on the hillside." And that's how we did it.

Me, I can't complain. I got a piece of flat land down near the well. Only thing is, when it rains hard like it did last winter, the whole place floods over, and your house is in the middle of a lake for a while. I like it down there, but Julia doesn't. She wants to be up where we're living now, up where her grandma and sister and all them are living. So that's how come we're living up here. I rent out the other place. And Julia likes it that way.

Though, as you know, when I first came here, it wasn't Julia that I was living with. I had another woman. Meches. We had two kids together, and I had Chico with me. Me and Meches weren't on good terms. I had gotten together with her up in Mesa Grande, and we were together in Santa Marta before we came here. She wasn't the woman for me. I knew that. I just wasn't of a mind to do anything about it right then. To be honest with you, I had someone else in my mind. No, not my first wife. I had loved her once, but it was over between us. The one I had in mind was someone else. The one over there making tortillas right now. Look at her—a woman like that stays in your mind once you've seen her, verdad? [Julia, overhearing Luis's comments, chuckles and shakes her head as Luis goes over to grab another tortilla. The rooster, as if on cue, follows him to the kitchen, and Luis tosses him some kernels of maíz. Then, lying back down in the hammock, Luis launches into the story of how he met and got together with Julia.]

I remember the first time I laid my eyes on her. It was up in the monte. She was a radista up there, and our units had come together for some meeting. I remember trying to start up with her, asking where she was from and that kind of thing. She sort of ignored me, and later I found out she had some guy up there—the one who is father of Margarita and José. So, I figured, not much of a chance there, though now and then she'd come back into my mind. The next time I caught a glance of her was in Santa Marta. I was there with Meches, and Julia was there living with her grandparents. I found out that she's alone, her guy from the guerrillas had gone his own way. And I was thinking, "Hmmmm!" I didn't have a chance to see her much or even talk to her up there, and then I got this call from a former compa that they were looking to repopulate down here in Comunidad Guazapa, and I figured, "What can I do?" I left Santa Marta with Meches and the kids, came down here, and started to settle in. And then you know what happens? I tell you, it makes me laugh—because what happens is that relatives of Julia, her father and grandfather, they show up here and tell us they're wondering about resettling. They don't like it up there in Santa Marta, they say, and they wonder if there's any room for them down here. And me, since I was one of those coordinating the effort to get people to resettle here, I say to them, "Yes, fellows, you are welcome. We need you. Bring the whole family, of course! I'm going to make sure you all get your lands. And don Miguel, I know he's a bit old now, but bring him and his family too. We'll take care of him." You know what I was thinking, right? I admit it. I knew Julia was living with her grandparents, and I was figuring Julia is coming my way, just like I was dreaming might happen. And that day when they came, I made sure it was me who was in the truck bringing them here. In the rearview mirror I could see her back there, and I kept smiling at her, and she was laughing. But later, when they got here, and she settled in with her grandparents and two kids, when I tried to start with her, she told me "no," she wanted no part of that. "And why?" I said. And she tells me, "You've got someone here, you don't think I know that? I don't want any part of that kind of thing, your woman coming after me, trying to kill me. No way!" "And why would she kill you?" I said. "I'm not living with her any longer."

You see, I had already moved into another place, I wasn't living with Meches. I was providing for her and the kids I had with her, but I was living by myself and with Chico. I tried to explain this to her to make her understand that Meches wasn't the woman for me, that only she was for me. "Look, I know you're a *mujerero*. I know about you." That's what she told me, straight to my face. And I told her, "You've got me wrong. I don't know what you've heard, but you've got me wrong. I'm loyal when I'm with the one who is right for me."

Well, she wasn't buying it—not right then. She didn't make it easy for me, and I was going crazy wanting to make her mine. So what I did is, when she wasn't aware, I knew where her milpa was—it wasn't far from mine—and she wasn't finding it all that easy taking care of her two little kids and farming at the same time. So when she wasn't up in the milpa, I'd go and take care of it, weeding and whatever. I didn't tell her it was me who was doing it, even though she asked me. I said I didn't know. Because, it really did bother me seeing her try to do all that work by herself, and I did want to help her.

Finally, little by little she started warming up to me. She let me visit her at her grandparents' house in the evenings, and when I was alone with her I treated her with respect—no smoking or drinking or anything else. Still, I could see she was afraid of me. I was an older man, forty-five years old, and she was only twenty-three. I mean, I was not too bad for my age. But like they say, you've got to be careful with an older man, because he's like an old bull. Still, I could see she was beginning to like me, and I told her, I promised her that I would never leave her, that I would work and provide for her, and she wouldn't have to work in the milpa. "But I like working in the milpa," she told me. So, all right, I told her she could work if she wanted, that was up to her. And she would take care of the money. And I wasn't going to tell her she couldn't leave the house—I'm not a jealous guy, and Julia isn't the kind to make a man jealous. So I promised her all that, I swore on it, and finally I told her, "I have never met a person like you, my heart is longing for you, and I can't see living without you." I don't know what she was thinking right then, but all she said to me was, "You men are all fanatics!"

And me, I'm going crazy wanting to be with her. I'm feeling miserable as hell. And then it's Christmas Eve, and I'm feeling so awful I decided to go with a pal of mine, and I get drunker than hell on a bottle of vodka. I'm no drunk, no way, but I was trying to get her out of my mind right then, and then sure enough, what happens is she comes along to my house and sees me there all soused up. Of all the damned luck, that's the night she comes to see me!

A few days later—by then I was back sober—she says she wants to talk to me. I knew she liked me, and she starts talking to me, saying, "I don't want to be responsible for anyone messing himself up, becoming some drunkard and doing himself in." I tell her she's got no worry there, I'm no drunkard and never have been and never will be. I mean, I'll have a few beers now and then, maybe to celebrate some occasion, but I don't drink like some people around here. And she knew back then I was not a drunk, but she tells me, "All right, I believe you, but if you ever turn *bolo* on me, you're out the door." I told her I understood her thinking there, and we came to an understanding—that we'd start being together. Not out public right away. In secret. And so we started.

I'd go over to her grandparents' house, and then I'd stay in a side room with her till dawn, when I'd sneak out like a rabbit and go to work. But after awhile I wanted the thing to be set straight, no hiding, and we agreed that I would go to her parents, in the way of respect, and I would ask their permission for her to be with me. One evening, then, I went over to their place, which was just a ways up from where Julia was living with her grandparents. I had a beer and then a little liquor before I went, you know, putting myself at ease, relaxed. And I brought some more along with me to Julia's parents. I knew Julia had followed me partway, close enough so she could hear whatever I was going to say. It wasn't so unusual for me to visit them, since I was active in the community, the president of the community, and I was visiting people all the time. Though not with beer and guaro. So I sat down, and they were there on the veranda sitting with me, and I gave them something to drink and even had a little more myself, and I could see they were feeling real relaxed and easy with me, and I turned to don Jorge, Julia's father, and I say to him, "Look, excuse me, don Jorge, with all respect, I would like to talk with you." "We are talking, aren't we?" he answers me. "Yes, of course," I say. "But what I want to say is that I come here tonight to be with you, the father of Julia, and you, the mother of Julia, because I want you to accept me as Julia's partner. I ask you with all due respect for this permission." And don Jorge says to me, "Look, this is real difficult. You had this woman down there, and you've left her, right? And this woman is going to have problems because you've got some kids with her." "Leave that to me," I say. "I'm not going to neglect my obligations. I'll do everything to take care of them. No problem there. And as for Julia, I promise you that I shall watch over her, take care of her and her children, and I'm not just fooling around. Trust me!" Don Jorge is quiet for a moment, and then he turns to his wife and says, "Look, old lady, what've you got to say? I know Luis is a hard-working man, a man of honor, and a wise fellow. What've you got to say?" And Julia's mother says, "Well, yes, since they're already like a pair, no? She's a grown woman, she can do what she thinks best, no? I know Luis is a responsible man. He can't marry Julia, he's already married. But, look, if that's what Julia wants and that's what you want, I've got nothing against it. I give her over to you, yes."

Bueno, I'm happy as hell to hear this, and I make a toast, and we all have a few more drops, and we are all feeling happy, real good. And I know

Julia is hearing all this a little in the distance, out of sight. I was real happy to get their permission, though truth is, I had planned to be with her no matter what. Yet I wanted to do it with respect, honoring them the right way, and it worked out just fine.

And ever since then I have honored my word. I've provided for Meches and the two kids I had with her, and I've taken care of Julia and our kids, the two she had before, my boy Chico, and the six Julia and I have had. I've never betrayed her, I swear. I took an oath to honor her, and I've stuck to it. [Luis lowers his voice slightly, even though Julia has retired into the house.] I've stuck to it even though there's these possibilities all around, temptations, but I've not betrayed her. Not once. I feel that I got real lucky to have her. I love her too much. Since the beginning I've never changed. I thank God, and I thank her parents that me, at age forty-five, I was able to have such a woman. So pretty and so modest and loyal; she's not looking around for another man like some women I used to be with. And you can say something to her, and it stays with her; she's no gossip like lots of others. She's the best woman I've ever known. The best! We've been together all these years, and I've decided that I want to make it legal. I'm thinking to get a civil divorce. My son Chico, now that he's a lawyer, he's telling me that he can arrange it for me. He tells me that his mother, the one I'm still married to by the church, she'll sign the papers so we can be divorced. I'm thinking maybe to do that, to remarry without the church, to go that way because I want to make my marriage to Julia recognized. You know, to get my papers in order so if I'm not here anymore, Julia gets the land, the house, and she's taken care of with no problems, right? We've got a bunch of kids to think about, so I've got to take care of it.

Things have gone real smooth between me and Julia. Never a serious problem. Arguments about small things now and then, but no real problems. Our only big problem was right in the beginning, shortly after we made it public that we were a couple. Then—maybe we'd been openly living together two or three months—I thought I was going to lose her. She scared the hell out of me. I'd been working up in the milpa. I come back to the house, and she's there inside lying on the bed. She tells me not to go near her. She says she's got this terrible fear inside her. She's never felt anything like this in her life, not in the monte, nowhere. I approach her, and she tells me to stay away. She's afraid of me too. And me, loving her like crazy, and there she is telling me to stay away from her. It was terrible.

So what I did is tell her I'm going to bring some doctor to see her. She says that's fine, she'll go along with that. The guy I brought was not a real doctor, but he was someone who people here in the community went to when they had a health problem. *El que cura*—that's what we called him. I knew him pretty well, since he was living with my niece. I begin telling him what's going on with Julia, and immediately he says to me, "Someone has put a curse on her." He says he's sure that's what it is. I knew he had been in Mexico studying this stuff, that he had some kind of knowledge about these things. And he tells me, "I can cure her, you'll see." I know this kind of cure is costly, so I ask him what he's charging, and he says, "Since you're a relative, I'll do it for one thousand colones." Me, I'm thinking that's a hell of a lot of money, but I had no choice. I knew I had to do something quick.

And so he came to the house where Julia was lying in bed. He says a few words to her, and then he tells us, "No doubt about it, someone has put a curse on you." He cleaned all around the house, and then he gave Julia some kind of medicines. Don't ask me what they were. I have no idea. He tells me I have to give him a photo of her and also a pair of her underwear. I've got no idea what the hell he did with these things. He didn't say, and I didn't ask. Then he lit some candles and put them on the table, and with the candle drippings he starts making some kind of drawings. He tells us that these are drawings of the hands and feet of the person who did the witchcraft. I can't say I understand any of it. Those were his secrets, he said, and he figured in a few days she would start feeling better.

He came back every day or so to check on her, and sure enough, in a week Julia already felt much better. She was weak, but she was no longer afraid of me or anyone else. The only thing el que cura said to her before he ended these treatments was that she should forgive this person who had put the curse on her. The woman was going to weep and repent, he said, and Julia ought to forgive her. Julia never said anything to anyone about who it was, but I knew it had to be Meches. I knew it because when I left Meches she had told me she wasn't going to permit me to get together with Julia. I told her that I would go on providing for her and the kids, but there was no way she was going to stop me from being together with Julia. So I knew it had to be her who did it, or she had someone do it for her. I went to her and cursed her out, and she was crying and denying it completely. But later on I heard that she told someone in the community that she was sorry for the whole thing. She never said a word of that to me or Julia, though. But what does it matter? The thing is, nothing like that has ever happened again. Julia and me have been strong together ever since. Julia had our first kid a few months after that witchcraft. The boy was healthy. And we've had five more since him, all healthy. And Meches, she's still in the community, but she's never pulled any of that crap again.

CHAPTER EIGHT

Julia

Comunidad Guazapa Then and Now

At the end of the war Julia found herself living in the dingy town of Santa Marta in the northern district of Cabañas. Once again, she was with her grandparents who raised her, but now with two small children. However, in 1992, with the peace accords about to be signed, an uncle told her and her family that he had found a more suitable place—Comunidad Guazapa. It was a four-hour truck ride away, below a volcano where she and her platoon had nearly been killed during an aerial attack by the Fuerza Armada. "The FMLN hadn't got the area secured right then," she recalls. "There was only something like twelve families there, and they were looking to repopulate it with our people." So she went, along with her grandparents and her two children. Her parents followed a month later, together with eight of her younger brothers and sisters.

And that is where she has remained for the past eighteen years. During this period Julia has experienced some rather dramatic changes in her personal life, and, similarly, Comunidad Guazapa has undergone some of its own striking alterations. In this chapter Julia recalls her beginnings in Comunidad Guazapa, her meeting and getting together with Luis, and their establishing a new family and life. She also reflects on the many changes that have come to the community, most important, the building of a school and the arrival of electricity and water to almost all of the houses. In her usual manner, Julia sounds an upbeat note about much that has happened, though in her equally usual frankness she also reveals some of the more difficult moments that she and her family have had to face.

Here are some of her recollections about this period, "the second half of my life," as she puts it.

For me it was a big relief to get out of Santa Marta. Too crowded and ugly up there. Better to try someplace else, I figured. At the time, I didn't know what we were going to, except what my uncle said. He'd told us that the new place had wide-open fields, lots of sugarcane, which is what the landowners had always been growing there, and that there was good water for growing crops. And right above you had Mount Guazapa, a place I'd known during the war. Sounded good to me.

Problem was, the negotiations between our people, the FMLN, and the government hadn't finished up. The final deal with the landowners here hadn't been made. And, really, it wasn't all that secure here. You had soldiers from the Fuerza Armada nearby, and they were still messing with people who they thought were with the guerrillas. For that reason, we didn't just come over here by ourselves. A few families came from Santa Marta, all of us in a truck with FMLN soldiers protecting us. Safer that way.

When we arrived, we came up the cobblestone road that leads from the main road into the finca. It's the same road that's still there today, the one that leads up to where we have the school today, right? Back then, of course, there was no school. Just broken-up buildings that had been the landowner's main residence. The place had been bombed during the war, and it was all messed up, not the kind of place that you could live in. But that's all we had back in those first few months. We stayed there until we were given some laminated metal and some boards and thick plastic. With that stuff we were able to move out of those collapsed buildings and up to the hillside, where we started putting up our houses. Nothing too nice. Not like we have today, with the houses made of concrete blocks and most folks having two or three rooms. Nothing like that in the beginning. Just these hot, laminated tin houses with dirt floors, like the way we were living up in the refugee camp in Honduras. It was good enough, though. And besides, you had all this open space around you, just like my uncle said.

I'm not exactly sure about the deal the FMLN worked out with the landowners. Luis and others know more about that. What I know—it was obvious—was that the landowners, the Morales family, they got to keep most of the good flat land where they had their sugarcane. And we got some flat land, but mostly land up the hillside above, where we've got our houses today. That's where each family could put up their milpa and grow their maíz and maicillo and frijol. And that's what we did, soon as we got our tools to work with and some seeds to plant.

In the beginning, those first few months, we didn't have the land divided out, you know, each family having its own plot or plots. Everyone was free to plant wherever they wanted. I mean, if nobody else had already been planting there, you could take the land and cultivate it for yourself. Me, I had no experience farming. I'd never planted a seed of maíz in my life up to then. My grandfather was the one who did that work when I was a kid, and after that I was in the monte for nine years. So I didn't know a thing about how to be a farmer. Not really. My grandfather had to teach me. And he did. I worked with him in the milpa, cleaning up the land, planting, fertilizing, harvesting. Everything. We'd work from dawn till about noon, and then you couldn't work anymore. The sun had you baked by then. Mamita Cecilia would take care of Margarita and José. They were, let's see, Margarita was four years old, and José was something like two years old. My grandma would watch over them, and she'd bring me and Papito our breakfast in midmorning.

I can't say I was all that good at farming. Papito Miguel had to teach me. We didn't have an ox to help plow the ground. So the way we did it was to use a sharpened stick to make holes, and we'd sow the seeds in those holes. It took me awhile to figure how to sow the right way, in straight rows. In the beginning I'd make crooked rows, and you don't want that, one row running into the next. You'd put two kernels of maíz in each hole. Frijol was easier because you planted it in the middle of the maíz rows, so I didn't get lost doing frijol. The hardest part was lugging water to the milpa. In the summer months you'd have to go way up the hillside to fetch water out of a pipe we had dug into the mountain to catch some underground water, and in the winter when it rained you'd go way down to the well. Either way, it was a long walk with the jug of water on your head. I'd do it five or six times a day.

Bueno, once you've had a season or two working in the milpa, it wasn't so bad. I knew how to do it all. And then when the community divided out the land so that each member had his own parcels, I got my own. Three manzanas, more or less, for every member. My grandfather had his own land, and I had mine, and I began farming my milpa by myself. I was pretty good at it by then. I only did it for a year or so by myself, but I had pretty good harvests. My grandfather had his milpa near mine, and my father had his milpa pretty close by too. Yes, we all got our own land, because the way it worked is that each family got their land. My father and mother had the same amount as me, even though they had three times as many mouths to feed. Pretty rough for them right then, no doubt about it.

The hardest part for my parents, though, wasn't the farming or them going hungry. Truth is—it's not so nice to say it—but it's the truth. My parents had problems between them. They didn't talk to any of us about it. Still, it was obvious. They were arguing and fighting all the time. And worse, they were having problems with some of my brothers. Several of my brothers have taken off for the United States, mojados. I suppose you know that, no? Right, they're in Virginia or maybe it's West Virginia. They've been up there for more than ten years. None of them got much schooling, so they're working up there cutting lawns or in construction. Illegal—all of them. It's good for my parents nowadays because some of my brothers are sending *remesas*, and that's helped my parents out. But back in the beginning, when my parents first got here, it was rough for them, and my brothers were growing up wild, like weeds. You never knew what one of them might do.

And one of my brothers, Marcos, he got into a real mess. Not so surprising, you could see it coming, sort of. He's the oldest of the boys. He went off to the monte, too. Like me, he was about thirteen years old when he took off from the refugee camp. I don't know all the details. He's never told me. I just know that soon after he'd got incorporated in the guerrillas, his unit was ambushed. Many of his compas got killed, but he managed to escape. And being just a kid, he found a place to stay with this woman. She put him up, and he worked helping her out. Then, in this place where they were living—I don't know where it was—the Fuerza Armada came along recruiting people. He must have been sixteen or eighteen by then. He had no choice. Either he joined up with them, or they might have killed him. My parents knew nothing about him, not where he was nor what he was doing. Nada, *nadita*. Then, with the war over and us settled in Comunidad Guazapa, one day he suddenly shows up. Says he wants to stay here. Not so easy, since he had been with the Fuerza Armada, right? Anyway, he's here just a short while, and he gets together with a woman who, we told him, was no damned good. He was stubborn—always has been—and he decided that things aren't going to be good for him in the community, so he might as well take off. He goes up to Chalatenango. Up there he falls in with a bad bunch. Crooks. You know, you hang around with people like that, you come out like them. So he got thrown into jail. And this woman he had, she got Marcos into even more trouble. She was passing him marijuana, and he was selling it. He got caught, and they beat the hell out of him, nearly killed him. And what does this bitch of his do? She and Marcos already had a baby, and with Marcos in jail she figures to get rid of it. She comes back here and leaves the kid on the veranda of my mother's house, and she takes off. Then—imagine this!— awhile later she finds out that Marcos had six thousand colones on him when he entered jail, and now the police are giving it back to whoever is taking care of the child. Hearing this, she comes back here, and when my mother is down by the well fetching water and the kid is alone in the house, she snatches the kid and takes off so that she's the one who wound up getting the money.

Me, I visited Marcos once when he was up there in jail, but only once. You couldn't talk to him; he wanted no advice from nobody. And damn, the way they searched you all over when you went into the jail, even pushing into your private parts looking for marijuana or who knows what, I told

Marcos I'd see him when he got out. Which he did a little while later. But he didn't stay here for long. Soon as he could he took off by himself to the United States. We heard from him later when he got there. And actually, he was doing all right. He got his own house. Near my brothers. They all are making out pretty good. But, I tell you, once a fool, then always a fool. Marcos just got arrested again a few months back. Driving without a license, since, being illegal, he's got no license. The police got him in jail now, and God only knows what they're going to do with him next. Ugly stuff, all that.

Anyway, let's talk about something else. Where was I? All right, you want to know how I got together with Luis, right? Well, there isn't all that much to tell. No flash of light, nothing like that. He's told you that he had his eye on me back in the monte and that he saw me again up in Santa Marta. That's what he says. But I never remember seeing him until I got to the community here. And when I got here, I surely wasn't looking for anything. I had my two kids and was living with my grandparents and farming my own milpa. Last thing I was looking for was some man to start up with. Besides, Luis was not alone. He came here with his woman, Meches, and they had some kids. And the man was twice my age, or almost that. I was twenty-three years old, and he was, like, forty-something.

Still, Luis is—you know him—he gets some idea in his head, and he holds onto it. It wasn't obvious to me at first. His milpa wasn't too far from mine, but he wasn't coming over to help me out. Not at first, anyway. Eventually, when my maíz was ready he came to help me harvest it, but that was all. He was president of the community then, and what he did was to come by chatting—like he was all business—with my grandfather. He started coming regularly, and then my grandmother began to sense that he was looking for something else. I sensed it too. And slowly, Luis started saying things to me, making it clear. Like I say, I wasn't interested. Not at first. Then, little by little, I found myself liking him. He told me that he and Meches weren't getting along, they were fighting all the time, and that he and his boy, Francisco, had moved out to another house. I listened, listened, and after awhile, him so persistent and telling me this and promising me that, I decided, well, I'll give it a try. Me and my two kids, we moved in with Luis and Francisco.

And that's how it's been since then. Luis and me have been together about fifteen years now. It was hard on Francisco, and it took him a while to get used to the idea. He was already sixteen years old when Luis and I started. These days, Francisco and me are on good terms. We're friendly and easy with each other. I've got a lot of respect for him. He's very clever, did so well in school and then university. He's a lawyer now. Luis is real proud. As for my kids, Margarita and José, they were small back then. For them, Luis is like a father to them. That's the way they see it. José has never seen his own father. Margarita saw him recently, but it's Luis who she respects as her father. And both my kids see Francisco as their brother; they get along real well.

Luis and I have had a whole bunch of kids since then. Six, altogether. More than I wanted, but that's how it is. They came easily, more or less, except for the first one we had. That was difficult. In a strange way. To this day, I still am not sure what happened. Back then, it was scary as hell. I must have been three months pregnant, and I started to feel all weird, like someone or something was grabbing me from behind. My eyes felt like they were popping out, my head was hurting, and I felt like I was going to faint. I lay down, closed my eyes, but this great fear had come over me, and it wouldn't go away. This went on for days. Finally, I was bringing lunch up to Luis in the milpa, and I felt this thing, somebody or some force, about to push me over into the gully. I was scared to hell. I told Luis. He answered me, "Look, I'm going over to el que cura." We had a *curandero* living in the community then, down by the soccer pitch where all the mango trees are, right down there he was living. Luis brought him to our house to see me, and soon as I answered a question or two, he said, "Someone has worked some witchcraft on you. But I can help you." Luis figured it was Meches who'd done it. He went over to tell her off, but she denied it completely—and she still denies it today, far as I know. Anyway, the curandero started working on me. He put together some herbs, stuff from the monte, and told me that each night I should bathe myself in water with this herb mixture. Seven days and seven nights. And after each bath there was another herb mix I had to put on my head. One of those nights he came up and lit some candles—red, green, and purple candles, I remember—and he said some prayers. I didn't understand what he was saying, maybe some Catholic prayers. And that was it. He told me I should start feeling better after that, and, you know, slowly I did start to feel better. I have no idea how it worked, how he removed that witchcraft. But he did fix me up. In about a month I was completely back to myself again. It cost me and Luis a lot of money, about half a year's cash money that we get from selling our extra maíz and frijol. It was worth it, though, because I was in bad shape. Something awful, really.

Since then nothing like that has happened again. Luis and I have had five more, and I never felt like that again. Everything has been fine, except with Dorita. I had her over in the hospital in Suchitoto. Dorita came out fine, and I figured, "Good, it's over!" And then the nurse says, "Hey, wait a minute! There's another one in there too." I didn't even know I was carrying twins—no idea. But the second was small, weak. She lasted only a short while, died soon after I'd got her home. Sad, real sad for all of us.

Well, apart from that time and the time in the monte when I lost my first baby, all my kids have been born fine. Usually with a midwife at home, not in a hospital. Let's see—yes, three in the hospital and the rest with a midwife helping me out at home. Do you know Lucita? She's the principal of our school in the community; grew up here, and now she's the school principal. Well, her mother is a midwife. She knows what she's doing. She's been the lady who's come over and helped me give birth to the ones I've had here. Never had any problems. That lady knows her stuff. No, she doesn't charge you for it. It doesn't work like that. You give her something, as a gift sort of. With my last one, Manuel, I gave her a chicken and a bunch of chicks. She liked that because all her chickens had been wiped out by some disease that was going around the community then. Mine hadn't been hit with it, so I gave her the chicken and chicks. And I'm always telling Manuel, especially if he's giving me a hard time, "You, you cost me a good chicken and a bunch of chicks!" Actually, he's the only one I remember paying for. The other times I think Luis took care of it. I think he gave her some colones. Back then we weren't using dollars, right? Twenty colones, something like that.

Yes, yes, I remember telling you back when we were first talking—ten years ago or around then—I remember saying I didn't want more children. Truth is, I'm worn out from all these kids. I didn't want any more. And I did try using some kind of prevention. I get my period real irregular, so there's been no way of planning around it the way some folks do. And those rubber contraceptives that the men use, we avoid that because they say it causes cancer. I don't know, that's what I heard. So I tried some pills—and that didn't work. And then some kind of injection that they gave me, but I hemorrhaged awful bad, nearly bled to death. So I don't know what to do. I've gotten old now, and I'm just hoping that nothing more happens. I had Manuel five years ago, and since then I've been fine. God willing, I won't be having any more. Like I said, I'm worn out as it is.

All my kids are still home. None have gone off yet. Only Francisco, Luis's boy, has gone to university and lives in San Salvador. The rest of my kids are still here. Though, thank goodness, they aren't just hanging around the house all the time. We've got a fine school here now, and Luis and I make sure the kids go. I had four years of school, including what I got up in the refugee camp. I could read and write when I was a kid. Luis, he never went to school. Never had time. When he came out of the monte and came to Comunidad Guazapa, he couldn't read or write. He was president of the community back in the beginning, and all he could do was sign his name. He'd learned that. But it was embarrassing for him. Little by little, he's taught himself. He didn't go to any classes; he just picked up some books and slowly figured it out. He can read some now and write a bit.

Having never had a chance ourselves, Luis and me tell our kids, "Look, you got your opportunity. Don't blow it!" The girls, they listen better than the boys. I don't know why that is. Margarita just graduated from high school, though unfortunately, she didn't get into university. She's talking about some kind of technical training, maybe in San Salvador. And Dorita, she's the one who's got her head fixed in the books. Margarita, the oldest one, has helped me a lot with the younger ones, and now that she's planning to leave the community, Dorita is real annoyed. She knows it's going to be her turn to help out, and she's always telling me, "Mama, I need to study. I want to get my career, Mama. I haven't time to be watching after anyone or doing sweeping up or any of that!" She looks at Francisco, sees what he's accomplished, and she tells me she wants to be a lawyer too. Maybe she'll make it. The teachers say she's very smart, number one in her class.

My younger boys, Manuel and Arturo, they're pretty good students too. It's the older ones, José and Roberto, who have never liked school. We've pushed them to go through eighth grade at least, but truth is, the only thing that interests them is playing soccer. Soccer in school, soccer after school. Francisco tries to talk to them, tell them that they need to continue studying, but they don't listen much. They are figuring to be farmers like Luis, I guess. I don't know what they've got in mind. They're just like my mother's boys, my brothers. None of them ever went past eighth grade, and most went much less. And my parents, my father, he doesn't say anything to them—not to any of his children. He doesn't tell them to go to school or stay in school. He doesn't give any advice the way a father should. Luis, one time, went to talk to my father about it. He told my father, "You've got to send your kids to school. That's the only way they're going to go forward and not become fools." Luis put it to him just like that. And what does my father answer? He says to Luis, "It's up to them to figure out what to do or not to do. They don't go to school because they *are* fools." And Luis said to him, "The real fool, I've got to tell you, is *you*! You're their father. It's up to you to show them the way, don Jorge! Otherwise those boys are going to go nowhere." But do you think my father took Luis's advice? No way. I told Luis it was a waste of time, but he figured he ought to go have that conversation, no beers or nothing, just serious talk. It didn't do any good, of course. But that's how Luis is. He's got something on his mind, he's going to say it.

The school isn't the only thing that we've got now that we didn't have when we first came here. There's been a whole batch of improvements. Like the medical clinic we've had for the past few years. It's over by the school.

There's a nurse over there every morning now in case you got a fever or something else wrong with you. Monday through Friday. We haven't got a regular doctor—not yet. No, no, we don't have our curandero around anymore. He's moved away. What we did have for several years—pity he's no longer around regularly—was this doctor who had gotten together with Amparo, a lady who lives in the community. They were lovers, something like that. And he'd be here many days of the week, staying over. If you had some medical problem and he was here, he'd see you for no money. A good guy. He's living somewhere else now; he and Amparo have split up. Still, he comes by now and then to see the kids he had with Amparo. Actually, he was just here the other day. Good thing, too, because Margarita was feeling sick. So he came by, brought her some medicine, and she's much better now. Too bad we lost him. Though we can count on the clinic being open, and if you got something serious, you can always go to Suchitoto.

Let's see, apart from that, we've also had some other changes. Ten years or so ago, when you first were coming here, we'd already changed the houses from laminated metal to concrete blocks, right? Yes, and they were just putting in those cement latrines instead of those rickety shacks we had before. And these days, lots of us got better furniture than before, and we've got a second room in the house instead of just one big room for everyone to sleep in. Nice, a lot more comfortable.

Of course, the main difference between now and then is having electricity and water coming to the house. Nearly all of us have got it now. Luis has told you about all that, I reckon. He was busy working these things out with the municipality of Suchitoto. I think it was six or seven years ago that we got electricity coming to the house, and we got water coming to the house just a little after that. The municipality of Suchitoto has an FMLN mayor, and they've been helping out some of the communities around the area, putting in projects, sometimes with money or help from international people. They came out and dug this deep well and put in pipes to every house—almost every house, because Mamita Cecilia doesn't have a pipe like the rest of us, since she's living by herself right next to us, so she can come get water from us. We've got this huge cistern, and we've got water flowing six hours a day if we want, dawn till about noon. That's a real big help. No more hauling jugs of water from the hillside or down below at the community's well. And you can wash up real easy now in this makeshift shower we've put up next to the cistern. Real nice.

And with the electricity, well, that's made a big change. Some folks got radios and TVs. We had a color TV, but it got ruined. My mother has one, though. She's living just a minute's walk from here. I go up there sometimes to hear the news—not every day, but sometimes. That's all that interests me. Margarita and Dorita and Luis too, they like to go and watch the soap operas at night. Especially one that starts at seven at night. I don't even know what it's called. Luis is real prompt. Comes seven, and he's up there watching and laughing. "It's about romances going on and old ladies fighting with each other," Luis tells me. "Very funny," he says. And me, I say to him, "Look," I say, "what do I give a damn about that stuff?" I don't care for it. Better to stay at home. Except I'm the one who gets called on to help the kids with their homework. Now that we've got electricity, the kids play after school and wait till night to do homework. Used to be at six or six-thirty it was too dark to do anything. All you could do is lie down and go to sleep. Now the kids are waiting till night to do their homework. That's good in a way, more fun for them. Thing is, I'm the one they want to help them with the homework. Luis has got no patience for it, and besides, he's watching the soap opera. "You help them," he tells me. "I never went to school." So, comes night, me lying there in the hammock looking to rest a bit, and I got my younger ones coming to me, saying, "Mama, come on, the lady teacher says I need to ask you to help me." Usually, since I'm the only one they'll go to, I help if I can figure it out. I can read pretty well and do my numbers. So with the younger ones I can help. With the older ones, they usually know more than I do. Not much I can do for them.

Only time I can help the older ones, sometimes, is when they get an assignment on politics or history. I know a little of that. In some of their classes they're studying about what happened here during the war. Some of the kids, they come to me and Luis and ask us about what happened. Francisco, the one who is a lawyer now, he was asking all the time. About *that*, yes, Luis likes to talk. The other day Arturo had this assignment and was asking Luis. Arturo sat there silently listening to every word, and then he said to Luis, "Papi, you just about got killed, right?" And Arturo said, "Papi, if the war happens again, are you going to go back fighting?" Luis told him, "It depends. If I have no choice, then maybe I'd have to go back fighting." And Arturo quickly answered him, "Papi, I'm not going! I'd only wind up dead. Don't tell me any more stuff. I'm just getting scared." You see, that's the way some of the kids are. They don't want to hear about what Luis and I went through. Margarita was like that too. She once had the assignment to ask her parents, and she never came and asked a thing. To this day she doesn't want to hear about the war. When Francisco is here, he likes getting into politics and talking about the past. I remember the two of them had this argument one time. Francisco was talking about this stuff, and Margarita—she's usually calm and quiet— she suddenly said to him, "Talk about something else!" He looked at her in surprise. And she said, real abrupt, "All you ever want to talk about is politics!" And Francisco turned to her and said, "Come on, Margarita, cut the crap! Don't you know that people eat or don't eat because of politics?" And Margarita answered him, "Well, if I've got to eat because of politics, then maybe I'm going to wind up starving!" To tell you the truth, I understand her. I'm interested in politics, yes, but I don't like talking much about the war. Margarita was up in the monte with me for a year when she was two years old or so, but I don't think she remembers any of it. And really, I prefer to forget about those times too.

The one in my family that likes to get involved in politics, besides Luis, I mean, is my mother. She's active in the community. For a time she was even president of the community—the first woman. Then she got pregnant, and she had to give it up. These days she's still active with a woman's group we have here. She's one of the organizers. I'm sure she'll tell you about it. She goes regularly. I think she does it to get out of the house; she finds it enjoyable. Me, no way. I went once, a few years back, and that was it for me. They were talking and talking about men and women having equal rights and women having to learn to value themselves and all that. I mean, it's not that they're speaking nonsense. I agree with that stuff. But I've heard it so much, I feel it's just a waste of time going over it again and again. So I avoid those meetings, and she's stopped asking me to join her.

Truth is, my mother and I don't spend all that much time together. I don't go over there and talk to her hardly at all. Never have. And with her mother, my grandmother Beatriz, I don't ever go there. She lives down the hill, not so far away, and even though she's alone by herself now I don't bother seeing her. When we were kids she never wanted me and my brothers and sisters around, and to this day I avoid her. I don't like her much.

The ones I'm close to are my sister Elena, who lives here in the community with her family, and, of course, Mamita Cecilia, who's living right next to us. Sometimes in the evenings Elena and I will go over to Mamita Cecilia's house, and we'll be there for hours "telling tales"—that's how we call it. Our grandma loves having us there, and she'll get into it too. Even when Papito Miguel was alive she liked having the grandkids and the great-grandkids over at her house. She'd cook for you—her *quesadillas* were about the best you've ever tasted. And no matter what, she was almost always in a good mood. Even these days, with my grandfather gone, she still is real pleasant to be around. Yes, he died—something like nine years ago. A stroke. He went suddenly. She was real sad, still is if you start talking about it, but with us she's always with a smile. My son José, he sleeps over there at night to keep her company. He's been doing it for years, even back when my grandfather was alive. He's like a son to her. He helps her out bringing water, making a fire, growing some frijol in her yard for her. She owns a milpa, the one my grandfather used to farm. These days she rents it out, but José is hoping to take it over soon.

"Hoping," I say. Because I'm not sure he's going to get it. My grand-father loved José very much, and he told him before he died—José was only seven or eight years old then—he told him that one day José would inherit that milpa. My grandmother says the same; she wants José to have it. But my father, who's her son, I hear he's already got the paperwork set up so that when Mamita Cecilia dies, he, my father, is getting the land. Ugly stuff, if you ask me. And I'm afraid it's going to get real ugly when she dies.

Bueno, aside from hanging out at my grandmother's house and being with my sister at her place, I pretty much don't go anywhere. I've got a couple of friends in nearby communities, but we hardly get to see each other. I go over to Suchitoto maybe once every fifteen days to pick up some supplies—salt, sugar, coffee, matches, soap, and maybe some vege-tables and fruits. That's about all. No, I've never been on vacation. Never been out of El Salvador, except when I was in the refugee camp. I've never even been down to the sea, except maybe once. Margarita's been there a few times, and so have some of the others in the family. I'd like to go, sure, but who's got the time for it? Only on Sundays I get a little rest. I lie myself down in the hammock, and I tell the others, "You take care of things, today I'm taking it easy."

There's some folks here that are going to church on Sundays over at that church in Suchitoto. I might go once a year, that's all. Or if a priest comes out to the community to give mass, which happens once in a while, then I might go. The ones who're celebrating mass out here regularly, or whatever it is they're doing, are the Evangelicals. Lately, they've been growing out here. I went once or twice to see what it was about. I don't care for their way. All that shouting and crying and noise they make, car-rying on like that for hours. No, no, that's not for me. Better to be Catho-lic. You go for a short while, say your prayers, and that's it. Simple. My kids feel the same. They don't go to any of those Evangelical meetings. They prefer to be Catholics. Just about all of them, starting with Margar-ita, have been baptized. Margarita made her communion and confirma-tion, and the others are doing it too. Me, I was baptized and confirmed, at least I think I was. Luis, who knows? He says he's a Catholic. We bought a Bible—twelve dollars, I think it cost—and Luis likes to try reading parts of it. And he likes trying to discuss it with me. He seems to understand it more than I do. I don't like trying to figure out this passage or that one. I believe in God, in Jesus, and yes, I figure there's a heaven and hell. More than that, I can't really say I'm interested in learning about.

And that's about it. That's the way I'm living these days. No complaints. Things are going well for us. Sometimes a problem here and there—that's life. I got this growth on my neck, you can see it real obvious. It wasn't there ten years ago when I met you, no. It started around seven years ago. I'm running around these days going to doctors. They tell me I got to get it removed. No, it's not a dangerous thing, like it's going to kill me. They say I've got to have this operation soon or else I might wind up not able to talk. I got to take care of this thing. Not a big deal, I don't think. A few weeks from now, I'll get it removed. I don't expect I'll be talking much right after that, but later on, I'll be all right. You'll see.

CHAPTER NINE

Mari

Julia's Mother

Mari Lopez is a silver-haired, broad-hipped woman of fifty-six years who carries herself with an air of quiet resignation. Mother of twelve children (of whom Julia is the oldest), she is now clearly the commanding presence in her house—not her husband, Jorge, to whom she has been married forty-one years. And it is apparent that she likes it this way. Perhaps more than any other woman that we met in the community, Mari is the one whose life has changed most obviously from her docile youth to her present position as community activist. In a word, Mari is a self-proclaimed feminist—and proud of it.

When we met her twelve years ago, she had already taken steps in that direction. At that time she was the coordinator of the community's *comedor* for small children, and she had just been elected as president of Comunidad Guazapa. It seemed like every time we visited the community she was not at home but rather out tending to one of her duties. And as she told us then, "I'm no homebody anymore. I like to keep on the move."

In this chapter Mari traces some of the events that led to her taking the feminist path and how she sees the change in the role of women in her community. In addition, she recalls some of the struggles and strife that she and her family have endured over the years. Never one to mince words, Mari was at least as frank and four-lettering with us this time as she was when we first knew her. And this was especially so on those rare occasions when nobody else—not Jorge nor any of the children—was there on the spacious veranda listening in to her pointed recollections.

I'm ready to talk today, but you've got to wait a minute. Sara, over there, is making the tortillas, and looks like she's having a problem. Damn fire seems to have gone out. Hold on. [Mari rushes over to the kitchen right off the veranda, where she has her comal. One of her sons is adding some firewood as Sara looks after the tortillas. Another son is grinding maíz in a hand-grinder. Jorge is looking on from his hammock strung between wooden pillars on the veranda, evidently with no intention of moving. After a few swift words to her children, Mari adjusts the wood and then the tortillas and finally returns to the table, where we sit with tape recorders ready.] I got them helping me out these days, sure do. But go try and get my sons to make tortillas. No way. They think of that as women's work. I tell you, some things here just haven't changed—not yet, anyway.

But it's a lot better than when I was a girl growing up. That's for sure. Back then, women were the only ones taking care of the house. Men wouldn't lift a finger to help their wives. A man worked his milpa, and when he got home he sat on his butt waiting to be served. And if he didn't like how the woman was going about things, he'd whack her around. Believe me, that's how it was. Women didn't dare open their mouths. They had no say in anything. Not at home, nowhere. They didn't even vote. What, a woman go off and vote? No way!

[Jorge, munching on his tortillas, gets up from the hammock. "Look, Mari, you've got that wrong," he says. "Women had the vote back then, same as men. They just didn't bother." "Come on, Jorge!" Mari answers. "Who was going to take them to vote? You tell me. How would a woman get to the voting place? Come on!" "Well, some men didn't vote then either," he answers. "Too far to go, maybe." With a somewhat disgruntled look on his face, Jorge goes and fetches some beans and then disappears inside the house, where the TV is booming out a soccer game.]

Jorge doesn't like hearing all that, but believe me, that's the way it was. We women lived in ignorance, our eyes closed. We were brought up that way. Our grandmothers, our mothers, they lived that way with their men controlling them. You never figured it could be anything different. It was years before things changed. During the war we opened our eyes. Before that we lacked "consciousness"—that's how we call it.

Look at what happened to me. [Mari glances down the veranda to make sure nobody is listening.] Listen to how it was. I'm not going to lie to you, no. Getting together with Jorge wasn't my idea. Truth is, I had my hopes on someone else. A fellow from the same community where we were living up in Cabañas. I was fifteen years old then, and I had a liking for some other fellow there. My grandmother and mother knew it, and they got my father to put an end to it. My father told me, "I've got someone else in mind for you—a better one." And that was it. My father had picked out Jorge for me. He told me Jorge was a good man, he knew how to work real hard, and that I was going to be with him. True, Jorge is a good worker, a good farmer. But I didn't like the arrangement. I just figured there was nothing I could do about it. My parents, my father, really, was the one who commanded the house, and I had to do what he said.

And that was it. I got together with Jorge. I went over to his house—he was living in the same village—and moved in with him and his parents. Jorge was working with his father in their milpa, and I was helping out Cecilia in their house. We didn't get along too well, me and my in-laws. Right from the beginning it was hard on me. I was only a kid back then, and Jorge was, like, twenty years old. He'd come in from work some days, and five minutes later, for some damned thing or other, he'd slap me across the face or he'd start pulling me by the hair. His father and mother would say nothing, and his sister wouldn't help me out either. In fact, it was the sister—she's gone now, the blessed Lord has taken her back—she was filling Jorge's head with talk like, "I haven't seen Mari around all day. Who knows where she's been?" Bad talk like that. And Jorge would get all jealous and all puffed up, and next thing I'd be knocked to the floor. I'm telling you, I don't think another woman could have put up with what I had to. That's how it was in those days. I was ignorant, asleep. You just figured there was nothing to do, you had to put up with it. And there was no protection for you. Today it's changed. Today a woman has got her rights. If a husband starts whacking her around, five minutes later she can have the police coming after him. And the men know it. You can hear them talking to each other about it these days.

Like I'm telling you, things were rough between me and my in-laws. It came to a head when I had my first child, Julia. I was sixteen years old, and we were still living with Jorge's parents. I didn't know anything about giving birth; nobody had told me. The day she was born I was working like usual, milking the cows and then helping my mother-in-law make quesadillas, which we were planning to bring to the priest. Then suddenly I had some sharp pains, and I didn't know whether it was *her* wanting to come out or what. Jorge took off to get the midwife, but by the time she came Julia was already out. Right there in my in-laws' house. The midwife washed the child, burned off the umbilical cord, and then wrapped her up the way we do. And the next few days, weeks, my mother-in-law helped me out with the baby. But there was something in it I didn't like. Cecilia was treating Julia like she was her own baby, her own child. And after a few months, one day we were having a conversation—I don't remember exactly what—and Cecilia tells me that since Julia was born in her house, she had a right to raise her as her own child. I didn't say anything to her, but I went to Jorge and told him this wasn't right; he had to do something to stop it. And what does he do? Nothing! He tells me that my mother-in-law doesn't have any more kids in the house, so let her keep this one. My first, and he makes me give her away! Well, right then I knew I had to get out of my in-laws' house. I wasn't going to have any more children taken away from me like that. So we got our own place, up the hillside and away from my in-laws. I figured I'd see Julia often, and I did. But my mother-in-law raised her as her own, just like she said she would. To this day I don't accept how that happened. Yes, of course, it's led to some hard feelings. You don't forget things like that, do you? We've gone on living nearby wherever we went—the old lady is by herself now in a house next to Julia's place. Me, I got my feelings about it all—still. I keep it to myself. I don't go into it with Julia or Jorge.

As I was saying, I had decided that I wouldn't be having any more children until Jorge and me got our own place. That's how it was. I had three more kids in the next four or five years, and we were living in our own place in Cabañas. My mother was living nearby, and her mother too. My father, well, he was dead. Jorge told you about it, no? Yes, shot by the Guardia. Terrible. He didn't deserve to be shot, but that was the Guardia. In the campo, if they caught you doing something like making liquor, they often enough would get you. That's how my father got killed.

It wasn't because of my father, though, that we figured we had to get out of the village. No, not at all. We had to move because of something else. Jorge's brother Pedro had done something, well, real dangerous. Pedro had got in his mind to start up with a young girl. Chusita was her name, and she was the daughter of a cousin of mine. My cousin was dead set against it. He swore he'd stop it. Pedro didn't care; he just took the girl to live with him right there in the village. My cousin was a man who drank like hell. Pedro the same. My father-in-law could see that something bad was coming down the path, that sooner or later my cousin was going to grab his machete, probably in some drunken rage, and he was going to come after Pedro. If you ask me, my father-in-law had it right. It would have happened. So my father-in-law, along with Jorge and Pedro, decided the best thing was to get rid of the land up in Cabañas and move somewhere else. The old man decided to go far off, down to San Vicente. He went with his sons and had a look, and when they came back Jorge told me, "It's a good place. We're going to have to dig us a well, but apart from that it's fine."

So we went to San Vicente. It was tough on me, since I had never lived out of that village in my life. I was twenty-two years old then. But I understood that we had no choice. The men bought some land to farm down there, and we got some small houses right next to each other. Jorge, me, and my three young kids in one house. My in-laws and Julia in another house. And Pedro and Chusita in their place. My cousin never came after

Pedro with his machete. But the damned truth is, my brother-in-law, within a month of getting there, he and Chusita had split up. Pedro was a lousy drunkard and was screwing around with other women, and when he wasn't doing that, he'd come home drunk and be jumping on top of Chusita. That's right, he'd be forcing himself on her. That's the way men are when they're drunk. I know, believe me, I've had the experience. Jorge was the same for a long while. He wasn't a drunkard like his brother—who's dead now, by the way—a man drinking himself to death day after day, a real bad character. Jorge would only get drunk once in a while. But when he did, that's how it was. He'd want to throw himself on top of me, saying, "Get over here, come on! You don't love me, do you?" All that kind of bullshit, as if the only reason a woman gets together with a man is for that! And never mind if I might be busy with something, like some kid or other I might be tending to. A drunk man doesn't care for anything except getting what he wants. Doesn't care if the kids are awake and hearing what is going on, nothing. Jorge was like that for a long while. He'd be fine if he was sober, which he's been for many years now. He changed up in the refugee camp in Honduras. Since then I haven't had to deal with that crap hardly at all. But those first years, that's what I had to put up with. I'm not going to lie to you, that's really how it was.

Well, I can't say I took much of a liking to San Vicente. Jorge and his father farmed their milpa, and I was taking care of my kids. Julia, at least, she was closer by, and I saw her regularly. She was going to school there, and I liked that, since I'd never had a chance to go myself. My mother-in-law was minding her, but not the way I liked. Cecilia, Miguel, they were neglectful in ways. If the kid was sick, they just let her be and didn't look after her. I remember this one time, I hadn't seen Julia for a couple of days. I decided to go see where she was. My in-laws were none too nice about my coming and visiting, but I decided to go anyway. So I went and poked my head in the door, and I said to my mother-in-law, "I haven't seen Julia going about these last days. What's going on with her?" Bueno, soon as I open my mouth, Julia cries out to me, "Ay, Mama, look at how I am. I'm dying, I reckon." And sure enough, when I go over to where she's lying, I see that my kid is burning up with fever and with measles spots all over her body! I knew I had to get her over to the hospital. My in-laws weren't going to do it, I could see that. So I grabbed her and took her to the hospital, and she was given injections and medicines, and all that my poor kid needed to get rid of that monster of a fever she had. Then I took her home with me and kept her there till she was feeling better, and then she said she was going back to her grandparents' house. She was eleven years old, and I wanted her to stay with me, but Jorge told me, "No, she's going back to their place!" "Why?" I said. "They're neglecting her. Look how sick she's been, and they were doing nothing for her, not sending her to the hospital!" "Well, maybe my mother doesn't know about hospitals, that's all," he answers me. "She's never been to one. How's she going to know?"

So that was it, Julia stayed with them—just like before. But it wasn't long after that time that all of us had to move on again. We saw that we couldn't stay in our houses in San Vicente. Too dangerous. This was the late seventies, and you know what was happening then, right? Lots of political problems then, and we were in the middle of it. For months Jorge and his father were sleeping up in the hills. Soldiers from the Fuerza Armada were coming around to houses at night and hauling off men, people they thought might be linked up with the FMLN. You see, there were these meetings going on in San Vicente. Jorge told me about it, since he was going to them with his father. At these meetings the organizers were saying things that we had never heard before. You know, how the land belongs to the ones who work it; how we've got to organize and fight for our rights. The army had decided to crack down. You'd wake up in the morning, and you'd find people dead in the streets. Or you'd be taking a bus somewhere—this happened to me up there—and the soldiers would come on the bus searching people. I saw with my own eyes how they hauled this poor young kid off the bus. She was carrying a pistol and must have been linked up some way with the FMLN. Well, they hauled her off and in front of everyone they ripped her clothes off, raped her, and then killed her. You couldn't do a thing. You just had to stand there and be witness to the whole thing. After that I knew we couldn't stay in San Vicente anymore. I was scared as hell that pretty soon one of us was going to have something bad happen to them. The men were figuring the same way. But where to go? We headed back to Cabañas. When we got there, folks told us that the same crap was going on up there. It wasn't safe anywhere. People were fleeing from there too. They'd heard about refugee camps just across the border in Honduras. Nobody wanted to leave the country, but we figured we had no choice. We had to go, like it or not.

For the next six years or so, that's where we stayed. Up in Mesa Grande, a refugee camp. I'm not going to tell you I liked it up there. No. But it was safe for us. And for me, it was a place where I think I can say I began opening up my eyes. I mean, I began to have a new way of looking at things. Here's what happened. I was up there for just a few weeks when this woman from Spain—she belonged to a group called Médicos sin Fronteras—well, she approached me and asked if I wanted to help out with the health committee they had up there. "Yes," I told her. But I said, "I don't think my husband is going to let me, especially if I've got to be there at night." "Why's that?" she asked. "My husband is the jealous type," I said. "He doesn't want me leaving the house. And if I leave at night, he'll figure I'm going to look for some other man. Like one in the house isn't enough to deal with, right?" "I see," she said. "I'll go have a word with him, all right?" "Yes, that's fine with me," I told her.

So she spoke to Jorge—I don't know what she told him—but Jorge agreed that I could join the committee. He wasn't any too happy about it, I could see that. Because, when I started going off to the clinic or meetings at night, he'd follow me to where I was. Then, when the meeting or the work was over and I'd go back to our shack, I'd go in the door, and ten seconds later he'd come walking in behind me. He never said a word. What could he say? I wasn't up to anything bad. And really, it was an important thing for me—the first time I worked at something outside the house. I learned a lot from that Spanish lady. I learned about first aid, how to give injections, and how to read thermometers. After a while I even learned to read written things. Up to then I couldn't read. But I started taking classes, and I picked it up. As I say, my eyes began to open up.

What also helped me see things more clearly were these classes, sort of lectures, that some of the international people and FMLN people were giving. All of us were told to go, women and men. And Jorge agreed to go with me. At those lectures I heard things—Jorge, too—that we had never heard anyone say before. Things like how God made both men and women with heads and hands, that just as women could use a gun and be fighters, so could men wash dishes or pick up a broom and sweep the floor. Never before had I heard this, and it made a big impression on me.

At the time, Jorge and I were still having problems. He even went for a while to live with his parents, who were up there. I had gotten fed up with his jealousy, his getting drunk every so often and then whacking me around. I told him that I wasn't going to stand for that crap anymore. Besides, they had rules up in the refugee camp that nobody was supposed to have liquor on them. That helped. I had some support with that. And you know what? Jorge stopped. He decided to come back, and he agreed to stop all that crap. We even got formally married up there after awhile. Some priest came by and married a whole group of us. No, there were no parties or rings or any of that. But you had a church marriage, something we hadn't bothered with before. And since then, since those years in the refugee camp, things have been better between us. These days Jorge might have a few beers, and even I have one now and then when my head is bothering me, but nobody is going around drunk anymore, and there's no more of that whacking me around.

So you could say that I, we, had it pretty good those six or seven years in Honduras. The bad part was that a few of my kids went off to the monte. Julia first, then her brother Marcos, and then Elena. The two girls managed all right, I knew about them. But Marcos disappeared. None of us knew anything about him. We had to accept that we lost him. Things like that happened during the war, right? We said our nine rosaries for him, and that was it. Later, Jorge got involved in it a little too. He didn't go off to the monte like the kids did. He was a courier once in awhile. He'd go away for a few weeks, and he'd help the guerrillas out by transporting supplies—food, armaments, whatever. He doesn't talk much about it. I don't know all of what he did. And me? No, I didn't get into it when we were up there in Honduras. I had young kids in the house with me. I'd had two more when we were up there. I just worked with the health committee and took care of things in the house. It wasn't till we left Honduras and came back to El Salvador that I sort of got involved with the guerrillas.

My involvement started when we got to Santa Marta. This was in '87 or '88. When we were up in Mesa Grande we heard that it was possible to go back to El Salvador. The FMLN were in control of some areas, and even though it wasn't completely safe, we decided to go. Santa Marta was a lousy place, but at least it was in our country, and you could settle there. The old folks, my in-laws, came there too, though not for a year or so. During that year, Julia came out of the monte, and I had her living with me. Her and her baby, Margarita. She'd got pregnant up there, and she came down to have the baby in Santa Marta. I helped her out. I knew that she likely wasn't going to stay too long. And sure enough, soon as she could, she went back to the monte, taking Margarita with her. That's Julia, right?

Jorge started working again as a courier, and I had joined up too. You know, help out when I could. They needed people to carry things from one spot to another, and we women—you know, carrying baskets on our heads the way we always do—we could help out in that way. I did it for about a couple of years or so. Never had any problem except once, near the time that they had started the negotiations for peace. The war was still going on, and you still had problems in the area. I had taken a bus to go over to Sensuntepeque to buy batteries and bring them back to Santa Marta to be picked up by the guerrillas. These batteries were used in the radio equipment, for flashlights, and to make land mines. I had just bought ten packs of these batteries and was about to head home when I got stopped by some soldiers. I think they had been eyeing me and were ready to pounce. They took me to their camp, and some sergeant or colonel or whatever the hell he was says to me real nasty, "And what the hell are you doing with these?" I answered, "They were on sale here for a good price. People use them for flashlights and recorders. I sell them in Santa Marta." "It's prohibited to sell batteries these days," he says. "Don't you know that?" And I say, "They are on sale here. How can I know it's prohibited?" He's looking at me real hard, and he says, "How many children do you have?" "I've got eight," I said, "and this one here." I pointed to my stomach because I was six months pregnant with Pablo. "And how many are with the guerrillas?" "Not one," I tell him.

This officer, whether he believed me or not, says nothing more. Just real quick and cold like he tells me to come back the next day, and they'll give me the money I paid for the batteries. Which is what happened. And then, because I didn't want to go back to Santa Marta empty-handed, I bought two packs of batteries, not ten, and put them in my basket under a lot of bread. I figured I'm safe now. But no! I get stopped by another bunch of soldiers as I'm on my way home. One of them tells me to show him what's in the basket. I remove the rag covering the bread, and then he tells me to dump it out. Thank God, there was another soldier there who said, "No, leave her be. She'll only ruin the bread." And they let me go. I don't know what would have happened if they caught me. Surely I would have had to face that devil in the army camp again. I don't think they would have killed me, no, but it might have got nasty. Who knows? I was lucky. I made it home with no more trouble.

As it turned out, soon after that incident we got word that the peace negotiations were going well and we could get out of Santa Marta. Some FMLN people came to us in Santa Marta and told us about the communities they were starting up around Mount Guazapa. I'd never been there. Jorge went over and took a look. His father and mother, along with Julia, had gone there a month before. When Jorge came back he told me, "It'll be fine. Nice place. I want to be over there near my father." I had never liked Santa Marta, so I said, "All right, let's try it out."

This was back in '92. I was, let's see, thirty-nine years old then. I had ten kids by then, counting Marcos, who had disappeared. The kids all came to Comunidad Guazapa. Four of them, including Julia, got their own places in the community. And five were still living with me. The community back then wasn't much more than a lot of brush and woods, with people living over in the broken-down buildings of the rich folks who used to have their big house there. It was pretty, though, you could see that. You had Mount Guazapa right in front of you. And people had started planting their maíz and frijol.

That's what we did. Built our house out of the materials the FMLN gave us. And we grabbed some land—later it got divided up evenly between all of us—and Jorge began farming again. He was happy with that. And me, I was back in the house making tortillas, sweeping up, taking care of kids, and wondering what I might do next.

And then I had the surprise of my life. Marcos shows up! Out of nowhere, like he was back from the dead, he shows up in the community. He'd been riding a bus, and an aunt of mine spotted him. At first, Marcos pretended like he didn't know her, that he had another name. But then he told her who he was, and he began asking about me. She told him where to find me, and, well, suddenly he was standing there in front of me at our house here.

I couldn't believe it! As I told you, we'd already said the nine rosaries for him. But he was alive! And then, slowly, he began telling me how it had gone for him the last eight years. What happened, he said, is that he had gone off to join the guerrillas. That I knew. He got his training at some camp up in the monte, learned to use a rifle, and then he got sent off to fight. Pretty soon after, his unit got caught in an ambush. Everyone scattered, and he was left alone with nothing but the shirt on his back. He didn't know where his unit was, and then, walking around, he came to the house of some lady. Turns out this lady's son had recently been killed—as a soldier or what, I don't know. She told Marcos that she would be willing to put him up. And what she did is arrange his legal papers, his identity card, so that Marcos took on the name and identity papers of her son. Marcos figured, better to stay with her than to go looking for his unit, especially since he discovered that the guerrillas had made a judgment on him and considered him a traitor. The woman really cared for him, he told me. There was a time when she had sent him to a store to buy some stuff for the cow she had, and on the way he got stopped by the Fuerza Armada. Marcos had been with the lady four or five years by then, and when the Fuerza Armada told her they were going to recruit him, the lady broke down sobbing. She didn't want to lose Marcos. So the officer told her that she could have him back. But a month later they came by again, and this time they did recruit him—never mind what the lady said. And that's how he wound up as a soldier with the Fuerza Armada. For three years, something like that, he was with them. He even got sent to Mexico for a while to get some additional training, the way I understand it. I can't say I know much about what he did with the Fuerza Armada. I had no curiosity about that, since me and the rest of the family were with the guerrillas, and, well, I didn't want to know about any of what he had done with them.

Anyhow, Marcos moved in with me and Jorge and the rest of the kids I still had at home—at least for a while. He didn't last long, though. I guess he didn't feel so good here in the community; it wasn't for him. And besides, he got hooked up with some young woman here, and the two of them decided to move up north. And now he's not in El Salvador anymore. He's in the United States. In Virginia. He's been there about ten years now. Marcos and three more of my sons are living up there. The last one just left a few months ago. As a mojado. That's how they get up there. I talk to them every so often. They've got their cell phones, and for a few years now I've got mine. So we're in communication.

Actually, it worked out pretty well for my sons in Virginia. They're having a tough time right now because the economy up there isn't too good.

They've got less work. But when they have work, they make out well. They've got their money. And they have helped us out too. You see, we've got a refrigerator and our color TV and our small truck. And for Mother's Day one of my boys just sent me a microwave. They've been a blessing for us in that way because it's hard to accumulate much cash when all you've got is your milpa and a few animals. Yes, their money has helped us out.

Me, I try to make a little money too these days. But most of what I've done here in the community doesn't pay. It's nice when you make a few centavos for your work, but really I don't do it for that. I do things in the community because, well, it's my belief that I've got to contribute. Back some years I was president of the community—bueno, that's not a job that pays you. Yes, I was the first woman who was president. Since me, there's been one more. I lasted only a year because I got pregnant with Sara, and I had to get a caesarean at the hospital and was laid up for a while. I couldn't manage it all, so I stepped aside. Still, I did manage to get some things done. We got some organizations, like IMU, to give us money to set up a kindergarten and a comedor right out here in the community. The kindergarten got built, but it never got started, since we couldn't get a teacher to run it. The comedor did get going, and it functioned for three years. I was the organizer of that. Each Sunday I'd go to town, often San Salvador, to buy all kinds of vegetables, fruits, and chicken and meat. Me and a few others did the cooking. Kids age two to twelve could come and have a good meal there every lunchtime, and their parents didn't have to pay one centavo. Me, I got a few colones for running the whole thing. Unfortunately, the organization that was paying for this said they had no more money, and that was the end of it.

Since that time I've continued to work in the community as secretary of our women's group. I've been doing that for years now. Part of what we do is have meetings where we women do this talking, what we call "consciousness raising." We've still got the problem of machismo going on—more in some houses than others. Me, I've solved that problem more or less with Jorge. No more of the old crap like I used to have. Others are still struggling with it. So we talk about these things. We've got a group of about twenty-five women who come regularly. And we also do certain projects together—things that make us a little cash. We've opened up a small grocery store run by women over near the school. We buy large quantities of things like rice and flour over in Suchitoto, we put it in small bags, and we sell it. Or we'll make tamales, say, and when there's a soccer match going on here we'll sell them along with soft drinks. We make a little cash for ourselves that way, and also it's a good way to get women working together, organizing ourselves. I like doing it. Since that time up in the refugee camp I've always been interested in this kind of activity.

For women of my generation, that's about all we can do. We didn't have the chance to get an education like the kids today. I never went to school, apart from when I had a few lessons up in Cabañas that some old drunk gave for a while. That, and what I picked up in the refugee camp. I would have liked to study, maybe be a nurse or some career like that. Now, what can I say? It's too late. And the pity is that my kids haven't grabbed the opportunity. For some of them, like Julia, it was too late. But my boys haven't made use of the schooling they could have gotten here. They prefer to work in the fields with Jorge or take off for the United States.

The one who I think is going to get some education, maybe go to university, is my last one, Sara. She's only ten years old now, but she's very smart. And very curious. She asks me all kinds of things: how women get pregnant, how they give birth, what menstruation is. Damn, when I was her age I never thought about this stuff. Today they get some of this information in school, and I think the kids today are growing up quicker. Their hormones are working on them when they're younger. Maybe all that snack food with the chemicals that the kids today are eating. I heard someone mention that, but who knows? They just seem to be growing up quicker. Girls nine or ten years old, they're already little women, no? Take a look at Sara. She puts on her shoes with the raised heels, puts on her skirt, and she's looking like a young woman. I talk to her. We're close. I tell her, "Sara, don't you get any ideas about marrying young! You finish your schooling, get a career, find a way to support yourself." She's smart. She listens. Says she might want to be a lawyer like Luis's son Francisco. That's fine with me. I'd like to see that. I'd like to have one of my kids go that way. I'm praying it works out.

CHAPTER TEN

Francisco

The Oldest Son

At twenty-six years old, Francisco (or Chico, as his family calls him) is the oldest son, and if Luis can be accused of having a favorite, Chico is no doubt the one. And just as Luis's life has been an unexpected odyssey, so too has Francisco's path been fraught with unforeseen and sometimes bewildering twists and turns. Born in the refugee camp in Honduras, he arrived in Comunidad Guazapa as an unschooled ten-year-old with the sole ambition of following in his father's footsteps to the milpa. However, as a product of the changing times and changing community, he began to travel on a road not taken—at least not by anybody in his family. And, as he relates in his story below, he became the first to graduate high school, continue to university, and take up his new profession in the capital, San Salvador.

When we first met Francisco in 2005, he had just begun his university studies. Luis had proudly insisted that we meet "my boy the lawyer," and, accordingly, Francisco showed up on the veranda of Luis and Julia's house. A short and skinny young man, Francisco appeared then to be three or four years younger than his twenty-one years and somewhat lacking in self-confidence. While it was clear that he wanted to live up to his father's lavish praise, he seemed at a loss for words as we tried to engage him in conversation. Instead, he sat there in a broken plastic chair, which was in stark contrast to the designer jeans and spiffy dress shirt he was wearing, and after fifteen minutes of nervous nods and one-sentence answers, he politely excused himself.

I mention this first impression of ours because four years later, when we met Francisco again in San Salvador (the first time we had seen him since that initial encounter in Comunidad Guazapa), he seemed barely recognizable—a new man, so to speak. He had put on weight, and his dark eyes glowed with an easy confidence. When he spoke, it was not in quick sentences but rather in paragraphs and with a vocabulary seldom heard in Comunidad Guazapa. We met with him several times, both in the city and in the community. On all occasions he seemed eager to tell his personal tale. And he seemed equally eager to inform us of how he sees the needs of the community and the country. "I'm no radical, but I have my dreams for the future here," he told us. "And I have every intention of playing a part in it!"

We turn, then, to some of Francisco's dreams—and also to some of his past nightmares.

Thank you, I appreciate your congratulations, but to be clear, I am not yet licensed as a lawyer. I've only finished the course work. I've made it through that hurdle. But I've still got a thesis to write before I'm licensed, and that's almost another year ahead of me. Meanwhile, I'm looking around me, trying to see what direction to take. A few doors have begun to open, such as the job I have now working as an assistant in the office of a deputy in the Asamblea Legislativa. Good work; I like it. You get a feel for how politics are conducted in this country. And I can see myself maybe taking that path, the political path, I mean. But I've got time, verdad? God knows, it took me time to get here, and when I think of it—as I sometimes do—it seems amazing that I am where I am today. Hard to figure it, really. It could have turned out a heck of a lot differently. I tell you, I've had my share of blessings. Truly, I have.

I suppose my father has told you about my childhood, no? Right, I was born in Honduras. That's what my birth certificate reads: born in Honduras but a citizen of El Salvador. Up in Mesa Grande, in the refugee camp, is where I was born to my mama, Flora, and to my papa, whom you know. You don't know my mama, do you? She's up in Santa Marta now, living with my older sister and my younger brother. She's living with some guy now but doesn't have any more kids. I see her quite often these days when I have a holiday or a long weekend. For years I sort of avoided her, but now I like going up there, seeing her and my sister. We're on real good terms these days. It's the way it should be. And after all, they were the ones I spent my first years with, and really, for me as a kid growing up in the refugee camp the first four or five years of my life, it was a pretty good life. I didn't know hardly a thing about what we were doing there or why, so for me it was fun.

When I think back on it, I can imagine that for the adults, my mama and others, it must have been difficult living in those makeshift houses we had, which were usually one huge room divided into three sections, with a separate family in each section. No privacy for them, right? But as a kid, what it meant for me is that I had other kids, not just my sister or baby brother, but kids from other families living right next to me. So I always had someone to play with. My mama tells me—you see, I've asked her a lot of questions about that period, which I don't remember so well, except for a few things—she tells me that I was a lively kid. I suppose I was what they call "hyperactive." It's hard for me to imagine it these days, but she tells me that when I was only three or four years old I'd want to drag her to every party or fiesta so that I could sing and dance. Supposedly, I liked being the center of attention. I don't remember that stuff. What I do remember is that up there in the camp we had a carpenter who knew how to make guitars and violins and that I had my mother get me both. I started learning to play them, and I had this dream of forming a musical group with my pals up there. But I didn't have the chance, I guess, because already at five years old I was leaving the camp and leaving my mama and sister and my pals.

How that happened I can't exactly say. I don't know all the details. But what I recall is that I chose to go with my father. For a boy of five years old, your papa is your hero. He's the one you want to be with, the one you love the most. At least for me it was that way, even though I didn't get to see him much in the refugee camp because he was off in the monte. I knew there was some kind of war going on, that he was involved in it, but I had no idea then what that was about. All I knew is that now and then he'd come back to the camp, and when he came he'd always bring some gift for me—some mangos or sugarcane or candies for me. And at night he and I would sleep together, me wrapped in his arms. Except there was a period when he came back and he didn't stay at our house—our shack, really— but he stayed somewhere else. And when I asked my mama why he wasn't with us she just said, "He has other things he's attending to." It turned out that he had another woman up there and that my mama and he had separated. I realized this because one day some people on the directorate of the camp, Mesa Grande, they came to me and said, "Who do you want to live with, your mama or your papa?" I was about five or six then, and I didn't quite get it. But it turned out that my mama and papa had split up, and my papa had decided to go to El Salvador with his new woman—Meches is her name—and I was being asked whether I was going to stay with my mama or go with my papa. Can you imagine it? What a terrible thing, no? The authorities in the camp were asking me since, if I chose to go with my father, they had to arrange my papers so that I could return legally, you see. And me, so tied to my papa like I was and not really understanding what it would mean to go back to El Salvador right then, I naturally told the authorities, "I'm going with my papa." My mama was very upset, of course, and she told me that there was a war in El Salvador, to which I answered, "Papa will protect me!" And then she tried to blackmail me a little by telling me that if I left, I couldn't take the guitar and violin with me, to which I answered, "Papa will buy me new ones." She really didn't want me leaving her. I remember that on the day I was leaving I went to say good-bye to her, and again she told me I could still change my mind. When I told her that I was going with papa anyway, she handed me a big package of bread so I would have something to eat along the way, and then she burst into tears. That I remember. What I don't remember—but she told me later—is that I answered her, "Mama, don't cry, I haven't died yet!"

I didn't see my mama or my sister or baby brother again for another three or four years. My papa and Meches, along with Meches's two older boys, who were five years and six years older than me, we all went to Chalatenango, to a place called San Antonio Los Ranchos, which is near the border with Honduras. It was, I imagine, a place safe enough for FMLN people. My father established us there in a house, and we even had a small milpa. He, my papa, was with us some of the time, and the rest of the time he was off somewhere doing things. What I realized later, and besides he eventually told me, was that he was carrying out various operations for the guerrillas. When he'd be back with us, he'd work in the milpa, and I would go off with him. I liked that. He didn't let me do any real work until I was seven or maybe eight, but as soon as he did let me work with him I really liked it. No, I didn't go to any school, hardly at all. My papa told me that I could go if I wanted to, but he didn't emphasize it. "It's up to you," he said. I had gone to kindergarten in the refugee camp, and I went for about a month in San Antonio Los Ranchos but then quit. I was satisfied to just be in the milpa or just fooling around with my pals I had there.

What I recall is that there was a period when my father brought me over to Santa Marta, where my mama was then. He told her and me that I should stay there for a few months, and then he'd come back and get me. I didn't know what he was involved with. He never said. In retrospect, it must have been some mission, but it couldn't have been the "final offensive," since he wasn't involved in that. I don't know. All I know is that he suddenly one day brought me there and left. My mama, she was overjoyed. And it was good to be with her again, though I had my mind on my papa, wondering where he was and if and when he was coming back. And eventually he did. After a few months, something like that. He came back and told my mama he was taking me with him again. She was not too happy with that, but that was the agreement between them. And for me, yes, I preferred it that way.

The problem then was that it was very unsafe to be taking the main road between Santa Marta and Los Ranchos. The Fuerza Armada was stopping buses, and they'd have the people get out—this is what my papa explained to me—and they'd have you take off your shirt. If they found some scars on you, bullet wounds, then they'd figure you were with the guerrillas, or you had been with them, and then things would go badly for you. So the only way to get back to San Antonio Los Ranchos was through the hills and trying not to run into any army patrols. It took us about three weeks or maybe more. A group of several people went, and one of the guerrillas served as a guide. You couldn't go during the day and sometimes not at night either. And sometimes we had no food, but the people in the hamlets up there would see us and feed us. It was exhausting. And at one point my papa said, "We're going to rest for a while up in a hospital that we've got in our control." And I was thinking, that's wonderful, finally a bed to sleep in and something good to eat! But when we get to this so-called hospital, it was just a couple of shacks with planks made of bamboo for beds and with wounded guerrillas lying there. I saw then something of what the war was like. And really, that entire trek through the monte, it gave me some picture of what my father had lived all those years. And I tell you, not only then but till this day I truly admire him—what he was willing to go through along with his compas in order to fight for a more just system here in the country. I didn't understand it all then, but I could begin to see what hell they went through. He'd done it for years. Me, twenty days or so was enough for me! I was glad as hell to finally get back to San Antonio Los Ranchos.

It must have been a year or so later that, with the war winding down and the negotiations going on for a peace settlement, my papa came and told us we were heading to a new place to live. Over near Mount Guazapa, a few hours' bus ride—or truck ride, the way it turned out—from where we were in Chalatenango. And so we went and came over to where my papa still is today. In Comunidad Guazapa. My mama stayed in Santa Marta, where she had settled in with my brother and sister and some of her other family around. She's still up there today. But I didn't go see her for years. We were cut off. It wasn't like today, when you pick up your cell phone and chat with each other. We were out of touch completely. And me, at ten years old I settled into the new community, living with papa and Meches and her boys and a couple of more kids that my papa and her had in the meantime. It seemed pretty good to me.

My papa had his milpa, and I'd work alongside him. I truly enjoyed it, getting up in the morning and going up the hillside and doing what you do to raise your crop. It's good work—enjoyable, if you don't mind working hard. And my father worked me hard. He has this way about him—how can I put it?—this way of letting you know what he wants and how he wants it. It's something in his voice, because he's not the kind to whack you around. I can't remember him ever hitting me. But now that I was no longer a little kid, he wanted me to carry my weight. Say, for example, I wasn't feeling so good, a toothache, say. And of course, I had toothaches, since we in the campo didn't go around brushing our teeth. But say I had a tooth hurting me, his attitude was, "Look, boy, if you're sick, then go to the hospital. If not, let's get to work." Mind you, if I was truly sick, like with pneumonia—which I once had—then he'd be the first to take you to the hospital and take care of you. But anything short of that, his attitude was one of ignoring you. He's someone who knows how to work hard, still to this day. And he expected the same from me, and I admit he did turn me into a good worker. In the milpa, I mean. He taught me how to farm, and if I do say so, I became a damned good worker; good enough, in fact, that already as a teenager others were even paying me to help them out, those that could afford it. Twenty colones a day is what I got paid. Good money in those days. And my papa, too, gave me a small piece of land, and he told me, "It's yours to grow your own maíz and frijol, and if you don't make a centavo, that's too bad, and if you do make some cash, you keep it." I was about fourteen then—going to school, yes, sometimes—but my mind was more on working to make money. Working in the milpa in the mornings and sometimes going to school in the afternoons—that's how I did it. I wasn't figuring to do anything with my life except be like my father. A farmer. That's the only model I had, and especially then—I had no mouths to feed, right?—I wound up with some money in my pocket. Money that I got paid from working for others and money that I got from the eight sacks of maíz and four of frijol that I harvested that year from my own little piece of land.

That money didn't stay in my pocket too long, of course. I spent it soon as I could. On clothing first—pants, shirts, shoes—because up to then I didn't have much, just like any other campesino. And then I went and got something I had been dreaming of—a bicycle. Back in that time, having a bicycle was really something. There was a bike shop in Suchitoto with maybe a hundred brand new bikes, one lined up after the other. "I'm look-ing to buy a bike," I told the owner. "All right," he says. "Come in and have a look." Bueno, the very first one he showed me, I see it's got a double seat in back, a water bottle on the frame, and I say, "I like it. How much?" "Nine hundred colones," he says. It was a lot of money, but me, I answer immediately, "Fine, I'll take it." No negotiating on my part, no looking at any others. Just like that I tell him, "Here's the money. Put some air in the tires so I can take it." And the next thing you know, there I am riding proud as can be all around Suchitoto, showing off my new bike in the park there, and then riding back to the community on this new bike.

That was a proud day for me. There I was, only fourteen years old, and I had my new bike and my new clothes. I felt great. Never mind that after sixth grade I had dropped out of school, that I wasn't going anywhere in life. Where was there to go anyway? I had no model except in my family. My father was my model. He was a hardworking campesino, and at that point so was I. I had finished sixth grade. I could read and write. And the truth is, I had been a good student. I liked school. Learning came easy to me. Math, the sciences—real easy. I was even known as the top student. I used to read books on the side, and I enjoyed getting into discussions with people who knew things. People like Joaquín, my father's neighbor. He reads a lot, and he knows what's happening in the world. He drinks too much, goes on these binges now and then, but that's something else. When he's sober, you can talk to him, and you can learn things. We used to talk quite a bit, and I enjoyed it. I liked learning, but still I didn't see myself going to more school then. Besides, I was making good money, and that's what interested me.

My problem back then was something else. My father wasn't getting along with Meches, and one day we come back to the house, and we find two rolled-up balls of clothing outside in the front yard. My papa's and mine. Meches had thrown him out, and me too. I can't say I understood at that moment what was going on, but my father said, "Fine, son, let's go put up our own house over in that small plot I've got." Me, I was thinking that was a good idea. I preferred living alone with my father, just the two of us instead of that whole brood over in Meches's house. Meches had never been a mother to me; I never called her "mama" like the other kids did. So it was fine with me. But then, little by little, I caught on to what was happening. My father had his eye on someone else. Julia. It was hard to believe. She was twenty years younger than him, and she had a couple of kids of her own. But my father, he had fallen for her, and he was going over there constantly. And me, instead of being number one in his life, now I had become number two or even number three. So when he came to me one day and said that we were going to move in with Julia and her kids, I felt, "No way, I'm not going." I was real upset. And looking back at it, I became something of a *llorón*. I started envying my friends who had mamas that took care of them, fed them something whenever they were hungry, or looked after them when they were sick or had twisted a leg playing soccer. I had nobody to look after me, and I began feeling all sorry for myself. And I began to think of my own mama up there in Santa Marta and how it had been five years since I had seen her or heard her voice. So I decided to go up there and pay her a visit.

It turned out to be a short visit—only a few days. As soon as I got there, my mama took one look at me, and she started crying. She couldn't stop. She came over and felt my ribs, and she said, "Aren't you eating down there? Aren't they feeding you?" My mama is a real kind person, very warm. She fed me, really spoiled me those days. But all the time she was weeping. I couldn't stand it. It was too much for me. I told her I had to go back, that I'd come see her again when I could, though it was years before I saw her again. Actually, it's only in the past three years or so, when I was already in the university, that I started visiting her regularly. Her and my sister and brother. They live a tranquil life up there in Santa Marta. My sister cleans houses and is still unmarried. And my brother, well, he's something of a playboy, going from party to party. Neither of them have much schooling. But they're fine. These days when I go up there my mama tells me, "You've filled out. I can see you're eating well." And when we walk through the town there she'll say to me, "Chico, all the girls here are eyeing you." And me, I just put my arm around her and tell her, "No need for that. I've already got my sweetheart—it's you!" My mama and I talk a lot, and she's filled me in on some of what happened between her and my father. I've been real curious about that. If you hear my papa tell it, he turned from her because she was with someone else. I don't believe that at all. I know him well enough now. I admire him, like I told you, but I figure it must have been he who started with someone else, maybe even more than one. He has his eyes open for women, or at least he did back then. That's how I see it. And my mama, look, she got together with someone, but she never had more kids. Really a shame what happened between my parents. They had loved each other, and it just didn't last.

Anyway, back when I was fourteen years old I didn't really comprehend any of this. All I knew was that I couldn't stay with my mama, and I didn't want to go back to my papa and Julia. I wasn't comfortable there. I told my father—I've always been able to level with him—and I decided that it would be best for me to leave Comunidad Guazapa and go over to the community where my grandma and grandpa were living. Yes, my papa's parents. It's a few kilometers from here. You've been there, right? Way off the main road. Today the place is more developed than it was back then. Same as Comunidad Guazapa. Back then my grandparents were living in this shack, and they had no electricity. I settled in with them and started to go to school there. But I tell you, it was boring as hell. My grandparents would eat their supper at four or five in the afternoon, and then soon as the sun was down they went off to sleep. Some folks there had televisions that ran on car batteries. My grandparents didn't. So I found myself going to sleep at six o'clock and then going to classes in a school they had there. Well, after a few months of living like that, I'd had enough. I figured, like it or not, I had to go back to my father's house and live with him and Julia. And that's what I did.

I returned to school in Comunidad Guazapa not so much because I wanted to study for some purpose. No, I went back because—I tell you, it makes me laugh to think of it—I went to school to see the *bichas*. That's what I had on my mind then more than anything else—girls, girls! Best way to meet the bichas was at school, and that was my main reason for going. You see, I had sort of entered a new stage. I was no longer a llorón; instead, I became a *rebelde*. With my pals I used to go out at night looking to mess around. No, nothing delinquent or anything like that. We drank beer or guaro, and we smoked. No, not marijuana. Nobody had access to it back then, though I suppose if one of us had got hold of some, I surely would have tried it or anything else then. I dyed my hair blonde and thought to wear an earring like some others were doing, but when I put some tape on my ear for a couple of days to see how it would feel, I decided against it. My father didn't know exactly what I was up to. I'd leave the house at night without telling him—he didn't say anything—and my friends and I would go out. One of us might have a girlfriend in another community, and we'd say, "Hey, let's go over and have a look at the bichas there!"

Needless to say, with all that gallivanting about I was not putting in much time in school. We had just started learning English that year—in seventh grade. None of us wanted to study English. My friends were all saying, "Hell, I'm no gringo. What do I need to learn English for?" And I didn't study it either, which meant that I failed the course. Almost failed, I should say. Because the principal of the school—not Lucita, she came later—this guy, don Abel, he liked me, and he told me that I'd better start studying hard, since English was an obligatory subject and I would not move on to eighth grade if I didn't pass. So I hit the books a little, and I passed. And I passed again in eighth grade and in ninth grade. That was the end of the line for those of us studying in Comunidad Guazapa then. Our school only went up to ninth grade, not twelfth grade like today. If you made it through ninth, your only way of continuing was to go to town, to Suchitoto, and study at the high school there. Looking back, I imagine that I never would have gone on. I'd have stayed in the community and been a farmer. I'd have just gone on working with my father, I expect. Yet something happened to change my outlook. A real blessing for me. This teacher, Kathy, a woman who was working with the Cuerpo de Paz, was placed in our school to teach English to the ninth graders. None of my friends paid much attention. They still weren't interested in learning English, no matter how she tried to interest them. I don't know why, but for me it was different. I liked how she was teaching, and I began to take an interest in the subject. I became the best student in the class. Then what happened is that there was a week or so that I didn't show up at classes. You know, for a campesino you've got these periods when you've got to work full time, sowing or fertilizing or harvesting, and you're busy from dawn to dusk. There's no time for anything else. No school, nothing. So for a while I was skipping classes, and Kathy began inquiring as to where I was, and then she paid me a visit at my home. We talked for a while, and then she asked me, "What do you prefer, farming or studying?" I told her I liked them both. And she said, "Thinking ahead, the future, what do you want to do, farm or study? You're going to have to choose." I told her that I would like to study. And then she said to me, "Look, Francisco, I don't usually make promises, yet this time I'm going to make one. If you decide that you want to study, I will help you. Probably not with money, but I will show you the way, and I'll open some doors for you." Me, I was astonished. One is accustomed to looking to one's family for support, and yet here was a complete stranger, an outsider, proposing to help me out. I didn't know what to say exactly, but I indicated that I liked the idea. And, you see, I didn't know it at the time, but that was the beginning of my taking a new path, one that I could never have dreamed of before.

From then on, Kathy began guiding me and helping me out, like she said she would. And I had a cousin, Lucita's brother, who also encouraged me. He was a bright guy—he's an accountant now—and he told me to take whatever help I was offered and continue studying. The major influence, though, was Kathy. She told me to think clearly about who my friends were. And she warned me not to hang out with those who were going nowhere with their lives but rather to hang with those who were serious, people who I could learn something from. My ears perked up, and I listened to that advice. She told me that she wanted to speak to my father, and she then came out to the house and had a talk with him during which she told him that if I were going to succeed in school, I could not be working daily in the milpa. I wasn't sure what his reaction would be, but he went along with it. So at that point Kathy arranged for me to get into a course to study English at the Centro Cultural in San Salvador. It was a bit intimidating, the mere thought of going to the capital, since I'd never been there in my life. But she escorted me there in the beginning, showing me how to manage with the bus connections. And then she helped me get into the high school in Suchitoto in order to finish my high school studies.

She was my mentor. Every young person needs someone like that. Out in the campo you don't have people who can guide you. At least when I was growing up there was nobody. Kathy did that for me. She helped me to believe that I might realize some of my dreams—if I was willing to work for it. You see, she was living there in a rented house near the ciudadela, and I used to go visit her after school. We'd practice English, she'd let me use her computer—it was the first time I'd ever had access to one—and we'd talk. Very interesting discussions. From her I learned about all kinds of things—the United States, the war in Iraq, [Osama] bin Laden, world affairs, everything. She even would cook for me sometimes, treat me like a mother would treat their own kid. It was wonderful for me. Except the bichas in the community started spreading rumors that Kathy and me were like a couple, that something was going on between us. Really, that annoyed me. I even began pulling away, not visiting Kathy so often, since I didn't want that kind of talk to continue. For her part, Kathy—I don't know if she had heard anything or not—but she acted normal, and she never shut her door to me. She continued to treat me with kindness and give me advice.

Meanwhile, I had become a diligent student both at the Centro Cultural and at the high school in Suchitoto. I was determined to do well. And what made me even more determined is that I realized that in both those places there was a real prejudice against those of us who come from the campo. At the Centro Cultural I was learning English alongside kids whose families were well-heeled, sons and daughters of diplomats, business people. None of the students there would believe that I came from the campo until the day I brought in a picture of me in Comunidad Guazapa. Many of those kids were Areneros, and of course we got into some political discussions, heated discussions at times.[1] Those kids knew nothing about what was going on in the campo. What they knew was vacations abroad, big houses or apartments with elevators in them—rich kids. And they tended to look down on me and my background. But it wasn't only there in the capital of the country. The same thing happened at the high school in Suchitoto, except there the kids knew exactly who lived in the town and who was coming in from the campo to study at the high school. And it wasn't just the kids that looked down on the group of us—maybe fifteen of us—who were coming in from the communities. The teachers too! They were usually prejudiced against you. You may not believe this, but they would check your hands, your fingernails, and your clothing right down to your socks to make sure you were clean enough to be in school. If not, you'd get tossed out that day. Can you imagine it? But at least there were some teachers who acted differently, more sympathetically. One of my teachers saw I was carrying a newspaper in my back pocket, and he asked me what I'd read that day. "The soccer scores," I told him. "No, no, my boy," he said. "Start reading the newspaper from the front. Start learning what is happening here in the country." And he directed me to watch that program on Channel 12, the news program that Mauricio Funes used to have—yes, the same guy who is now president of the country, he used to be a news commentator—and I started listening regularly to these discussions of politics. It opened my eyes, truly it did. I became more determined than ever to prove to everybody there at that high school, prove to myself really, that I was a top student. I studied hard as I could and even worked for a while in one of those restaurants in Suchitoto so I could pay for my things, books, bus rides to the capital.

I knew how to work hard. My papa had taught me that. Now I applied that to my studies, and I succeeded. When it came to taking the national exam that you need to enter the university, I did real well. My grades were good enough to get into one of our universities.

Actually, Kathy and I had been talking all the while about the possibility of my going to the United States to study. I had learned English well enough, and I liked the idea. She had returned to North Carolina, and she had the intention of opening doors someplace there for me. But it didn't turn out. It didn't pan out because the date I had to go get a student visa at the U.S. Embassy—yes, I had my mind set on going to study, and my father told me it was all right with him—well, a month before you had September 11. The terrorist bombings in 2001. And to put it plainly, the gringos weren't handing out visas right then. My meeting at the embassy got put off for months, and I decided that maybe it was better to try to get into university in El Salvador.

Which is what I did. La Universidad Nacional. It's a fine place, a sort of leftist university, and one that gave scholarships to some of us from the campo and other kids who can't afford tuition. Me, I only had to pay five dollars a month tuition. And they took me into the Law Faculty. And that's how I began—five years ago. Seems like a long time ago. A lot has happened since then, to me and to El Salvador too, verdad? But that was the start for me of a new kind of life, the kind of life I'm living now. I tell you, hard as I worked to bring it about, I couldn't believe it when I got into the Law Faculty. And my papa, he was already telling everyone—you included—that I was a lawyer, even though I was a hell of a long way from that. A long way!

CHAPTER ELEVEN

Luis

Time to Sow, Time to Reap

It was mid-November, the end of the rainy season, and the noonday sun was again burning down on Luis's milpa. The week before there had been a hard and steady rain that had caused mudslides throughout the country, devastating some areas to the south and turning Comunidad Guazapa into a mucky mess. The rain destroyed much of the bean crop that Luis and others were just about to harvest. As Luis scrambled like a mountain goat up the hillside to his milpa, passing through the two-meter-high stalks of maicillo (which had managed to stand tall throughout the inundation), he cursed softly to himself and to me, as I tried hard to keep up with him. "Damn rain, look at the frijol. Brown and moldy. A few days later and we would have been all right. Now most of it is finished. Nothing you can do."

But with a resignation that perhaps only a fellow campesino could fully understand, Luis simply shrugged and patted his mongrel dog, Flaco, warmly on the head. "We still got our maicillo and our maíz, so Flaco and the rest of us are still going to eat. Ol' Flaco here, he likes his tortillas!" And with that, Luis's scowl turned into a grin as he scanned the five or six manzanas of his and Julia's milpas, which rose from where we were standing to the very foothills of Mount Guazapa. "Dawn to dusk, this is where I am every day. Not bad, no?"

Indeed, except for the browned-out beans, the whole area seemed like a miniature paradise. Yellow, blue, and purple flowers bloomed from the edges of the milpa, and from the milpa itself I looked straight up at the towering Mount Guazapa, now a dormant volcano but whose lava rocks still were scattered throughout the fields below. And facing below, in the direction of the community's houses and beyond, I saw a panorama of every conceivable shade of green in the trees, fields, and distant hills that stretched out fifteen kilometers away to the vague blue of Suchitlan Lake. Luis, who was seldom at a loss for words, simply stretched out his arms all around him, and at least for that moment his rotted frijol crop was completely forgotten.

"See that maíz growing over there next to my milpa?" Luis said. "It belongs to my neighbor, an eighty-year-old guy. Ol' Jacinto is up here every day with me, still working his milpa. No problem. The old guy works dawn to dusk. Nothing stops him." And at that moment one knew—if indeed one had any doubt—that Luis was talking not so much about his neighbor as about himself, and that no amount of rain or lost crop this season or next was going to stop him from coming up to this milpa and go on working here in his newfound paradise for as long as he, himself, went on living.

Sí, hombre, this is where I am every day of the week, except Sundays, which mostly I take off or at least only work part of the day. Or some days I've got some kind of work to do, political things in the community, or going to Suchitoto to buy my fertilizer or pesticide. Things come up sometimes that take me away from the milpa. Or talking to you, right? [He laughs loudly.] No, don't get me wrong, I like this talking, gives me a chance to remember some things, verdad? But if you ask me where I like to be most, it's up here. I figure if the day ever came that I couldn't work up here—like what happened to my papa when he got his stroke and was just like a rag sitting on his veranda—if anything happened that I couldn't come up here, I don't know what would be with me. Maybe just die, that's all. But, hell, I'm a long way from that and am not planning to ever get there if I can help it. I still got my strength. Still do. So I'm up here working same as I've been working since we got to the community.

These days I got my boys, two or three of them working with me. My oldest boy, José—the one who Julia already had when we got together—he's dropped out of school, so he's sometimes working with me. The other two, they come up with me in the morning and then leave to go to school in the afternoon. So I've got my help, you see. And way back when we just got started here in the community, Julia used to come up and work with me. She liked it that way until we started having kids, and then she had to stay around the house. Nowadays she just comes up and brings me something to eat for lunch. And then she might carry down some firewood that I chop down right over there. [Luis points to a wooded area near his milpa.] She's a fine worker, but I don't need her up here with me. Never did, really. It was more her idea.

The one I miss having up here with me is Chico. He hasn't been here with me for some years now, ever since he started at the university. Even

before then, he was studying so hard he couldn't help out like usual.
A real good worker, Chico! From the time he was just a little kid—just like
I was with my papa—Chico was the same with me. He wanted to work
with me. The only problem with him back then was getting him up in the
morning. The kid liked to sleep. It would be six in the morning, and I'd
have to shake him, "Come on, boy, get up already!" Once he got going, he
was a good worker. No arguments, nothing. Whatever I'd tell him to do,
he did it. He was hardworking, nothing lazy about that boy once he got
up there with me. Except the thing with Chico, unlike with any other kid
I've had, is that he was always asking me questions when we were taking
a break or even when we were working. When he was just a little kid he
used to ask me all kinds of things. He wanted to know how many days in
a year or in a month. Or he'd ask me how come there's a sun or stars or
a moon. I didn't know what to tell him. I'd have to take out a Bible back
in the house, and we'd look it up there. Or sometimes, later on, he'd start
asking me about the war—you know, there were some terrible battles
right where we are now, right here on Mount Guazapa—and he'd want to
know about weapons, like how many rockets you could fire with a rocket
launcher or cartridges with a rifle. Some of that I knew, of course. Not
like the moon and the stars and the sun. I didn't figure what was going
on in this kid's mind—just that he was different in that way from others.
And anyway, long as he was working as hard and good as he always did,
I figured his questions were no real bother, verdad?

The way I'm working now—not just me, all of us here in the community—
it's different from the way I worked as a kid. Look, we're still growing the
same things, more or less: maíz, maicillo, and frijol. But back then we
didn't have some of the advantages we've got today. That land my papa had
up there in Cabañas, what he had inherited from his father, well, it wasn't
much good. Reddish land, like clay. Land that didn't produce much. We
didn't have fertilizer or pesticides—none of that. And the land was worn
out, not giving you much of a crop. That's how come me and my papa were
going in the off-season to cut sugarcane and pick coffee, because without
that extra cash we would have starved. I'm telling you, lots of people back
then did die of hunger. In our family, we barely got by. We had only one
harvest per year of maicillo, maíz, and frijol. And let's say you had bad
weather like just happened to us now, some flooding or a drought, sí, hombre, you were out of luck. You might have a few animals or catch some
birds or fish, but you were on your own, no help from nowhere.

Today, it's a whole lot different. Back then, I knew what my papa taught
me, and he knew what his papa taught him. Today you've got some information out there teaching you how to go about things. I even took some
classes that some agriculture expert gave way back here in the communities.

You learn things that way. Today I am a professional; I know what I'm doing. First of all, the land we've got here is much better than what my family had in Cabañas. But any land, no matter if it's good land, you've got to treat it right if you want to have a good harvest. You've got to know what you're doing. These days I get two harvests a year of maíz, two of frijol, and one of maicillo. The maicillo is mostly for feeding the animals, though you can make tortillas from it if you're lacking some maíz. Not so tasty tortillas from the maicillo, but you can eat them fine if you have to.

What we've got today is more knowledge, better land, and also other things. Like today we prepare the land by cleaning it, chopping down the old stalks and weeds with our machetes, just like we used to do; but today we are using pesticide to kill off any diseases that might get to our seeds and plants once we start sowing. And today, you see, the seeds we're using now, the maíz seeds, they're what you call a hybrid seed that we didn't have when I was a kid. These seeds produce better and bigger cobs, but to get these fine cobs you've got to use fertilizer, two different types of fertilizer, one when the first maíz shoots come out and a second type when the plants have been growing maybe thirty-five days. With the maíz—like what you see right over here in Jacinto's milpa or way over there in my milpa—once it's been growing about ninety days and it's turned yellow, then you double it over and let the cobs dry on the stalk. You can see, even with all that rain we just had, it didn't do any harm to our maíz. This week me and the boys have got to harvest the cobs. We haul them down to the house, and nowadays we've got a machine that degrains them. Never used to have any such machine when I was a kid. You used to have to do it by hand with a stick or knife—rraaaaz!—stripping the kernels off the cobs. It took the whole family days to do it. Today we've got two machines, one over in the ciudadela that belongs to all the communities; that was given to us by the Lutheran Church. And we've got another one right here in Comunidad Guazapa owned by somebody who bought it with money he got from some relatives in the United States. So you haul your cobs over to the machines, bring along some huge sacks that can hold two hundred pounds of kernels, and—rraaaaz!—the machine strips the kernels off, and they pour into your sacks. You pay one dollar for each sack of kernels, that's all. And it's a hell of a lot easier this way.

Once you've got the sacks, you haul them back to the house, and we pour the kernels into these huge aluminum containers. You've seen them, no? Right there on my veranda. You've got to put some kind of pesticide in with the kernels, or else bugs or rats will feast on your harvest. Some folks use these poison tablets. I used to put these tablets in my containers too. But then I learned from one of these courses—like I was telling you before—I learned that these poison tablets are not just killing the pests, but they might also be killing you someday too. Cancer! Those tablets are brutal stuff and no damned good for any human being. So now what I do is put in some five or six onions, depending on the quantity of maíz I've got in the aluminum container. And those onions do the job, keep out the rats and other insects. And with my containers of frijol, I don't use any of those poison tablets either. I crush some garlic, one whole garlic for every two hundred pounds of frijol, and I've found that the garlic does the job too. So you see, there's a new way of working that we have now, and we're getting much better harvests and eating better now. Nobody starving in my family, no, hombre!

No, I'm not growing any vegetables or fruit. Not these days. I tried it. Tomatoes. Watermelons. Some avocado and lemon trees. But it wasn't worth it. The big problem there is that soon as you've got your vegetables or fruits ready to harvest, some crooks come along, and quick as hell they make off with your crop. Hardly any of us farmers here are growing vegetables and fruits. The same reason: too many people coming by and grabbing what doesn't belong to them. We had the same problem with our animals—cows and goats. We used to leave them out at night in the pasture, but it's easy for crooks to come by and just grab them, even butcher them on the spot, and you're left with nothing. Several of us, me too, lost our animals that way. Hell, my father-in-law, who's got a whole lot of cows—well, back some time he even had his own son, that boy Marcos of his—and that son was behind some robbing there, taking his own father's cows. You just never knew who or how or when you would lose your animals. So these days the way we do it is we take the animals to pasture during the daylight, but when it comes dusk we bring the cows or goats back into a small corral that each of us has next to his house. Lot safer that way. Me, I've got a fine cow; gives us milk each day, and we make some cheese. And my cow has given birth to two calves. And I've got a couple of goats, too. I'm beginning to build up a little livestock that way. Each year I'm adding one or two more. With whatever cash I can save from my harvests, and after I've paid off the bank for the loans they give me each year to buy my seeds and fertilizer and pesticide, with that money I am adding some animals. Good money in that. If you've got yourself some animals, you can live real good.

Except, of course, you've got your setbacks, like what just happened to my frijol crop. That sets you back a little. But, never mind, we'll manage it. The thing we really need to smooth our way some is for the government to get on the banks, you know, get them to lower the rate of interest we're paying each year for the loans they give us. Right now it's nine percent. They need to lower that. And they need to get the price of fertilizer and pesticide and seeds to be cheaper. With that ARENA bunch, you had no chance of that happening. They weren't interested in helping the poor people. Only during the weeks before an election, then the ARENA people would come out and give the campesinos a bag of fertilizer or seeds or whatever, and some folks would figure to vote for them because of that. Well, now they're out of power. The FMLN has the presidency, and we've got some hope now. Perhaps those changes like I'm talking about are going to happen. I even heard that the government is thinking of reimbursing us farmers for the losses we just had due to the rains and flooding. I'm hoping so. Some people got hit real hard. Lost everything— crops, houses, everything! Something has got to be done for those folks, don't you think?

So much depends here on what happens politically. Since the war ended in '92, we've had one ARENA president after the other. They treated their own, the rich people, just fine. But they were no good for us. Here, I'll give you an example. It happened back in 2004, during the government of that ARENA guy Antonio Saca; he was president then. Those bastards tried to rob us of the water—yes, our own water—that we have here in the community. And they damned near succeeded, and they would have succeeded if we hadn't fought them like we did. I'm telling you, it was almost like back in the days of the war. You see, those ARENA people, they are all capitalists. They wanted to privatize everything, and all for the benefit of the *ricos*. That year they tried to privatize the health system in this country, take away social security from us, but they didn't manage it because the people demonstrated like hell. And they also decided they would privatize the water supply system in the country. For us, what that meant is that they were going to take away the water system that we in the communities had set up for ourselves. We did it with the help of some organization from Spain. Set up the wells, the pipes, and we had this fine, clean water coming into the communities. Just about all the houses in Comunidad Guazapa have their own supply of water coming to their yards. We pay for the pumps, the electricity out of our money, but the water is ours. Fine water. And you know what that Saca and his buddies wanted to do? Take that water away from us. They had a company, a Japanese company that was going to bottle our pure water and sell it abroad. We would still get water, but we'd have to buy it from some big company operated by people that the government likes. Well, of course, we told them, no way we'd go along with that. So what Saca did is try to take over our water by changing the laws. Not just *our* water. From communities all around this area. His plan was to change the laws to fit his scheme. We got word of what was happening, that they were going to sign an agreement over in Suchitoto. Hearing this, we got the folks together from all of the six communities here, and we were heading over to Suchitoto to demonstrate. And what does Saca do? He decides to use force against us. We gathered at dawn over by the ciudadela, planning to head to Suchitoto, and we're met by a sea of military police blocking the road, blocking the paths through the fields, and refusing to let us go protest. "You sons of bitches," they tell us. "You try to go there, and we're going to kick your asses." Hell, we weren't going to take that crap, and we decided we'd kick their asses instead. I'm telling you, we were really pissed off. We went and got our machetes—though we weren't going to use them unless we had to—and we got rocks, lots of rocks, and sticks too. And we started battling them. They had their helicopters flying overhead, but they weren't firing on us. The police on the ground were firing tear gas at us, and that stuff is real nasty. All day long it went on. We had lots of people, hundreds maybe, and they had plenty of men fighting against us. Some women, like my mother-in-law, Mari, they were bringing buckets of water to throw on us when we got hit with the tear gas. We weren't about to stop until we got them to retreat. We didn't kill any of them, and they didn't kill any of us. They arrested a few of us. No, not me. Later they tried to convict them as terrorists. That's right, in El Salvador we've got an antiterrorist law that ARENA put in after the gringos had that destruction of their twin towers in New York—when was it?—2001 or thereabouts. So they accused *our* people of being terrorists. Nonsense! Anyway, they got out of jail, the ones who were arrested. And Saca and his Areneros saw there was no point trying to take our water away from us. We wouldn't just sit back and let them intimidate us. Hell, no! We'd go on fighting them. So they backed off. And we've still got our fine water the way we had before.

So you see, that's why I'm saying that so much of what happens is due to politics. As long as the capitalists had their party in power, we poor folks were going to be abused. For us, the way to change things, to get the laws more fair and more on our side, is to get political power. And that's what we've done. Several of us here—me, Joaquín, and others—we're actively involved with the FMLN political party. The fight now is not in the monte. That part is over. The fight now is to get people aware, reach out to people, and get them to understand how things work here in the country, how the whole system—laws, everything—is for the rich and not for the rest of us. That's what we were doing for a long while, and finally just this year we got our first FMLN president. Before that we had victories in many of the smaller cities and towns, like Suchitoto. We got our FMLN candidates elected as mayors. And we've got a good number of members in the Asamblea Legislativa. But we hadn't won the presidency, the number one job. Not till this year.

Me, I was taking every spare moment I had, even neglecting my milpa or leaving it to my boys, in order to go around and campaign for Mauricio Funes, for the FMLN. Not just here in the community. All over the area. Once in a while Margarita would even come along with me. We'd go out at eight in the morning, take a break at noon while people were eating their lunch and resting, and then continue until six at night. Door to door, we went. My job was to get the message across. What message? Simple! Telling the people that the ARENA Party didn't represent anybody but the ricos—the people who've got the wealth of this country in their hands. The big landowners, the owners of the big businesses, all that bunch. And all of them supported by the United States and their capitalist interests. These people haven't helped us; they're too busy helping themselves. They build factories here and pay the workers as little as they can get away with, and these foreign companies walk away with the money. Them and the ricos here who they're working with.

During the election campaign, what me and our people were telling folks is that there's got to be a change. You know, you've seen it for yourselves, I'm sure; you've got people around this country that have nowhere to sleep at night, that don't have a centavo in their pocket to buy even a tortilla. That's what is still going on here. Yes, yes, some of us, like us in Comunidad Guazapa and the other communities around here, we've had some good things happen for us. We've been real well organized— I'll explain that to you in a minute—and we've been able to get support from the Suchitoto municipality, which is controlled by the FMLN now, and from other organizations too. But even here we haven't got what we need. We've got our school; we worked real hard for that. But, you know, some families don't send their kids because they can't afford to buy the school uniforms or shoes or even the pencils and notebooks that the kids use. And there's lots of families that still don't eat well enough—even out here, which is better than lots of other places.

So what we told the people during the campaign is that as long as ARENA is in power, nothing's going to change. Some folks, many, were real receptive to our message and told us, "Yes, we're with you. Don't worry, we're with Funes!" Others, well, they just told us to get lost, they shut the door on us. All right, so some people don't support the FMLN. All right. But you know what those bastards in the ARENA were doing? They were running a campaign of lies. That's right, pure lies, trying to scare people and make them think that Fidel Castro is about to take over in El Salvador, that Hugo Chávez [president of Venezuela] is coming to town. Complete bullshit! Look, if you ask me, sure I admire what they've done in Cuba—the way the poor get free education and health care. Sure, I want to see that happen here for all Salvadorans, rich and poor. And yes, I like the way Chávez is trying to help out some poor folks here in El Salvador, trying to send us cheap gasoline, cheap fertilizer. The ARENA people have blocked it, but you tell me, why shouldn't we get those things from Venezuela if they'll help out the poor people here? So, sure, I want to see us have closer ties with Cuba and Venezuela. But the truth is, we're just in the beginning of some big changes here. It'll take years—maybe ten or fifteen years. It can't happen right away. I know that. Others don't. That's the problem we've got, you see. Now that we have an FMLN president, people are going to want to see changes overnight. People don't give a damn about theories. They want to see results. More doctors and medicines. Better education. Cheaper loans and cheaper fertilizer and pesticides and all that for us farmers. Better pay for workers in the factories. That's what folks want, and they want it right now.

The way I see it, things are going our way. We've been planting the seeds for change a long while now, and we're beginning to see the results. That president Bush was completely against us, but you've got Obama now. I think he'll be with us, or at least he won't line up behind ARENA the way Bush did. I'm not worried about the United States bothering us now. The United States isn't going to stop us, I figure. The gringos thought that we—I mean us who went to the monte—they thought we were fighting just because we wanted to get land to farm. Sure, that was part of it. But we were fighting for a lot more: to change the whole system here in this country. You've got the capitalists here running things for themselves. All the injustices here. Not much has changed there—not yet. But that's what we wanted to change when we went to the monte, and that's what we're still fighting to change. And I think we will. The gringos, well, I figure they won't like these changes, but with Obama in there now, he'll leave us alone. The gringos don't scare *me*. I tell you, the ones that are scared here now are the ricos. They've been taking their money out of the country for a while now. Those that got big landholdings, they're worried as hell. Many of their lands are not being used, and we've got lots of campesinos who have no land and need some to feed their families. So why not get that land to the poor folks? I'm not saying, look, just go in and take it away from them. No, let the government give them some money for it. Like the way we did it here. The government bank paid off the Morales family, and we got the land. And they still kept the best land, the flat land where they're growing sugarcane, they kept most of that for themselves. We aren't about to get that land, no. It's just thirty-five manzanas. Even though we could use it for the community, which is growing each year, still we're not going to get that land. It's the big landowners, those with hundreds of manzanas, that's where it's got to start. It'll take time, but that's what I'm hoping will happen.

The main political stuff I've been doing since the war ended wasn't what I was just talking to you about. Those are my political ideas, the way I've learned about how the country works. During the elections I go out and campaign, that's all. For me, the main political stuff I've done—really it's more practical things than anything else—is the things I've worked for here in Comunidad Guazapa. Local politics, you can call it. We've got a directorate that runs the community. Twelve members and a president. Many people here in the community don't want to be involved in this, even though it's necessary to get what we want for the community. Take Julia, for example. You can't get that woman to participate no way. Her mama, Mari, she's another story. She was even president of the community for a year or so, till she got pregnant again. Jorge, her husband, he's like Julia. Can't get that guy to do anything, go to meetings or any of that. Everyone's got their own way.

Me, I feel I've got to be involved, even with all those meetings and going to talk to people in the municipality in Suchitoto and all the other stuff that's a pain in the ass. Still, I feel I've got to do it. Or at least I felt I had to do it for a long while. Now I've taken a rest from it. I was president here three times. Started back in the beginning. Joaquín was the first president, and then I got elected. I did it for two years—which is all you're supposed to be in for—but the people pushed me into staying a third year. Right, I think that's when you first came out here to the community, verdad? I was just finishing up my third year, and Mari was about to take over. Well, since then I was elected twice more. I would have preferred to just participate, maybe be part of the directorate committee. Easier that way. But I got pushed by folks into doing two more terms. I guess they figured I knew how to get some things done. And, bueno, the truth is, we did get some good things done.

Let's see, well, in my first term we got our houses built. You know, the ones we have now with the concrete blocks instead of those shacks we were living in from the time we first got here. To get the materials you've got to work with outside organizations, work with the municipality. Meetings here, meetings there. And me, I'm trying to work my milpa at the same time. You don't get a centavo for this work as president. You volunteer your time. Pure volunteer work. But it's a satisfaction to get things done. That's how I see it. That's why I agreed to do it a second time and then a third time too. And in those two periods we were able to get the electricity for the houses. No, we didn't have that back in '97 when you were first coming here. And then the water project like I was telling you about, the one we got done with some international group, a group from Spain. That took some doing. And then those bastards from ARENA wanted to take it from us. Of course we fought them off! Let them keep their own damn water and leave us with our good mountain water. That's the way we've got it now. And finally, in my last term—which just ended a few months back—we got some good things going for the youth in the community. We could see that we had to have more activities—sports, dancing, that kind of stuff—and so our directorate has put some of that in place. Or at least we've started to do it. And we've got the project of building a good road all the way out here to the community. The municipality of Suchitoto is helping us with the materials, and we men, when we're not busy in the growing season, we are putting down that road. A little more time is what we need, that's all.

The ones who are going to see that project through, and really they're the ones who've got to start taking over here, is the young people of the community. Our kids. The ones that have grown up here and had schooling here, even gone to university. Now they're the ones who are on the directorate. And the new president is my nephew, Balta, the accountant. He's a professional, an accountant. He went to school with Chico, and he's Lucita's—the school principal's—brother. You didn't know we were relatives? Bueno, he's my brother's son, though my brother is over there in another community with my mother. Never mind all that. The boy is here, lives here, and he's the new president. Bright as hell, that kid. Like Chico. Except Chico is now in the capital, so he's not part of the directorate or any of that. So Balta and some other young people are now taking over. They wanted it that way, and we older people agreed. It's a good idea. That Balta has already got a few new things in place. During my time as president I helped to get the community store going, the one just down below where the houses are. Nobody got paid for working there; they just took turns. Now Balta has got it set up professional-like. People, young people mostly, they get paid, and things bought and sold are accounted for. He's an accountant, right? So he's got it going right now. And I understand that he's got some other projects, things for the young people in the community, he's got that kind of stuff starting up. Dance groups, organized soccer games—that kind of thing. Me and some of the older people who've got our experience on the directorate, we give them some advice now and then. But they're the ones running things now. Better that way.

And for me, it's good too. I can just keep my mind on my work in the milpa. And a little work for the FMLN when it's needed. I'm not so busy as before. Even get to take a little siesta in the hammock these days. On Sundays, mostly. That's enough for me. I can't set too long, you see. It isn't my way. I like to keep moving. I've always been like that, and I'm planning on staying that way as long as I can.

CHAPTER TWELVE

Margarita

The Oldest Daughter

We first met Margarita back in 1997, when she was a seven-year-old girl, a bright-eyed and shy child who, somewhat hesitantly, showed us her new first-grade schoolbooks. "She's been pushed into first grade," her mother, Julia, proudly told us. "They said she was already reading, so they wanted her to skip kindergarten and move up with the older kids." And indeed, we could sense a certain maturity in Julia's oldest daughter, despite her bashful manner, as she darted away to take hold of her baby brother, who was crying on the veranda. "My second pair of hands," Julia told us, again with a touch of pride. "A good kid! She helps me whenever I need her."

As if time had stood still, twelve years later, when we came to interview Margarita for the first time, there she was on the veranda with another brother, the youngest, resting in the hammock on her shoulder. Julia was off somewhere, and Margarita was minding the house and watching over the smaller children. At nineteen years old, she was now a young woman in full bloom, with a radiant smile and an easy self-assurance. She beckoned us to sit down and said, "My parents will be here in a moment, and then we can talk." But, as it happened, we only managed a brief interview with her that day. Julia needed Margarita in the kitchen, and so we decided to meet with her another day—in San Salvador, where she was exploring the possibility of entering a university.

While our first talk with her had been understandably rushed, and Margarita was cautious in her comments, the second interview went on for a couple of hours, and she was unexpectedly frank. And this frankness remained when some months later we interviewed her once again. What follows, then, are some of Margarita's reflections on her family and friends

133

and also on Comunidad Guazapa, where—as she pointed out—"me and my classmates represent the postwar generation, the first ones to grow up out here in peace."

It's strange, you know, whenever I'm asked about being in the monte. It's hard to think I was there with my mother. I didn't even know about it till I was an older kid. My mother never mentioned it. Luis neither. My great-grandmother Mamita Cecilia, she's the one who told me. My mother is real close to her, much more than to her own mother, Mari. And so am I, and José, too. Anyway, it was my great-grandmother who said to me one day that I was born up there in Santa Marta, in Chalatenango, and that my mama had taken me back to her unit in the monte when I was like a year or so, and that I had gone around with her up there till I was two or three, until José was born. Then my mama quit the guerrillas. That's what I was told. When I asked my mama about it, I could see she didn't want to talk. I know she's told you guys about her years with the guerrillas, but with us kids she doesn't say much. All I know is that she was a radista with the guerrillas. I don't know for how long or even what it was she did. Really! I didn't even know who my father was—not until recently. She didn't say and, I figured, it was better not to ask.

It was only, let's see, only about three years ago that I found out who my natural father is. And that was by accident. Nothing planned. It just happened. I was visiting up in Santa Marta. I had gone there to see my cousin. My aunt and her husband from here in the community were going up there, and I had a few days' vacation, so I went along with them. When we got up there my uncle told me—this was the first I'd heard about it—he said he knew who my father was. By then I'd heard that my father was probably living up there, but I still knew nothing about him. No, I had no idea of meeting him. Not until my uncle said, "I reckon I can find him up here if you would like to meet him." And me, I didn't know what to say. "Well, in a way sí, and in a way no," I said. You see, I wasn't at all sure I wanted to get into it. But thinking it over, I figured, why not? So my aunt's husband went to get him, and then he came back and said, "He doesn't want to come see you." No, I wasn't offended. I mean, who was I to him? My father told my uncle he was busy working, constructing a wall someplace in the town. He had no time to come. Then my father's wife came over—a real nice lady—and she came along with a friend of his. We talked a little while. And then the two of them went to talk to him, and according to his friend, he told my father, "Don't be such a coward." And so my father said, "Look, I'm busy like you see, but if she wants to come see me, bring her up here." When they told me that, I can't say I had a lot of desire to go see him, but they began talking about him a little, and then I decided, all right, I'll go. "Out of curiosity, I'm going to go," I told them. "I just want to see who he is." When I got there he came over and shook my hand. He was trembling, I could see that. He didn't know what to say. Me neither. My uncle started to talk, explaining that I was Julia's daughter and that I had another brother José. My father listened, not knowing what to say. He asked me if I was studying, and I told him, "Yes, in high school now." He nodded and didn't say anything more. Didn't ask anything about José either. And that was it, like, hello and then good-bye. As we were walking back, my aunt's husband told me that my father was afraid I'd come to ask him for money or report him to the family court or something like that. I couldn't believe it. I had nothing like that in mind. When I got back home to the community, I told my brother José and my mother. She didn't say anything one way or the other. And José didn't want to hear about him much either. "I don't want nothing to do with him. Nothing!" José told me.

I didn't see my father—the one in Santa Marta, I mean—I didn't see him again for quite a while. Then some months back I was up in Santa Marta again visiting my cousin and with some friends of mine. My father heard I was in town, and he sent word that he'd like to see me. He surprised me. I hadn't expected that. And this time he was different from before. Friendly like. He even asked about José. And especially, he wanted to know about my mama. "She's together with someone, right?" he asked. And when I told him how it was with my mama and Luis, he said, "How would it be if one day I came to Comunidad Guazapa and paid a visit?" "That depends," I told him. "If it's to see me and José, bueno, there's no problem with that." "And what about seeing your mama?" he asked. "Well, that's something else, isn't it?" I said. "Might be a problem there." "Yes, I guess you're right there," he said. And then he began to tell me that he had really loved my mother, that it was because of the war that things happened, that they had pulled apart. And he had met this new woman, his wife, and they had three kids, and so on and so on. Finally, he said to me, "Look, when you come back next time, maybe bring some photos of the family, you and José and the others."

Later, when I got back home, I told my mother and José. My mother just looked the other way. And José, like before, said he didn't give a damn. "But you know something, José," I said, "me and you, we both look just like him, especially you. He's tall and thin and light-skinned, almost the exact image of you." José got a bit pissed when I told him that. "What rotten luck!" José said. "Now that you tell me that, I want to see him even less. No, for me he's nobody."

I understand my brother, but I don't feel the same. My father, well, if he wants to keep some connection, then why not? I mean, like they say, if it wasn't for your father and your mother, you'd never be born, never be in this world, verdad? I mean, it's not like I see him as a father, no, not at all. He's a person, a new person who I met, that's about all. If it turns out that I never see him again, that's all right with me. It's not like I'd miss him or anything like that. Like with Luis, if I go away for a few days on vacation—Luis never goes on vacation; the most he's gone is a day or two to see his mother—if I don't see Luis for those days, I start missing him. I'm used to having Luis around me. To me, he's my real father. Always has been, and always will be.

I was six years old when my mama and Luis got together. I had been living with my great-grandmother until that time. Me and José both. Then, when my mother got together with Luis, we moved in with him. With Luis and his son, Chico, who's about five years older than me. Chico became like a brother to me, and Luis is my papa. Yes, sometimes I call him "papi," but mostly I call him "Luis" or even "Campos," the way my mother sometimes does. In this community, sometimes if I or José refer to Luis as "papa," some people get it in their mind to remind you that he's not your *real* father. So I guess that's why I prefer "Luis."

Anyhow, to me Luis has been a fine father. To José also. He treats all of us—the kids he's had with my mother, Chico, and me and José—all of us the same. No preferences, *igualito.* The only preferences I've seen from Luis is every time my mother gives birth, he pays a lot of attention to the baby. He's sweet with them, rocking them to sleep and playing with them. There's not a lot of men here—you know, this is still a macho society—so men aren't usually going around holding onto babies. But Luis, yes, he's like that. And also, he feels he's got to help my mama out. He's good that way.

The way I see it, he's been very good to my mother. You can see he really cares for her. If she's sick, say, he'll be hanging over her, making sure she's got her medicines and is on the mend. Even if he's busy up in the milpa, he'll come down to the house checking up on her. She's the kind that'll neglect herself, but Luis, he won't neglect her. He's good to her. Not like some men around here who neglect their women or go around hitting them. Not Luis. I've never seen him lift a hand at her or threaten her or anything like that. I've heard some people say—even Chico has said it—that Luis is, or rather that he once *was,* a womanizer, and now and then Luis will joke around about how he used to be a ladies' man. I can't say I like hearing that stuff, but the way I see it, it's all talk. He isn't serious; it's his way of joking around. My brothers find it funny. He entertains them like that.

Like sometimes when we're up in the milpa during harvesttime, me and my brothers, Luis will start telling stories about how he used to chase women. He's told us things like how with this one woman, in order to convince her that he cared for her, he put Vicks—that stuff for your lips—he put it into the corner of his eyes so when he talked to her, tears would be coming out, and then she would believe his words. And my brothers, laughing and laughing. That's Luis, always telling stories and joking around. And I admit, when you go spend some hours with him up in the milpa, it goes by like minutes, with him filling your ears with his stories and jokes.

But he's got another side to him, a very serious side. There's plenty of people here in the community that are a little afraid of him. They don't want to cross him. He's got this way about him—how can I put it? Let's say that you don't deal with him respectfully, then he won't have anything to do with you. Treat him with respect, then he's good to you; treat him bad, you're going to have trouble with him. With us kids, he demands respect. The only time he ever hit me was once when I talked rough to him. He grabbed a stick and whacked me. I admit it, I deserved it. He didn't want me going out with certain people; he told me it wasn't good for me. And when I answered him, "Never mind, I'm going anyway," well, he got furious and came after me with a stick. Looking back, though, I deserved it. And with my brother José, thank God Luis was there to keep him in line. José was hanging out with some bad folks, and Luis got him to stop it. He filled José's ears, got his attention. The way I see it, if it hadn't been for Luis, my brother would probably have wound up as some kind of delinquent. Luis is the one—not my mother—who straightened him out.

That's the thing about Luis: he'll talk to you, reason with you. I love my mama, but she's not one that you can talk to. That's the truth. It's Luis who you can go to if you've got some problem. He'll be understanding. Like the time I got in trouble at school because I'd skipped out that day. They told me to bring in my mother. But I didn't want to talk to her about it. I knew she'd get pissed and wouldn't even go speak with them. So the person I went to was Luis. He told me to tell him why I'd skipped out. "Because my friend had a birthday, and we wanted to celebrate it by taking the day off," I explained to him. "That's the truth. No other reason," I told him. Luis told me he believed me. He knew, just like I did, that sometimes kids skipped school to go off into the hills and fool around, you know, to have sex up there. But I wasn't into that. And Luis trusted me, and then he worked it out with my mother that she go and straighten the thing out at school.

Luis—he's a big supporter of us kids going to school. He wants us to do well there. He says that he never had a chance, and now that my generation has got that chance, he wants us to take advantage of it. My older brothers only finished eighth or ninth grade, except for Chico, who is some kind of genius, real bright. Chico is about to finish university and become a lawyer. The rest of us aren't like that, except maybe for my younger sister Dorita; she's a top student. Me, I was pretty good, maybe a little lazy sometimes. I can remember some days, cold mornings when I didn't want to get out of bed and go to school. Luis would come along, shaking me and forcing me to get going. Funny when I think back on it. It sort of tells you how times have changed, no? Back when my mama and grandma were growing up, none of their fathers would have chased them off to school. The opposite! But Luis, he's a believer in education for girls just the same as for boys. And really, I'm grateful to him for that.

Back when I started school here, things were much different from the way they are now. We hardly had any classrooms, and no desks or blackboards. Schoolbooks were scarce. We didn't even have real teachers. I mean, teachers like we have now, with training at a university. Back then, you know who my teacher was? Lucita, the woman who is principal of the school now. She's from here in the community. A real bright lady, like Chico sort of. She's only thirty years old, I think, or maybe younger. Back when she was my teacher in kindergarten, she was only fourteen or fifteen years old. She knew more than us kids, so she was teaching us how to read and write. I liked her. She promoted me into first grade; I didn't have to spend the whole year in kindergarten. I caught on quickly how to read, and they said I made my letters real well. And I could do the arithmetic, too. It was easy for me in the beginning.

These days the school is much bigger and well organized. It's over at the ciudadela. When I started, there were only three grades. Now we have all grades, right up through high school. Almost all the teachers come from the outside—even as far away as the capital. We still don't have any teachers from here in the community, except for Lucita. These teachers we have now, they know their stuff. And they are strict! You've got to come to school in your uniform—blue skirts for the girls and blue pants for the boys, and white blouses and shirts. And you've got to be there on time, no excuses. Except in the winter when it rains real hard, then they'll tolerate your coming in late. I mean, no exaggeration, if it rains hard, there's rivers that form in the gullies between where we live and the ciudadela. You've got to take your shoes and socks off and try to make it through. I tell you, one time it was so bad that we felt like we were going to drown passing this one place. And you know, Lucita herself, she was coming along, and she almost did drown, with the rushing water knocking her down and carrying her off till she caught hold of a branch, and some of the boys had to pull her out.

But, no, that's not the way it usually is. That time was unusual. I mean, it's not like we had to swim our way to school, verdad? And I can't complain about the classrooms or the way they have it organized now. It's strict, but really, you've got to have it that way or some kids will go a little wild. These days we have kids coming from all six communities in the area. Our school is the center. We've even got computers in the school these days. A whole classroom with them. Real different from the way it was in the beginning.

I just graduated a few months back, and in a way I'm glad, sure, but in another way I'll miss it. I liked a lot of what we studied. Not everything. But things like literature or social science, or courses on health. I feel I learned a lot, some things that I never figured to hear about. Like what? Well, for example, they talked to us in health class about the whole process of getting pregnant and giving birth, all that stuff. And they even went into the ways of preventing pregnancies, using contraception. I knew a little, what you hear outside, but I learned a lot from what they taught us. Important stuff, I think. Important because, let's face it, there are girls who don't know how to take care of themselves, and we've had cases of girls getting pregnant real early. Nobody from my class, but some girls from other classes. We even had a girl who was pregnant, and she came to school and gave birth in the bathroom. Nobody knew about it, but they found the baby—it was premature—they found it in some basket in the school. Terrible, no? So I say it's good that they talk to us seriously about these things and teach us how to protect ourselves. Not everyone agrees with me, including some parents. They complain that teaching this in school is only going to pervert the kids. "Pervert"—that's the word they used. I don't get it. Seems to me they should be glad their kids are learning these things instead of having their daughters wind up with stomachs because they were ignorant, no?

The stuff that I didn't really like learning—but that's my problem, because I understand they have to teach it—it was about the civil war we had here in El Salvador. I don't like going over that material. My mama, she doesn't go into it at all. Luis, yes. He'll talk about it if you ask him—or even if you don't ask him. Chico likes hearing about the war and talking about it. Not me. I figure that was the past, and now it's the present. Besides, I've seen how some of the adults here who were in the war, when they begin talking about it, it shakes them up. They get all sad. So I try to avoid it. Though in school they have to talk about these things, I guess. It's part of what you learn in social studies. My teacher in that class, he got all emotional talking about the war. The main thing I remember him saying is, "You can't imagine what it was like, just how bad it was trying to go from place to place, how dangerous it all was." He reminded us of how things had been in the ciudadela just a couple of years back, the time they had to close the school down for a few days. I suppose Luis has told you about it, no? There were lots of soldiers here trying to prevent people from demonstrating. I don't know the exact details, but I remember the government was trying to take over control of the water supply in our community, and Luis and my grandmother Mari and hundreds of people were battling here with the soldiers, throwing stones and being hit by tear gas. I had never seen anything like it in my life. Ask Luis, he'll tell you about it, I'm sure. That's the first time I had any idea of what it was like for a battle to go on. And I remember our teacher saying, "Bad as that was, it was nothing compared to the civil war. To live in those days, that was something else, something terrifying." Me, I don't really want to know about it. Maybe that sounds strange to you, with my whole family having been involved, my mama and Luis up in the monte for years, but that's how I am. I don't want to hear about the war. Not at home, and not in school either.

Like I say, though, school was usually interesting to me, and I had fun there. I liked studying and learning new things. My problem with school was something else. You see, I wasn't free like some other kids—some of my friends or my sisters and brothers these days—I wasn't able to put time into learning when I wanted to. I couldn't just say, like my sister Dorita says these days, "Leave me alone, I've got to study! I haven't got time to make tortillas for you all!" Dorita doesn't even know how to make a good tortilla! My mama calls on her to help in the kitchen or sweep up, and Dorita ducks into the house. I never could have gotten away with that. I mean, I like being the oldest in a way, but in another way, when you're the oldest, what happens is that your mama is calling on you to help her out. That's how it was for me. Many days I didn't have time to do my homework or just read or hang out or do whatever.

From the time I was a small kid, that's how it was. My mama used to like working up in the milpa with Luis. Besides, he needed her help. Between the two of them, they have more than six manzanas, and so she'd go up there most days to work with him. Well, once she began having more kids, she needed me to help her around the house. And me, what was I? Maybe six or seven years old. Bueno, from that time on I was doing a lot of the housework—sweeping up, making tortillas, cleaning dishes, and washing clothes down at the well. We didn't have a cistern in those days, with water in the house. I'd have to get up early in the morning and go down to the well with a heap of clothes. And when I'd come back dead tired, often enough there was nothing to eat because my mama hadn't had time to cook before going off to the milpa. So sometimes I'd just go hungry rather than start cooking. I remember telling my mama at one point, "Mama, if you have one more kid, I'm leaving home!" I wasn't serious, of course, but that's how I felt many days.

The worst of it, though, was when one of my brothers or sisters got sick. I'd be the one left to take care of them. Roberto was a kid who was always getting sick, and it was usually me who minded him then. Some folks in the community used to say—they still do—that I'm Roberto's mama. And for years, Roberto would only go to sleep if I lay next to him.

The problem was that at ten years old, well, what did I know about taking care of a kid who was sick? Nobody told me, and I was scared. Maybe something bad would happen. And once it did! With Dorita's twin sister. When my mama brought her back from the hospital that little baby was already sickly, and the day she died it was me who was minding her. My mama was off someplace. I could see she was doing real bad, and a neighbor said that maybe someone had put the evil eye on her and that I had to take her to el que cura. But el que cura wasn't around either, and that poor little baby, my sister, died there in my arms. When my mama got home, we had to tell her that Dorita's twin was dead. Awful!

Back then, when I was real young, it seemed overwhelming to me. These days it's easy enough. I know all about managing a house. And, you know, in a way that's good. Most of my friends, they don't have the slightest idea how to take care of a house. They come to me sometimes and ask me, "Margarita, how do you do this? How do you do that?" And in a way I'm proud that I know. I'm proud that I was able to do it. And at least back when I was a kid and feeling overwhelmed, I had my great-grandmother to help me out. She still tries to help me even though she's an old lady by now. She lives right next to us. She's the one who raised my mama, and we, José and me, lived with her and my great-grandfather back before my mama got together with Luis. Later, when my mother gave birth to more kids and I had to help out and I was working like a burro, and I might not have breakfast or lunch, Mamita Cecilia would show up with food. A real kind lady! And even though she hasn't got money, now and then she'd manage to get me and José and the others some little gift or something. I love her. José does too. He even sleeps over there at night, every night, and he watches over her. Which makes my grandmother Mari a little pissed. My great-grandmother Mamita Cecilia is her mother-in-law. And my grandmother Mari has always been a little pissed at the way Mamita Cecilia favors us. I won't go into it, but there's some bad blood there. Maybe my mama has told you. Yes? So you know. My mama's got some problems with her own mother, and that's the story. Me, personally, I don't avoid Grandma Mari. I go up to her house with Luis sometimes— especially these days when we no longer have our TV—and we watch the soap operas at night on Grandma Mari's TV. Luis likes them, just like I do. It's fine with my grandmother. We're on talking terms, of course. But still, you can sense there's some kind of bad feeling. What can you do? Every family's got its problems, verdad?

Actually, it's not just families who've got problems. Communities, too. Our community, to me, it's a wonderful place. I like it here. No offense, but I prefer it to the big city, to San Salvador. But even here, we've got some real problems. Not as bad as in the big cities, where you've got all the gangs messing with people. Little by little, though, we're getting infected by the same problems. These days, even out here in the community, we've got some robbing and all kinds of bad things beginning to happen. I don't remember that kind of problem when I was a kid. You always felt safe. These days, not so much. Like, if I come back to the community at night, I don't feel safe any longer walking through the fields. Luis always comes and meets the bus, and he escorts me back. But even in the daylight sometimes, you no longer feel so safe. Especially during the sugarcane season, December and January, when the stalks are high. When I was walking home from school, I was fearful that somebody could come up and grab me from behind and haul me off into the tall sugarcane. The guys who were cutting the cane made it even worse. They'd take to calling out to you, all that macho stuff. They'd even find out your name—maybe one of the students might tell them—and they would call after us. "Hey, Margarita, come over here, let's have a talk!"—that kind of nonsense. I'd ignore them, but still it got me unsettled.

And you know, just last year something bad *did* happen. To a friend of mine. This friend, Juana, decided to go home at midday and skip the afternoon session. We had science lab that afternoon, so the rest of us were in school. Normally, to be on the safe side, we head back to the community in groups, especially when they're cutting sugarcane. And what happened is that as she was passing through the sugarcane fields, someone grabbed her. I heard about this when I got home later. Someone who knew her name grabbed her. She didn't know who he was, since he had a mask over his face. She tried to break free, to make it back to the community's houses, and she almost did. But she slipped—that's what she told me later—and he put a machete to her and threatened her. And then he raped her. One of the ladies in the community said she had heard some screaming going on, but she figured it was normal. There's always a lot of noise, laughing and yelling, when we return from school. Only afterward that lady realized it must have been Juana screaming. Juana was all bloodied up. And they had to rush her to the hospital. She's only eighteen years old, and she's been messed up. I don't know how she'll be in the future. I mean, how do you get over something like that? I don't know what's going to be with her. It scares me to think of it. You can't feel safe anymore, even out here in the community. I think the community directorate is taking some measures to give us more protection. We have to do it, because it's no longer as safe out here as it once was.

No, no, that doesn't make me think I want to move out of Comunidad Guazapa. I still love it out here. In my view it's preferable to living in a big city like San Salvador. You've got the mountain and the trees and lots of open space. And I've got so many friends and my family out here. You're never alone, there's always this one or that one you can go chat with.

I wouldn't have anything like that if I lived in the city. My brother Chico, now that he's a lawyer, he likes the city, and he's going to stay there. Me, no. I don't think so.

What I wished would happen is that I could get accepted into a university, get my degree as a teacher, and then come back to the community and work here. That's been my dream. But unless you're real smart, it's hard to get a scholarship, and my family hasn't got money for that. And it doesn't look too good for me these days, since unfortunately I failed the exams—twice I failed them—to get into La Universidad Nacional where Chico went. And at another university, La UCA [Universidad Centroamericana], I also didn't get a high enough grade. So what I'm beginning to think is that maybe I can get some other career. I know this institute where they teach you things like "culinary arts"—that's what they call it. I figure I could become a cook and then maybe work over in Suchitoto, where they've got a number of restaurants and hotels. I'd like that. Suchitoto is only ten kilometers or so from here, so I could work there and go on living here.

It depends, though, doesn't it? I'd have to marry someone who's from here or at least would be comfortable living out in the community. Some of my friends have already got married to guys from here, and they've got babies already. I'm in no hurry to do that! I guess I had enough of that most of my life, so I'm not going to rush into that any too soon. And when I finally do have kids, no way I'm going to have a bunch like my mama did. Three or four—that's the most. I don't have any serious boyfriend right now. And I'm not exactly looking for anyone. If it happens, it happens. But I'd prefer to wait. I've seen how things develop with some of my friends. They start going out, and next thing you know they're living together. I'm going to take my time. Try to get some career, even if it isn't teaching, and then have a way of making some money and enjoying my work outside the house. My generation, we've got a chance that my mama and others didn't have, and I plan to take advantage of that if I possibly can. And I think I can, but it's hard to plan it all out. I mean, sometimes things happen, verdad? You just never know.

CHAPTER THIRTEEN

Lucita

The School Principal

A kilometer up from the main road, where the former landowners once had their ten-bedroom house, there stands today a spread of twenty or so blue-and-white buildings that serve as the school for the six communities in the area. It has been built up slowly from the rubble it had been after the war. These days it serves some five hundred students from nursery school to twelfth grade in morning and afternoon sessions. On any given school day you can see the blue-and-white-uniformed students seated behind desks in their classrooms, or playing soccer on the small cement soccer pitch, or crowded into the computer room, which now boasts twenty-three comput-ers. Perhaps most striking (at least to a visitor) is what sits smack in the middle of the three-acre school complex, namely, the remains of a Fuerza Armada helicopter propped up on two white pillars—a rusty reminder of what once took place in this very schoolyard.

A few paces away from the helicopter monument there is a small admin-istrative office that can be distinguished from the other blue-and-white buildings by the dozens of plants hanging from a rafter of the tiled roof or lined up along the small patio. Here in a corner of this small building is Lucita's office, which is as plain and unadorned as the thirty-one-year-old woman who sits behind an old wood-and-metal desk, meeting and greeting the steady flow of students and teachers and parents who visit her daily. In the midst of this seeming chaos, Lucita is a calm and steady presence, and one can easily imagine why the six-community committee chose her last year to be the new school principal. "They knew me, I guess," she states in her modest style. "I suppose because I'm from here—grew up here, went to school here, and had been teaching here over the years. So they asked me to do it, and I felt I wanted to give it a try."

As it happens, Lucita is one of only three teachers in the school who actually live in the six communities, in her case, in Comunidad Guazapa. For the time being, the remainder of the fourteen-member staff are outsiders who come from Suchitoto or San Salvador, although it is Lucita's hope that some of the more recent graduates will finish their university studies and eventually return to work as teachers in the school, just as she has done. "I'd like to see that happen soon, and I'm sure it will. Meanwhile, we're doing fine, and, if I can say so, I think we are improving every year. Personally, I'm planning to be here the rest of my life. I love it, ever since I began teaching here seventeen years ago. Yes, back when I was fourteen years old I started teaching. Strange in a way, sure, but you've got to understand how tough things were in the beginning. We were lucky to have a school at all after what we'd been through. Here, let me tell you."

And so Lucita, in her direct and frank manner, began her story.

What you see here today, the school we've got today, is a far cry from what we had in the beginning, back in '92, when we first arrived here. You've spoken to other people here, like Luis, right? He's an uncle of mine, by the way, but that's another story. What I want you to know is how we started and how it came about that at fourteen years old I was teaching already. The simple reason is that we had no alternative. We had kids in the community, dozens of them, and the parents decided to set up a school, even though we had no buildings, hardly any materials, and hardly any teachers. It took us about a year to get the school going. Me, I had arrived in the community, along with my mother and five brothers and sisters, when I was thirteen years old. I had only finished first grade at the time. What did I know? Nadita! So along with some other kids from Comunidad Guazapa, I went to a school a few kilometers from here. In a year I managed to get through second and third grades. I was eager to learn, and I worked hard at it. With my mama's support! That's the key, you see. If the parents are behind a kid, then that kid goes forward. If the parents don't care one way or the other, then the kids don't care either.

Anyhow, what happened is that after a year we had the very beginnings of a school starting up here. Nursery school through sixth grade. I entered fourth grade, and I guess because I was a pretty good student, I was selected along with another girl to be a *maestro popular*. We had a couple or so trained teachers coming from the outside, but it was decided— the Lutheran church nearby came up with the idea—to have some community people, kids like myself, to teach whatever they could to the younger kids. That's how I started—as a maestro popular. In the morning I was a teacher of nursery school kids, and in the afternoon I became a student in the fourth grade. I mean, at the time it was the only way we could have done it here. To me, it was a great pleasure, even though, frankly speaking, I had no idea what I was doing. That first year nobody told us how to teach; we just figured it out for ourselves. We didn't even have a real classroom in the beginning. I taught my kids under a tree; if it rained, we went to somebody's house nearby. For desks, we used huge stones; and instead of a blackboard and chalk, we used sticks to draw letters and numbers on the ground. Later we got some materials from the Lutheran Church, and, more important, me and the other maestros populares began to get some training. On Sundays a trained teacher would come out to the community and help us prepare lesson plans for the coming week. That's how I got my first teacher training, you could say. And I continued that way, teaching at the same time as I was a student, eventually teaching older children—fourth and sixth grades—as I went on getting my own education and finishing high school. That was when I was twenty years old. I had been teaching for six or seven years by then as a maestro popular. And I knew then—or, really, I had known right from the first year I started—that this was the thing I wanted to do with my life. Teaching kids—I love it. Always have. And I tell you, the person I have to thank for that is my mama. She's been behind me all the way. To me she is, bueno, she is my hero. Me and all my brothers and sisters wouldn't have gone forward if it hadn't been for her. She's a person of real strength. She had to be strong; otherwise, none of us would have made it. And really, it's just by the grace of God that we did, considering what she—and we—went through.

Looking back at it all, I'm amazed. I was too young to know what was happening at the time, but little by little my mama has filled me in on the details. I wanted to know. I wanted to know why I had no father, why we had no house, why we got stuck in that refugee camp. I was only one year old at the time, so how could I have remembered anything? This was back in 1980, back when the war started. I had an older sister who was four and a younger one who had just been born. But I have no memory of my father. And I've never seen a photo of him, though they say I look like him—the same dark features, the same broad face. Just like him, they say. But I can't remember ever seeing him because—this is what my mama explained to me—he had already become incorporated with the guerrillas. He was hiding out, since the Fuerza Armada was rounding up men in our area in Cabañas, taking them off at night, and that would be the end of them. And it was while he was out somewhere that suddenly my mama and we kids and everyone in our area had to leave our houses and take off, or else we would have been killed by the Fuerza Armada. That's the way my mama explained it to me.

We all took off to the north, to Honduras. I can't imagine how it must have been for my mama—three small kids and nothing to feed them. It must have been awful. I've got no memory of this, but I was told that we made it just over the border to a small town in Honduras. We were stuck up there for two months. We had nothing there to eat, and my sister tells me we were dying of malnutrition; we were nothing but stomachs and backs, the way starving kids look. Some folks up there gave us food out of pity, and at times we grabbed whatever we found nearby so as not to starve to death. From things I was told, it's a miracle that I'm alive here telling you the story.

The one we lost, though, was my father. He had come back to our home in Cabañas, and when he saw that everyone was gone he came looking for us. Both him and my uncle. They were frantic, I suppose—so frantic that they didn't even bother removing their green guerrilla uniforms. And that was a big mistake. They ran into a Fuerza Armada patrol and were captured. My uncle is the one who told me all this. He and my father and several others were taken to a Fuerza Armada encampment in the mountains, and all of them were shot. Six shots to each one, according to my uncle. My father was killed that way. My uncle got hit in the ear, just a scratch, but he fell down as if he were dead, and more bodies landed on top of him. Eventually, when the soldiers left, he managed to get away and go where my aunt was. He's alive today. But my father and two more of his brothers got killed.

It was only later, when we were in the refugee camp—Mesa Grande, you've heard of it, right?—it was only then that my mama found out. She was a young woman then, just twenty-two years old, and with three kids. From what she told me, she and my father had loved each other a lot, and they had gotten married legally and were living fine together up to then. But that was it—at twenty-two years old, a widow. Imagine it! I can't. I suppose the only good thing was that up there in the refugee camp her kids and she were safe. I mean, as long as you stayed within the wire fences of the camp you couldn't be shot. Step outside, and you were dead if they saw you. The Honduran soldiers would shoot you. Inside the jail— I call it a jail, because in a way it was, no?—inside we were safe. Food, plenty of food. Some kind of roof over your head, and schools for the kids.

Seven years, until '87, we were up there. For kids like me, it was pretty good. In the mornings I'd go to a nursery school or later to kindergarten and first grade. In the afternoons or whenever, there were always lots of other kids around to play with. All kinds of games, like kids have—tag, singing games, and even softball. For me, it was sort of fun, really it was. What was bad is what was going on with my mama. I don't know exactly when it happened, but she got together with Antonio. Not married, like she'd been with my father, but together as a couple. You know who Antonio is, no? Yes, Luis's brother—his younger brother who was also in the guerrillas. When he'd come back to the camp, like the guerrillas did at times, he was with my mother. Antonio was not a good man. He's not like Luis. I know Luis now, I know him well, and he treats Julia with respect. But Antonio was a different sort. With my own eyes, I saw him whack my mama, kick her; and with my own ears, I'd have to listen to him cursing her out, telling her that she was nothing and worthless. I knew it was bad, but apparently it was even worse. She told me more later, that he had abused her nonstop, that he was running around with several other women up in the camp. By then she had three kids with him, and she had six mouths to feed. She put up with it as long as she could, and then finally in '87, when she heard that it was possible to go back to El Salvador, she took off with all six of us. Told him square to his face that she was leaving him, leaving the refugee camp, and he needn't bother following her. Which he did a couple of years later when we were in Santa Marta, back in El Salvador. But she told him she'd had it with him; it was done and over. She was keeping the kids, and he could go wherever he wanted, but not with her. If you ask me, it took a lot of guts on her part, because she had to raise us by herself from then on.

And she did. Up in Santa Marta she put us in school, and she went out to work doing whatever she had to do to feed us. Cleaning houses, working in a store, whatever. During the harvest of maíz she would work the cobs, removing the kernels by hand—we had no machines for that—and getting paid just two colones for a full sack of kernels. And somehow she had managed to buy a small piece of land, which she was working by herself, growing maíz. That's how we got by. We weren't eating all that well, just tortillas and a little con qué. Just enough to survive, that's all. But somehow we made it through those years. Four or five years up there in Santa Marta. Then, thank goodness, we got word that they were looking to repopulate over in new communities near Mount Guazapa. And my mama, she leaped at the opportunity. Grabbed the whole bunch of us, and we came over here. It was in '92. Like I told you, I was thirteen years old then—and at the moment with little idea what was going to happen next.

I expect you've heard from others how it was in the beginning here in Comunidad Guazapa. From Luis and Joaquín, no? For us it was the same as for everyone else. You received materials to build your house, and you got your land and some tools and seeds. My mama did all this by herself. Built our house, a shack really, by herself. And she worked the milpa by herself. She also became a partera, delivering babies. We had very little in the way of health services back then. Some folks from the Lutheran church in Suchitoto arranged for a few women from the communities to get training as health workers and parteras. They set up a course in Suchitoto, a course run by doctors, and my mama learned how to be a partera. She's been doing it ever since. Not for money, really. She doesn't charge anything—not back then and not today either. She says, "The people don't have money to pay, so I can't be setting a price for it." That's her way. Often, someone will give her something—vegetables they might be growing, a chicken, whatever. But she goes on doing it, since she likes being helpful in that way.

And with us kids, she encouraged us all to get whatever education we could. She wanted us to go forward, and she had the foresight to understand that going to school was the way to improve your life. Many parents, most back then, didn't look at things the way she did. They didn't see any point in sending their sons and daughters to school. You couldn't make a living from anything you learned, they figured, so why bother? Better to keep the girls at home helping out with housework, and better to have the boys working in the milpa. My mama, she saw it differently, and she pushed us to get as much schooling as we could handle. One of my brothers is an accountant now, and several others have their high school diplomas. Me, I gravitated to teaching. To see kids grasp what you're teaching them, see their excitement, it has always moved me. Always.

So what happened to me, like I was telling you, is that I finished high school when I was twenty years old. I did my high school classes over in Suchitoto. We didn't have a high school here like we do today. I got a scholarship to study there in a kind of intensive course. I finished seventh through twelfth grades in three years. Not easy, but manageable. Especially if you had support at home. And I had my mother behind me. And not only her. My husband was behind me, too. Right, right, I didn't mention that, did I? Well, I had got married when I was eighteen years old. Yes, to a fellow from out here, from a community next to ours. He's a couple of years older than me. I met Rodrigo when I was sixteen. I was working in the store over in the ciudadela. It was a tiny place where women of the community took turns selling things. I was doing my turn, and in comes Rodrigo. We chatted a little, and I guess he took a liking to me. He kept seeking me out, wanting to start up with me. Truth is, I wanted nothing to do with him. It wasn't that I didn't like him. It was just that I had my mind on my studies in high school, and I didn't want any interference. But the man didn't give up. He kept coming after me, and, well, eventually the magic hit me, and I started falling for him. And, bueno, we decided to get married. He hadn't finished his high school degree; he still hasn't. I encouraged him to finish, but he didn't want to do it. Instead, he got interested in being a mason, building houses. He's pretty good at it, and at this point he's got lots of work and even hires some of the boys in the community to work with him. He's done real well. His parents are a little miffed with me, figuring I was the cause of his not getting more education. But Rodrigo doesn't feel that way. He's happy with what he's doing, and right from the beginning he has supported me in my studying and my work. Rodrigo is no *machista*. He's a good man. Back when I got pregnant and had my first child, Quique, he was there in the room with me giving me emotional backing along with my mama. Yes, right, she was my partera. Calm, cool. I don't know how she could do it, you know, watching your own child in pain like that. But she, she's a real professional. And so it was a bit unusual, you could say—my husband right there and my mama delivering my baby.

So here I was with my new baby and still in high school. Rodrigo, though, was true to his word. He encouraged me to continue with my studies, even taking care of our baby on some days when I was off studying. And my mother helped me out too, of course. And on those days when neither was available, I just took the baby with me to class in Suchitoto. Sounds unusual? Yes, I suppose. The teachers and authorities in the school didn't mind. They told me it was all right with them. And that way I managed to get my high school diploma and at the same time also continue working as a maestro popular in our school in the community. Lots of support at home—that's what it took. Rodrigo was behind me all the way, even though I wasn't making a centavo teaching here in the community. I was still working on a voluntary basis. Until ten years ago, that's the way it was. Until then, I never got paid a centavo.

Anyhow, after I had my high school diploma, I decided to go ahead and get a college degree as a teacher. In San Salvador. It was a three-year program, and it was structured in such a way that I was able to continue my work in the community and also get my degree. Very hectic, you could say. But again, it all comes down to whether you've got support at home. I did. On those days when I had to take off from home at dawn, Rodrigo would walk me to the bus stop on the main road; and on those nights when I came home in the dark, he'd be waiting at the bus stop to walk with me back to our house. Not too many husbands would have done that.

I never had to stop teaching here at the community school. Even when I had my second child, Rosita, I was able to go on teaching—you know, with a little time off to give birth and take care of the baby. No, my mama wasn't my partera the second time. I mean, she helped me during the pregnancy, but then it became apparent there would be some complications, and so, rather than take any chances, I went to the hospital. Rosita turned out fine, though. She's four years old now, in nursery school. And my son is twelve. I think it's a little hard on them having me in the school right there with them, especially now that I'm the principal. And for me, it's a little difficult too. For me, the problem is—I guess it's a problem that all of us mothers have when we're working out of the house—my problem is that I don't have enough time to be with my kids. On school days I'm off early in the morning. I take Rosita with me to nursery school, but when I get home at, say, seven at night she's often sleeping already. I have a neighbor who comes in and does the cooking and cleaning and looks after the kids. Problem is, I'm not around enough, that's how I feel— you know, to play around with them, help with the homework, and all of that. It's a big worry of mine, even though when I'm there I am involved with them, and they know it. My daughter tells me that when she grows up she wants to be a teacher like me. My son, I don't know. He's a bright boy, very good in math. I don't know what he'll go on to do, maybe something involving math. But I think they'll both go on and get some university training. I hope so, anyway.

For me, despite this guilt I have, I'm committed to continuing my work at the school. I'm proud of what we've done here. Since 1994 our school has been fully accredited by the Ministry of Education, and I feel we're doing a good job. And each year we're getting better. We've got a computer lab now—since 2002. We bought a few computers from our own budget, and an outside organization donated several to us. It's for the high school students only at this point. They're the ones who need it most. We've got someone here, an expert, teaching them computer technology. Me, I've not been involved in that. I prefer to teach younger kids, especially sixth grade, which is an important grade in our program, since there is a national test after sixth grade before they go on to junior high school. I've taught it for years. No, I didn't teach my own son, but of course I've taught many of my neighbors' kids. Yes, some of Luis and Julia's kids too. Francisco, no. I heard about him from my colleagues, of course. He's something special, always at the top of his class, the way I heard it. One of his sisters, Dorita, is something special just like him. I'm sure she's going on to something in the future, maybe studying law like Francisco. Margarita was also a student of mine—a good kid, but, frankly, not in the same league as Francisco and Dorita. She had to work hard at it, and she did manage—last year, if I'm not mistaken—she graduated high school. I don't know what's happened to her since then.

Naturally, not all our kids go on to university. Let's see, last year we had thirty who graduated, and nine of them are going on to university. All on scholarship, and all to La Universidad Nacional. The Lutheran Church provides them with scholarship money, between forty-nine dollars and sixty dollars, according to their needs, and tuition at La Universidad Nacional is almost nothing. The rest of the students? Well, they either stay at home working with their mothers or in the milpa with their fathers. Or they try their luck finding work in the cities somewhere as police or office workers, or some of the girls become *muchachas*. And many of the boys, they go mojado. I don't have any statistics on it, but I'd say at least half the boys from Comunidad Guazapa go on to the United States, figuring they can make some money up there. Make some good money and send some back to their families here to help out.

You see, it's not so easy for our children out here in the campo to get through high school. Many don't have the support at home. Their parents don't give them the support they need. The parents can't help them with their homework because they don't have their own education. So we get lots of kids dropping out, even though we try hard as we can to convince the parents to encourage their kids to stay on. With some we have success, and with many others there's just no way. They can't manage it. And the fact is that you've got to apply yourself nowadays, study pretty hard, to make it through high school. The Ministry of Education sets the program, and we out here in the campo have the same program that others have in the cities. There's a large body of material that the kids have got to learn—memorize, really—to get a good grade on the matriculation exam, which you need to go to university. Nothing easy there. At least we've got good teachers, dedicated teachers, who come out here to teach. And that makes a big difference. We try to make the courses interesting for the students, even with all the memorization they've got to do, and I think we're doing a pretty good job of it.

Here, I'll give you an example. We've got a new course going on now— one that was not taught back in my day, I assure you. It's called Orientation about Life, and in this class we discuss with the students subjects like gender, sex education, and family planning. Many students like it; they're hearing things they don't know about. Some kids, I know, don't much want to hear this material. But, the way I see it, it's excellent that we're teaching it. It's necessary, I feel, because the fact is we've had problems with students here, girls that suddenly drop out, and when we inquire about it, it turns out that the girl sometimes has gotten together with some boy, and she's pregnant. Recently, we had a twelve-year-old girl drop out for just that reason, to go with her sixteen-year-old boyfriend and have her baby. A child raising a child! And the thing is, they did it with the consent of their parents. And we had another case of a girl in fifth grade hanging around the schoolyard embracing her boyfriend, and when we called in the parents they told us they'd given their permission for the couple to acompañarse. So what we try to do in this new Orientation about Life course is give the kids information and also explain to them that there's a time for everything: a time to get engaged, a time to get married, and a time to be in school and study. We can't force anything, especially when parents are teaching something else at home.

What we *can* do—and we've done it—is enforce some rules here in the school. No kissing, no embracing in the school. Because once we let one couple do it, others are going to think, "That's cool, I'm going to do it too." The way I see it, our job is to get the kids to think, to discuss, even if they don't always agree or like it.

Another area where we try to get the kids to think and discuss is in the area of politics. The Ministry of Education gives us certain materials that we have to cover, yet our teachers have the freedom to discuss some of our history, including the civil war, together with the students in a way to get them to think. When ARENA was in power our kids were hearing some things that were different from the government line. We try to do it in a way that is not some kind of propaganda but rather by posing questions that get the kids talking, debating. Again, we find that some students enjoy this more than others. It may be surprising to you, but a whole lot of our students don't have a real idea what went on here during the war. The students will say, "Me, I'm with the FMLN!" That's natural, since almost all their parents or grandparents were involved with the FMLN during the war. Still, the kids have little idea of how the FMLN was formed or what the war was like. That's because their parents don't discuss it with them. They consider that it was something in the past, that they don't want it to happen again, and better not to talk about it. My feeling is that students *would be* interested in hearing about it if the parents did talk. I know that for me, personally, I lived through the war period, but it was only when my mama explained to me what went on that I understood more, and I did find it interesting to hear from her what our family went through. So, again, it's a question of getting the students to think, and fortunately we've got the kind of teachers here who are trying to do just that—along with the memorization stuff, of course.

For me, this is the first year I'm not teaching. Being the principal doesn't leave me time for any teaching, which is really too bad. I knew that would be the case when the committee asked me if I'd take on the job as school principal. I didn't want to say no. It's a heck of a challenge, and I wanted to give it a try. There's a lot more responsibility with this job. I no longer have just one class, my sixth graders, who I'm responsible for; now, I've got the whole school to deal with. So far, I'd say that I like the job. Most of the time, anyway. The administrative part—scheduling and all that—is easy. But there are other aspects of this job—I can't say I was fully aware when I took it on—that for me are difficult. Which aspects? In one word, "discipline." You have kids that are breaking the rules, and it falls on me to deal with these things. Like this one kid we had who was bullying smaller kids. We talked to him about it, told him it had to stop, but it didn't. So I had to suspend him from school, go talk to the parents, and for the time being the boy has changed his ways. No, we don't physically punish the kids; we don't whack them on their hands or on their butts the way teachers did in previous generations. It's against the law, and we don't want to handle things that way. If talking doesn't work, then we have them stay after school and clean the classrooms, and if that doesn't work, then I suspend the kid. I can't say I enjoy this; it's a part of the job that I do because I have to.

What we've done recently is apply to the municipality in Suchitoto to get a psychologist to come out here regularly. We've got some students who are badly neglected at home, and we need some psychological assistance for them. Like one boy—I think that he was abused at home—he was taking a needle and pricking himself with it, and he was cutting his wrist. This is a kid we've got to help, I feel. And for that we're trying to get a psychologist.

The students who give us the most problems are in junior high and high school, not the younger kids. They start rebelling once they hit adolescence, and sometimes it gets out of hand. We had a bunch of young adolescents recently who were hanging around the school—they had dropped out, you see—and they were threatening kids, causing problems, and we knew we had to do something about it. What we did is create a group from the communities, and we confronted the kids and more or less negotiated with them. We got them to stop hanging around and threatening other kids, and instead we've created some activities for them—sports activities and some workshops for them. And thank God, they've gone along with it. To me, that's the way we've got to solve things with these kids who are school dropouts and are getting involved with delinquency. And as you know, we've got an enormous problem with delinquency and gangs throughout the country. Many of these delinquent kids come from homes where the parents are neglecting them, and since there are no work opportunities and not sufficient activities, sports or other cultural activities, what's left for them? The kids are wandering about aimlessly, and then, the next thing you know, they get involved in delinquency.

In our area, from the six communities here, we don't have a problem. Like I said, when we had the beginnings of a problem, we solved it. What we have now—and this is a worry for all of us—is delinquents, gangs, coming from the outside. We've had robberies here in the school. It's real easy to just hop over the fence, break in, and steal things from the classrooms or cafeteria. Now just these last three or four months we've got a new phenomenon. Gang members from the towns around here are coming out to our communities and extorting money from residents. That's right, they come to the houses and tell you that you've got to pay such-and-such an amount, or they'll make you sorry you didn't. Some folks pay up, and some are taking their chances by refusing. Real bad stuff, I'm telling you!

We've reported this to the police, but I think what we've got to do is get together—all the communities—and figure out how to provide security for ourselves. I'm not sure how we are going to go about doing this. It's complicated. You can't just take the law into your own hands, and yet neither can we go on living with the kind of fear that is beginning to set in here in the communities. I tell you, for the first time, I begin to be scared just walking back to my house through the sugarcane fields at night. We didn't have this before. Now we do. It's going on all over the country, and our new government is going to have to act on it. I'm hoping they will—*soon!*

Despite what's been going on lately with the delinquency and all that, I am not pessimistic. I believe we can solve our problems. Here in the community, at the school, and I hope in the entire country. We've got a new government and an FMLN president, so let's see what can be done. As for me, I'm happy with what we're accomplishing at the school. We've done a lot, and I believe we can do more. You say you first came out here twelve years ago, verdad? Well, come out here twelve years from now, and you'll see. Me, I'll still be here at the school. As the principal or as a teacher, I don't know. I just know that since I was fourteen, I felt that I was settling in here for good. I like the community, and I like what we've been able to develop at the school. And when I think of the future, I'm sure that we'll be even better equipped here at the school. We'll be turning out more high school graduates. No doubt about that! The trend is already in that direction. And you know what—this may surprise you—but I figure we just might have a new college out here. A technical training institute or some kind of college. I think we will. That's my vision, anyway. What do you think?

CHAPTER FOURTEEN

Francisco

Looking Forward

It was six days before his graduation from law school when we interviewed Francisco once again in San Salvador. He was wearing a black suit, a white shirt with light-blue stripes, and well-shined leather shoes. He had his tie neatly tucked into one suit pocket and a cell phone in the other. If it were not for his youth and the utter sincerity of his smile, one might have mistaken him for a member of the Asamblea Legislativa. "I'm having my picture taken with my graduating class this afternoon—thirty or so of us. Next Friday it'll be in the newspapers. That's what they told us, anyway."

So for a final time, we sat down with the first and only lawyer from Comunidad Guazapa—or, for that matter, from any of the six communities in the area—to hear a little more about how he had traveled on this road not taken by others, where he thought it was leading him in the future, and where he thought his family, his community, and his country were also heading. Not one to hide his thoughts or feelings, Francisco was candid and clear in presenting his case. For an hour and a half, stopping only for moments to sip his coffee, Francisco went on. And in the end, one could not resist the thought that perhaps one day, and not too far off, this young legislative assistant was going to have his photo in the newspapers on a regular basis—and, hopefully, without having lost the sincerity of his smile.

I appreciate it. Thank you for your congratulations. Yes, yes, now I finally am a bona fide lawyer—in six days, anyway. That's when we're having the graduation ceremony over at La Universidad Nacional. All the faculties are part of it, so it'll be packed with people. Each of us was given only two tickets, and me, I was thinking who to invite. My papa for sure, and then I figured I'll invite my mama too. The two of them haven't seen each other for twenty years, though they've spoken—a few words anyway—on the cell phone. Sometimes, you see, when I'm out at the community I'll call my mama up in Santa Marta, and a couple of times I just passed the phone over to my papa and told him, "Why not say hello?" And he did. I guess it was a little awkward for them, but I figured, why not do it, no? So I decided to invite them both to my graduation, but, as fate would have it, just a few days back she fell into a ditch of some sort and got all cut up and damaged her leg. She's still recovering from that, and as a result she's not going to come. Too bad. I would have liked it if they were both there, but some other time, I guess.

As for me, bueno, this is maybe the most important day of my life so far. I've been waiting for this day for years now—ever since Kathy put the idea in my head that maybe I had a future going to some university. I had wanted to go to the United States to study, but, like I told you, I couldn't get a visa. So I stayed here and got into La Universidad Nacional. The truth is, I had no idea at the time what I wanted to study. That was six years ago. Coming from the community and with no real experience in life, what did I know? I was thinking maybe I'll study computer technology or maybe engineering. I had no clear idea. But the decision was resolved for me, since the only faculty that was open to me, that would accept me right away, was the Law Faculty. I wasn't sure that studying law would be interesting, but I met some guy who was a lawyer, and he showed me some of his books, and he began telling me that it was interesting stuff, and, well, I figured I'd give it a try.

Today, looking back, I feel it was a good choice for me. I've enjoyed my studies, and I can see there's a good future in being a lawyer. I'm not going to tell you that every course I took was a pleasure. It wasn't. Some of the professors, including some famous guys—whose names it's better not to mention—were terrible. They were boring and obviously uninterested. But some of the other professors were good, and I feel I got a good education. I managed to take some courses in philosophy and economics and sociology, too. Interesting stuff. I didn't go in for all the theory—you know, Plato and Marx—no, no. What interested me more was the kind of subjects that pertained to our reality, how we are living today in El Salvador. I liked constitutional law, for example. And I liked the courses that dealt with how laws were applied, how the legal system actually functioned today in El Salvador. You see, I was looking for a practical way that I could use my knowledge to get involved here.

I was fortunate to have some financial help from people. Kathy was sending some money to help me each month, and then I managed to find odd jobs here and there—painting houses, cleaning pools, cutting grass, that kind of thing. And a classmate of mine, a guy who came from a well-to-do family, had a house he was living in by himself, and he offered me a room in the house. That was how I managed to get by. I was able to buy my food and clothing, my books, and in the first year I even managed to get a real nice cell phone. One of the latest models. I really liked that cell phone, but, well—I don't think you know this, unless my papa told you—I got robbed by a bunch of maras. He didn't tell you? When he saw how they had busted up my face he got so damned angry that he wanted to come to San Salvador with some of his buddies from Comunidad Guazapa and go after the crooks. But there was no way of finding them—fortunately! My old man would have just gotten into trouble, verdad? The one who could have told us the identity of those maras was the bus driver. That's where it happened, on a bus here in the capital. The bus drivers know who these maras are because they themselves are having to pay protection money so as not to be robbed. But they keep their mouths shut. This is happening all the time here. I just happen to have got hit because I was using my cell phone before I got on the bus, and I must have been spotted by this bunch of maras. They got on the bus, a couple sitting behind me and a couple in front. I had no idea they were crooks. Then, suddenly, one of them sitting behind me grabs me in a stranglehold, and since I couldn't breathe I started struggling, and then the two in front start punching me in the face. Finally, they grab my cell phone and take off. No, nobody on the bus tried to help. The bus driver himself quickly exited the bus until the whole incident was over. That's how it is here. Everyone just runs when a robbery takes place. The victim is left alone. Me, I was bleeding all down my face and shirt. I had to go to the hospital and get my lip sewn up, and I had to take care of a broken tooth I had. What can you do? That's El Salvador today. It's one of the biggest problems we have—maras all over the country hitting on people day after day. People want the situation solved, but the question is, What can be done? It's a hell of a problem.

At this point I think I've got a pretty good understanding of this problem. I've looked into it. I did my thesis on penal law and penal reform. I think it came out well, my thesis. It took me not quite a year, and at least the professors felt it was a good piece of work. Anyhow, by doing research in this area I had to go to several prisons and also interview a number of inmates. Really, it was an eye-opening experience. I found out a hell of a lot of things. For one thing, our prisons are crammed full of inmates; we've gone beyond our capacity to house the large number of prisoners that we have. And for another thing, we do nothing in the way of rehabilitation. No workshops, no training, so that the criminals can have a way of making a living when they get out. So, naturally, they go right back to crime. I know, I know, this is not just a problem in El Salvador.

But what we have here now, more than in most other countries, is the problem of delinquent gangs. This didn't just start now. The media would have you think that the problem has got much worse now that we have the FMLN in power. But that is—excuse my language—that is complete *bullshit*! The media are controlled almost exclusively by ARENA people, and back when we had presidents from their party, they had an understanding to play down the amount of crime going on. They wouldn't report it as much, and they wouldn't show the gruesome photos of the victims. Now that the FMLN is in power, the media are exposing it more. But this problem has been going on for years. And it's a very complicated problem, with many causes.

Look, I could go on about this for hours, but let me just sum it up quickly. Think about it: who are these maras? They're kids from the poor, crowded neighborhoods, kids who've been absolutely neglected by their parents. The father has usually abandoned the house, or he's gone off to the United States. And maybe the mother has joined him there, too, while leaving the kid in the care of a grandmother. So nobody is controlling these kids. They drop out of school, they start drinking and taking drugs, and the easiest way to get money is to rob. They join gangs, and— here's an important point—the gangs serve as a kind of family for them. The kid needs a little money for food or for a smoke or whatever, so his fellow maras share with him. And the kid feels that finally he's got someone who's looking after him, that he belongs somewhere. Of course, once he's into the gang he's tied in real solid, no easy way out.

Now this problem didn't just start yesterday. It is, the way I see it—not just me, others who've investigated it too—it's a problem that came out of the postwar situation. You see, the reconstruction that took place after the war had to do with the physical rebuilding of the country—houses, roads, commercial centers, and all that. But there was no emphasis on the psychological reconstruction of the people here. For twelve years, both in the guerrillas and the Fuerza Armada, you had young people who lived and died by the gun: you solved your problems with force, with arms. When the war ended, many of these people had no way of making a living. My papa and others, yes, they got their lands, or some got business loans, and they were able to go back to work. Others, many young people, got nothing. So what was left for them? Many of them went as mojados to the United States, and once they got there some of them joined gangs or formed gangs. They knew how to use weapons, and they became real skilled as criminals. And then what do the gringos do? When they catch these guys they deport them back here. And these criminals—highly skilled criminals, I should say—they went back to the poor neighborhoods throughout the country, and they began recruiting. Not just to commit petty crime. No, they started getting involved in the drug trade. Lots of money in that. Enough to pay off poorly paid and corrupt police. And so now what we've got is not only maras who are dominating poor neighborhoods, who go out and rob people in the streets and in their houses, but now we've got a whole system of more sophisticated criminals involved with the drug trade and some of these groups of maras working with them.

And what's the solution? Nothing easy, that's for sure! The thing I learned by going to the prisons and talking with the criminals is that the idea of having stiffer laws and greater repression—the hard-fisted approach of the previous ARENA government—is not one that is going to have good results. The citizens here want that kind of approach. Shoot the criminals, kill them off—that's what the public says it wants. But, I'm telling you, that's *not* the ultimate solution. To me, the emphasis has to be on prevention, not repression. Sure, you can put more police on the street, even a few thousand soldiers, but that won't stop the crime. The answer lies in improving conditions for the young kids, the ten- and twelve-year-olds, in these poor neighborhoods. Keep them in school if possible, and for those who drop out there needs to be vocational training and even more recreational activities. In these neighborhoods there's no place to even play a little soccer or basketball. And no clubs or activities at all. It's these kids who we've got to reach before the gangs reach them. Those already in the gangs, those in the jails, it's going to be very hard to rehabilitate them. We need to try. But the emphasis now—and what needs to be a major area of involvement and investment for our new government—is setting up alternatives for those young kids *before* they get drawn into the gangs. Will the government do it? I have my worries. But I am convinced that this is the best way to slow down the growth of gangs and begin to correct the problem.

No, no, I'm not planning to go into the area of criminal law—not as a defender and not as a prosecutor. Politics? Well, yes—maybe that's where I'll wind up, or at least give it a try. I don't know. I'm just beginning to feel my way around now, see what I want to do with my law degree. There's several possibilities. But the thing I'm planning on right now is to get my private life on a stable footing. And that's going fine. I'm about to get married. Yes, really! To a woman who is graduating next week with me. Eugenia—a classmate of mine. Yes, she's a lawyer, too. I haven't told you about her? No, I guess I haven't. Well, that's what's happening. We're planning on getting married fairly soon. I've been with her a while, sort of on and off, but about a few months ago we decided to get married.

She comes from a different background than me. She's a city girl, born and raised here in the capital. Her mother is from the campo—she and

I get along super well—and her stepfather is a businessman. Eugenia, she's had a different kind of life. She never was out in the campo really until she met me. And actually, it wasn't until we had known each other for a couple of years and I saw that she might be the girl I wanted to marry, not till then did I bring her out to the community. It was a shock for her. The first time I brought her out to meet my family it was in the rainy season, and the whole area, like you know, it gets muddy and all humid and with the mosquitoes biting nonstop. If you're not accustomed to that, then it's pretty uncomfortable. And Eugenia, she's a city girl, and she could hardly tolerate it; she got bitten up so bad that her skin was red all over. Truthfully, it was terrible for her. She didn't say so, but you could sense it. Since then, though, she's gone back with me many times, especially on the weekends when I go there to play soccer with my brothers. She knows my papa and Julia and the whole bunch. And they all like her, same as her family likes me. Things are good now. Even my papa is enthusiastic about her—which is saying something, because he's always been my biggest critic. From the time I started up with girls, back as a teenager, he was always warning me. "Listen here, Son," he'd tell me. "Girls come easy and they go easy. Don't get yourself all messed up with this one or that one!" Looking back on it, I figure he was warning me—without saying so directly—not to do what he'd done, running after this bicha and that bicha the way he'd done as a teenager and, really, the way he'd done when he was already a good deal older. No, he never sat me down and gave me any advice about how to protect myself; no, nothing like that. Because the truth is, he never protected himself, never bothered using contraception. I know this because it's been *me* who has gone to him and given *him* advice about contraception. When I learned a little about it in school and then started reading up about it, and I could see he was having one kid after another—all those mouths to feed—I talked to him about contraception. I mean, we didn't have any huge conversation, but we talked, and I could tell he hadn't even thought about using anything. All he told me was, "Son, you're going to complicate your life. Watch out!"

　　And I guess I did give him some cause to worry. Not that I was running around with bichas when I was a teenager. Later, well, yes, I did some running around. Even after I'd met Eugenia—and there was nothing serious between us—I was a bit of a mujerero. Now, no. And as a teenager, no, not really. But what I was involved in—I guess I can tell you, since Eugenia knows now, I've told her the whole thing—back when I was seventeen I got involved with a woman in the community. You probably know her or have heard of her. She's a wonderful person, still lives there in the community with her three kids. She's all involved with politics, a real smart lady. Bueno, she's the first woman I was ever involved with. It went on for four years, till I went to university. She's older than me, something like nine years older. She had three kids when we started up, but she and her husband had split up. I used to like talking with her, and then one thing led to another, and we became lovers. I fell real hard for her, but she was direct with me right from the beginning. "Look, Chico," she said. "Don't get any ideas that you're going to acompañarse with me, because I don't want to have kids with you. If I'm having more kids, it'll only be with my husband, if he comes back. So don't start having any illusions, understand?" At that time, hell, I was only a kid myself, so whatever she said was all right with me. But for my papa, once he got wind of what was going on, he started giving me hell. "What are you doing messing around with that old lady?" he said. That's what he called her, "an old lady." He was damned annoyed with me, but even though I respect him and all that, I wasn't about to listen. Of course not. I was real attached to her, and the thing is, I got a hell of a lot out of that relationship. She taught me many things, smart as she is, and it was a wonderful experience for me. Weird thing is, just a couple of years ago, after we'd no longer been together for quite a while, she came to me and wanted to start up again. Her husband had come back, but again he left her; I guess she'd had it with him. And so she came to me, and we did get involved again. But this time it was me who had to put conditions. Now *she* wanted to acompañarse with me, and I had to tell her, "No, you've already had your children. I'm still young, and I'm looking for a woman who doesn't have kids and who'll be mother to my kids. I'm grateful to you for all you gave me back then, but there's no way you and me are going to get married." She listened—I guess it was tough on her—but she understood. We spent a little more time together, as lovers, I mean, but then it came to an end. These days there's no hard feelings between us. The opposite. There's a lot of mutual respect, and we're friends. She's even helped me out. Involved as she is with politics, she knows many folks in the FMLN, and she's even introduced me to some important party members. In fact, it was her who put me in contact with the deputy in the Asamblea Legislativa, the one I'm working for nowadays. I owe that to her. Because how else would someone like me, a law student, wind up knowing someone like that, verdad? Real lucky for me!

The way all that happened is that the deputy was visiting out here in the Suchitoto area, and my friend took me to meet her. I liked the deputy, and she seemed to like me. I told her what I was doing in law school, and I volunteered to help her out with any tasks she had. She told me thanks, but no thanks. At the time she had an assistant, and she didn't need any further help. But the good thing was, she took my name and phone number. I didn't figure anything was going to happen with that, and then suddenly one day a year or so ago, I get a call from her. "Francisco," she says to me, "if you're still looking for some work, I can use you. Be at my office tomorrow, and we'll discuss it." It surprised the hell out of me. I was busy with my studies, and I had no idea how to get to her office, which was in another district, quite far away. But I got myself over there. Sure did. And immediately she told me that her assistant had left, and if I wanted the job, it was mine. I was shocked. Me, working for a deputy in the Asamblea Legislativa! I couldn't believe it. And even though at first all I was doing was running errands for her, a kind of messenger boy, that was fine by me. Lately, though, she's given me more and more responsibility. She's a lawyer too, and she can't handle all her clients, so she's turned some of that work over to me. I do the paperwork, and she signs, and I'm beginning to make some good money, which I can use, because as a law student I've been fairly broke.

But besides the chance to make a little cash, what I'm getting now is a real insider's view of how the government, the law functions—or doesn't function—in our country. You can't learn this from books or classes. Not the same way. You've got to be up close, see how the legislators work, how they cut deals. Then you begin to know something. You expand your horizons. What I've come to see is that, yes, we have a fine constitution in this country and, on the whole, a good legal system. It promises a fair deal, protection and security, to all our citizens. In principle, it all looks good. But in practice, we are in a mess. Why? It all comes down to politics and the fact that the wealthy people in El Salvador have used the laws to benefit themselves—tax laws, land distribution laws, you name it. The rich have it figured, often quite legally, how to hold on to their money and not allow the poor to benefit enough. And then, too, we have widespread corruption. To put it simply, there's too many politicians on the take. Let's say a particular politician is responsible for building some infrastructure. Well, he cuts a deal with a company that will benefit not only the citizens but also himself. And I'm not talking just about politicians from the ARENA Party. I'm talking about politicians that come from every political party. From the FMLN, too! You talk with my papa, and he'll tell you that the FMLN is clean and ARENA is filthy. Not so! My papa would vote for any fool that the FMLN puts up as a candidate. He's still living the ideology of the 1980s. Bueno, that's his experience. It's not mine. Some Areneros are decent politicians, and they do good things, and I say, when they do good we need to back them. And some from the FMLN are in politics in order to enrich themselves. People say that when you get political power it corrupts you, it can make you lose the social values you used to have. And I've seen that. I've seen that some of those same guys who were *comandantes* with the FMLN during the war, well, now they're wealthy politicians or wealthy businessmen—big houses, cars, and with four bodyguards. These guys took care of themselves once they got into power, and they no longer are looking after the very people they had fought for during the war. And where is Luis Campos these days—still in his milpa! Still having to work his butt off to support his family. But try to go tell this to my papa! I've tried, and what he tells me—and not only him, others there in the community—they tell me I'm talking like an Arenero. Not so. I'm talking about what I see now that I'm there in the Asamblea Legislativa working with the deputy. I'm not saying that I don't support the FMLN. I do. They're the best of a bad bunch. But I will say this: I'm glad we've got Mauricio Funes in there; he's a good man. I'm just skeptical about how much he can do and how quickly he can do it. He's got to work within the system. He can't pull a maneuver like that Hugo Chávez—and good that he can't. We need to keep a good constitutional system in this country—no dictatorship. But to work with all the political elements here, including the rich, is not so easy. Funes is trying. He's done some fine things—more housing for the poor, improvements in the education system, and other things. The media aren't covering that. They talk about crime, not the good things that Funes has done. And that's a major problem for the FMLN right now. People aren't clear about what is going on here, and it's not at all certain that the FMLN is going to stay in power. When Funes's term is over in 2014, we may very well get a president from another party. Maybe a new political party. Not the FMLN, and not ARENA. It's not like my papa thinks. It's not at all certain that the FMLN is going to stay in power. At least that's how I see it.

For the time being, I'm still learning. I've got my eyes open, and I'm seeing what direction I might take. Meanwhile, I just want to get myself established. You know, get married. Eugenia and I have known each other for three and a half years now. In the beginning we were just classmates—pals. She was hesitant to get too involved with me, since, to put it plainly, her background was different. Her friends were telling her, "No, not with that one! Choose someone else." And me, being from the campo, I was hanging around with kids who were more from my background. But as I got to know her and she got to know me, we got closer—and then even closer. She's good-looking, but really, there's lots of good-looking women out where I came from. What I was looking for was someone who had a good head on her shoulders, someone sociable and who would be a reliable mother for children. Someone I could talk with, you see. And Eugenia is all of that. You'd have to ask her what she saw in me, but I guess she liked me well enough to start up, and, well, now we're real solid. We haven't rushed into the thing; we've talked it over plenty. And we see that we want the same things. Soon after we're married we're going to open up a law office together. In her parents' house, that's where we'll do it. They've got a big place, seven or eight rooms, and we'll be living on one floor of their house, with the office down below in a corner of the house. Once we've got some money, sure, we'll get our own place here in the capital. Meanwhile, we both like the idea of starting at her parents' place.

Like I was just telling you, when Eugenia and I started thinking seriously about getting together, well, she wasn't all that happy that I came from the campo. Even going out visiting with me to Comunidad Guazapa was not something she liked. Too many mosquitoes and all that. But once she saw that my being out there was important to me, she began to change. And she sees that I have no intention of living out there. Neither of us wants to live out in the campo. Still, that's where my family is, and when I have free time, sometimes on weekends and vacations, that's where I like going. Seeing the family, my brothers and sisters. I like visiting out there, and besides, I feel a kind of responsibility these days to help them move forward. My papa, he can't do it. He's got no money to buy things for them—even some necessary things. And the way things are now, it's me even more than him who can talk to my brothers and sisters about getting their education and not being lazy. With José it's too late. He's dropped out of school. But with Roberto, he had dropped out, and all he was interested in was playing soccer. "Damn it, Roberto," I told him. "You can't make a living playing soccer. You've got to study!" I bought him some soccer shoes, yes, but also school supplies, and now I've got him going back. We'll see if he sticks to it. And with the younger ones, like Juan or Dorita, it's easier to convince them. They're listening real hard to what I'm telling them. Juan was screwing around, getting involved with kids who were going nowhere. All he was interested in is getting the latest cell phone and getting an earring put in so he'd look like his buddies. I understand Juan real well; he's thirteen, and when I was his age I was the same. I talked and explained all this to him, and I got him to forget the earring and the cell phone and to put whatever money he's got into stuff for school. He's listening now. And with Dorita, I don't even have to say a thing. She's a natural; she studies hard and always has her nose in a book. This summer I paid for her to come to the capital and take some course in English. She's real smart; she's even talking like someday she wants to be a lawyer. We'll see. The main thing is that she is heading for university; I can see that. But the one who may be heading nowhere, I'm sad to say, is Margarita. She didn't pass the exams to get into the university, and nowadays she's talking of maybe taking up some technical training. Maybe. She's a bit lazy, doesn't apply herself. I've talked to her—yelled at her, really—that if she doesn't figure some way to support herself, she's going to wind up a housewife who's dependent on her husband, and she knows damn well that if that happens, she might end up with a bunch of kids and some guy who leaves her, and then where the hell will she be? She gets pissed at me when I talk to her like that, but she knows what I'm saying is true. God help her, that's all I can say.

It's true, I've sort of become like a parent to my papa's kids. But my papa and Julia, they don't mind. No, no, they're behind me one hundred percent. They see that my brothers and sisters, at least some of them, listen to me. And they want their kids to go forward. And yes, it takes a little money—not much—to buy school supplies, books, clothes, and all that. I tell them, "Take advantage of me now, because when I get my own kids I may not be able to help out so much." My papa and Julia, they're not like others in the community who've got money coming in from relatives in the United States. Many other families do. Which is helpful, but it also has spoiled some of those families. I've seen kids here in the community who've got a brother in the United States sending remesas every month, and those kids buy whatever they want and figure they don't have to work or study; the money flow, the one hundred dollars a month, is all they'll ever need, or if they need more, then, hell, maybe they can go as mojados too. They become lazy, spoiled. It's hurt them as much as it's helped them. So at least in my family, I'm the only one with some spare cash; and even while I'm helping out, I don't have so much, and I've got no intention of spoiling my brothers and sisters. Julia and my papa see all this, and they understand. Yes, there's a good understanding between us these days, and they're grateful for what I'm trying to do.

And me, I tell you, I appreciate how they take seriously the future of their kids. If you ask me, they had too damn many. But, all right, now they have this whole bunch, and, unlike some other families in the community, they don't neglect their kids. Julia and my papa are real good about it. Yes, yes, it's true that in the beginning when Julia got together with my papa, well, I was angry. I even ran away. But one grows up, no? You get older, and you see things more clearly. And I can see now that Julia and my papa have been very good for each other. They've got a good relationship between them. If you ask me, looking at it from my papa's side, I think Julia saved him. The way I see it now, if he hadn't gotten together with her, he would have wound up bouncing from one woman to another and, in a way, all alone. Since the truth is he was *not* a responsible father with several of his kids. With me, yes. And with the ones he's had with Julia, yes, definitely. But with my own mama's kids—no. And Meches's kids—no. They don't see him as a real father. Without Julia my papa would have wound up like my uncle Antonio, isolated and with kids that don't recognize him. Without Julia my papa would only have had me. I'm the only one who would be respecting him. And I do respect him. Not in everything he thinks or has done, no. But as a man, I admire a lot of what he's done, and I respect how he's opened his mind to see some things, like the importance of education for his children. We're like good friends now. We talk openly with each other, and there's a lot of mutual respect.

I'm just hoping that when I make a little money I'll be able to lighten his burden a bit. My papa is sixty-one years old now. He figures he can work forever, but who knows how long he can keep it up, going to the milpa from dawn to dusk six or even seven days a week? It's damned hard work, even for a guy like him. I know, because I've worked up there plenty, as I've told you. Maybe he's someone who's got to stay there forever. I think he is. But even he wouldn't mind taking it a little easier in the coming years. The man has never taken a vacation. I'm not sure if he's ever been down to the sea. I've told him that once I get a little more money, soon as I can afford it, I'm going to buy a car—a pickup that will enable me to get out to the community even in the rainy season. And then I'm going to take him and Julia and my brothers and sisters on a vacation. We'll be able to go to the sea. And then—this is my idea—I want to go on a trip alone with him. I've told him about it, and he seems to like the idea. I want us to go north, back to some of those places where we lived during the war. Like Los Ranchos and Santa Marta. And back to Talpetates, where he was born. And even up to the refugee camp area in Honduras where I was born. I want to see those places with him. My papa says he'd like that. Take a trip back to our past, you could say. It'll be good for both of us, I think. Pretty soon—once I've got a car. I'm looking forward to it.

CHAPTER FIFTEEN

Luis and Julia

A Final Word or Two

It seemed fitting that, in the final chapter of a book based on oral histories from them and members of their family, Luis and Julia ought to have the final word—or two. Over the dozen or so years that we had known both of them, several times at their house in Comunidad Guazapa we had heard them talking with and teasing one another. However, these conversations were invariably interrupted by a child, a neighbor, or even a rooster, turkey, or goat that strayed between them. Thus, in an attempt to get the two of them to sit together for an extended dialogue, we convinced them one Saturday to come with us alone to the nearby restaurant, Guazapa Café, and submit themselves for a final time to an intrusive question—or two.

Much to our surprise, as we entered the restaurant, passing by the display of wartime memorabilia—the rifles, the uniforms, the radios, and various other pieces of equipment of both the Fuerza Armada and the guerrillas—Julia told us that she had never been here before. "I'd heard about it from Luis—he's a pal of the owner," she told us while standing wide-eyed before the prolific collection. "But no, no. This is the first time I'm here." Then, after quickly examining an item or two, she added, "Brings back real bad memories. I can't say I like seeing this stuff again. No, not at all." At which point all four of us moved off to an isolated table at the other end of the restaurant beneath a tiled roof and with a couple of hammocks hanging invitingly from the rafters.

For the next two or three hours, with tape recorders running most of the time, Marta and I engaged Luis and Julia in a kind of rambling dialogue. As might be expected, Luis did most of the talking, but (with an occasional prompt from us) Julia joined in too. We paused for a lunch of grilled chicken and a few beers, followed by the best quesadillas that any of us had ever tasted. For the most part, the mood was light, though the subjects discussed were often serious—the war, the community, politics, their children, their extended family, and, of course, their seventeen years together as a couple.

What follows then is a (necessarily) abridged version of that Saturday conversation, held far from the madding crowd.

JULIA (J):   Good to lie down in a hammock. Yes, it is. That stuff at the entrance gave me, I don't know, gave me a rotten feeling.

LUIS (L):   Me, no. I wouldn't want to be back in uniform, hell no, but I don't mind seeing the stuff again.

J: Those uniforms were different from what I wore. We were always in black uniforms—black shirts, black pants. You never seen me wearing black since then, have you? Nor pants either. The day I came down from the monte I told myself, it's no more black and no more pants, whatever color they are. And I've stuck to that, haven't I?

L: Sí, sí. [He then turns to us.] I understand her. I haven't kept anything, not even a photo from those days. I don't want it around. And no green shirt either. That's the color we wore. I don't want anything from those days, no, hombre. But just to see the stuff like at the entrance, I can't say I mind.

QUESTION (Q): You both have told us that your children don't know much about what you did during the war. Do you prefer that they don't know?

J: I don't prefer one way or the other. They learn some of these things in school. I just don't go into it much with any of them. They don't ask much, and I don't care to discuss it much. The one who likes to discuss these things is over here. Luis. He likes talking about the war, don't you, Luis?

L: It's something they ought to know about. That's the way I see it. The kids need to know how we got to where we are today, how so many of our people died struggling to get to where we are. Problem is, many don't take an interest. Only some do. Like Chico, yes. He's the one who was always asking me. Even today, now that he's older and might be getting a car, he's telling me that he wants us to go back and visit some of those places where we were living during the war; even the refugee camp up in

Honduras he'd like to see. Being the oldest, he remembers some of those years. He was wandering around with me near the end of the war, back when he was about seven or eight. And when he got a little older, he started asking me all about things. How I got the bullet holes in me, what I did, all of that. I told him. Not every detail, but a lot. And he was asking Joaquín and others too. That's how the boy is. Always wanting to know things. And now that he's a lawyer, he's into everything. Knowing about this politician, about that one. He's no boy anymore. Him in his lawyer's suit and his tie and all that—the kid's a professional, and he knows things. I'm proud of Chico, sure I am. Way I see it, he's a good example to our other children.

J: That's for sure. Chico grabs hold of all of them and tells them that they got to stay in school. That's where their future is. With Roberto, he was real tough. Roberto wasn't going to classes. Chico got hold of him and talked some sense into him. Roberto decided to go back, try it again. And the younger ones, they all are listening to him. Dorita— she's in eighth grade now—she's figuring to do like Chico, go be a lawyer. This past winter Chico was paying for her to take English lessons. She was going a couple of times a week to the capital, and I guess she's pretty good at it. She got the highest marks in her class. Smart kid, sort of like Chico.

L: My boy has got me convinced now that school is the future for our kids. I see where he's gone with it. He's got his work now, some cash in his pockets. He's not just spending it on himself. He buys schoolbooks for his younger brothers and sisters. Shoes, school uniforms, even toothbrushes and toothpaste—Chico buys it for them. And he's got his influence on them. They see what he's managed, so they listen.

J: Except for José. Chico came along too late for him. José dropped out awhile back, and he won't continue. He's nineteen now. God knows what is going to happen to him!

L: He should be inheriting his grandmother's land, that's how it ought to go.

J: But you know that isn't going to happen. No way!

L: Because of your father, his wrong way of thinking.

J: Both him and my mother! [She turns to us.] I reckon you know what my parents are going to do with my grandma's land when she dies. My father's going to keep it for himself. Even though it's José who is taking care of my grandma—sleeping there, fetching water for her, and food. And even though my grandpa promised José the land. Never mind, my father has got the legal right to it, and José is going to wind up with nothing. Awful, no?

Q: So what do you see him doing? Going to the United States?

L: If he could, yes, that's what he'd do, I figure. Maybe Roberto would go with him, even though he's studying now. But you've got to have a whole lot of cash to pay the *coyotes*. Costs several thousand dollars. Where is José or Roberto going to get that money?

J: Not from my brothers, that's for sure!

L: Julia's got four brothers that have gone mojado. Living somewhere in Virginia, I think it is. Three have been up there for years, and one just went a few months back.

J: Not four, Luis. Just three. You're forgetting about Marcos, who just came back.

L: Sí, sí.

J: The damned fool got caught for driving without a license. Spent eight months in jail up there in Virginia, and then the gringos deported him. He's back in my parents' house now.

L: He's not about to stay, though. Even though the community wouldn't mind nowadays. Before, yes. The guy fought with the Fuerza Armada during the war. He wasn't welcome here. Now if he wanted to stay, nobody would mind. I think the guy has wised up some. Not the fool he was before. So if he wanted to stay here, raise a family here, no problem. But I figure he'll go back soon as he can.

J: He's got connections with the coyotes up in Mexico. Don't ask me how, I don't know. He says they'll get him over for hardly any money. So I reckon he'll be going.

Q: And it's your brothers who are sending the remesas to your parents and helping them out, right?

J: You've seen what my parents got in their house, no? A refrigerator, a stove, a TV, even a microwave oven. And my father's got a herd of cows. I don't know how many, but he's got a bunch.

L: A dozen now. That's what he's got, and some other animals too. That's fine. Let him have what he's got. Let them have whatever they got. But what angers me is that, all right, the brothers send to their parents, but why don't Mari and Jorge help out Julia with something? Why, if you've got all that, why not let José inherit the grandma's land?

J: Because that's how they are. My mama resents that my grandma is close with my kids and not hers. She's got her reasons, she says. So let it be. They've got what they've got, and we've got what we've got. And we're doing fine, right?

L: Actually, we did have a TV. That was a year or so ago.

J: Right, but—

L: But unfortunately it didn't last. Chico had bought it for us. An old color TV. Problem was, you couldn't see too clear, and next thing we knew it went on us. You'd push the buttons, and nothing worked. The kids were real mad. You know, they had got used to it, watching their soccer games or whatever for a couple of months, and then the damned thing died on us.

J: So tell them what the bichos did.

L: Well, they got so pissed that they dragged the TV out into the yard. It was a huge thing, that TV, like a one-hundred-pound animal. They dragged it out, grabbed some sticks, and beat the hell out of it. Made a mess of it. I wound up having to take the damned thing on my back and go bury it over there in the underbrush. Yes, where I caught the armadillo—down there.

J: I can't say I miss it much. Except for the news programs. I liked seeing that. All the rest of that garbage, the soap operas and all that, who needs it? [Julia smiles and points to Luis.] The one who watches the soap operas is right there. He's the one who likes them. Him and Margarita. Tell them the truth, Luis! Go on!

L: You mean that one at seven at night? *Doce corazones* [Twelve hearts]?

J: And that other one right after, at eight—*Fuego en la sangre* [Fire in the blood], no? Whenever you've got a chance, you're up at my mama's house watching them, aren't you?

L: Why not? They're entertaining. And you learn things, verdad?

J: Sure!

L: You see things on those shows that you can learn from. Like how to talk sweet, how to approach a woman, all kinds of things. You learn, really. But [he laughs] it's a little late now. I mean, I wish I knew that kind of thing back when I was fifteen or twenty. Then the girls, bueno, the girls would have appreciated it. Now it's no use. I'd like to be that way now, you know, all the sweet talk and warming up stuff, but she's not interested. [Luis laughs again, but louder.] Maybe I've got to go practice elsewhere.

J: [She shakes her head as if annoyed.] You go out at night all the time. Who knows what you're doing! Maybe you're already practicing!

L: She doesn't sound too worried, does she?

J: I'll worry when I've got something to worry about. I got other things to worry about than that.

We stop briefly as the somewhat baffled waiter stands there with menus in hand. Luis takes a quick look at the menu and immediately orders some lunch to go along with his beer, and Julia and we do the same. There is a long pause as Julia seems to contemplate the flowering bushes and shade trees, and then she begins talking in a serious tone.

J: The thing that is worrying me these days is Margarita. More than a month now, I haven't heard from her. She just took off. I know where she is—up in Chalatenango with a cousin. But that's all I know.

I don't know what she's doing or what's in her head right now. Since she failed the exams to get into La Universidad Nacional, she's not saying what she's got in mind. Only God knows what's going on with her, what's going to happen with her.

L: You see, even though she didn't pass those exams, all right so she didn't—

J: I'm telling you, she wasn't studying hard. The night before that last exam she was hardly looking at her materials. I told her, "How are you going to pass if you're just spending a few minutes studying?" She didn't say anything. Maybe it was just too hard for her.

L: All right, so she didn't get into the university. But she had the chance to work in Suchitoto, right? She could have had some work in the social services over there in the municipality. But she turned it down.

J: Yes, I know.

L: What happened with her was that she fell in with some friends who are giving her bad advice. That cousin of hers is no damned good. I know her, she's a relative of mine, that cousin. And she's got Margarita thinking it's fine to just be fooling around, no work or nothing.

Q: Do you think that there might be some boyfriend up there in Chalatenango?

J: Who knows? She didn't say anything about any of that.

L: No, that's not what it's about. Look, awhile back here in the community she had some guy who wanted to marry her, and remember what she told him? She said, "I'm not about to marry anyone. I want time to have some fun first!" And that's what's got into her head, just to fool around doing whatever she wants. She doesn't want to work at anything, the way I figure it.

J: It's true, even back a few years she was complaining to me that I was working her too much. She wanted a rest from it, she told me. But I told her, "Look here, Margarita, look at how old I am, and I'm still working like always, because in this life if you want to eat, then you have to work. I'm the one who took care of you when you were young, and now I need you to help me with the younger ones." But she wasn't listening to any of it.

L: I remember that. I remember her telling me that we had exploited her—that's the word she used, "exploited"—because she was the one who had to take care of Roberto when he was a baby, rocking him to sleep, minding him like she was his mother. And we had her doing the wash and cooking and cleaning and all that. And she was tired of it, and she wasn't going to go along with that. Well, that got me real mad, and I told her that in this house me and her mother are the boss. Not her. She wants to stay here, she's got to understand that.

Q: And how did she react?

L: She was quiet, didn't open her mouth. And that was it.

J: She continued to help me out, even while going to school. But lately she's been saying that it was Dorita's turn. Again, I was getting the complaints from Margarita. And when I turned to Dorita, she says to me, "Look, Mama, your Dorita wasn't born to be making tortillas! No, Mama, I was born to study!" And it's true, she's a much better student than Margarita was. Dorita's got her nose in a book all the time.

L: Yes, but she also does her share of the work. Just now when you were in the hospital, Julia, having that operation on your neck—

J: [She turns to us.] I had this tumor, nothing real bad, on my thyroid, so I had to be in the hospital a couple weeks. Things go slow here, right? Months to get into the hospital, and then when you finally get a bed there, it takes days before they operate on you. But I'm fine now, nothing bad at all—

L: Well, like I'm saying, Dorita's got her nose in the books, but she was the one who took over, making tortillas, washing, all that. It's Margarita that's gone rebel on us. Vaya pues, what happens to her is out of our hands now. I figure she might get knocked up, pretty as she is, but that's her business now. If she screws around and then comes back here to the house, well, she can come back. But not with those ideas that she's not going to do any work here. If she hasn't got her husband, she can be with us—but working like before. Not with that bad attitude, see?

J: God alone knows what's going to happen to that girl, I'm telling you.

Fortunately, the lunch arrived at this point, and we were able to turn off the tape recorders. The mood lifted, especially when the quesadillas later arrived—apparently one of Julia's favorite foods. "Used to make them with my grandma," she said. "On those days, we forgot about tortillas!" Luis, too, was feeling relaxed, not drunk, but pleasantly awash with his beers. And after a brief siesta, we turned the tape recorders back on.

Q: We heard from Chico and you too, Luis, that you might be getting your divorce papers from your first wife and are thinking of getting legally married to Julia. Is that so?

L: Sí, I reckon so. I just don't know when. [Julia smiles sheepishly but just shrugs her shoulders.] The problem, you see, it's the difficulty of getting the church divorce. I'm still married to my first wife, according to the church, and I've tried to get that changed. Must have been maybe three years ago, I went over to the church in Suchitoto, and the priest there sent me to another priest over in Aguilares. And then that priest sent me to the archbishop. And the archbishop told me to write up why my wife and I got split up, and what's been happening since then. I got all that written up, and I brought it to him. And the archbishop says to me then that I've got to get the godparents to sign some papers. But how was I supposed to do that? Those folks have been dead for twenty-five years now, maybe more. So finally the archbishop tells me that he can arrange it, but it'll cost me something like six hundred dollars. Bueno, at that point I realized what kind of business the whole thing was, and I figured to hell with it. I just let it go.

Q: And a civil marriage, is that possible?

L: Chico says there's no problem there. I'm not in communication with my former wife, but Chico tells me all that has to be done is for her to sign some papers agreeing to a divorce, and that's it. Chico says she has no problem with that. So I figure one of these days I'll get to it.

J: To me, look, if Luis gets his papers, fine. If not, fine too. I never cared one way or the other. We're married the way we are, ajuntada, and it's all the same to me.

L: No, it's important to get the thing straightened out. With all the bichos we've got, I want my papers in order. If something happens to me, just so there's no problem with the land and the house, I want the papers to be set straight. So now that I've got Chico able to take care of it quick and easy, I'll get around to it one of these days. Because who knows what could happen? I mean, I'm not planning to die so quick. [He grins mischievously.] I'm still strong as before, if you know what I mean. Probably we'd be having even more bichos if Julia here wasn't taking something against it or whatever she's doing.

J: Listen to him, he's entered his "golden years" and he's talking more bichos.

L: Stop with that—you know well enough what the truth is. I'm still like I was when I was twenty-five or thirty. Even take that tree over there, that tall one. I don't need any ladder, I could climb right up it just like a kid.

J: Sí, sí, I know. [She then speaks to us.] Truth is, there's still some old guys here in the community, seventy-five years old or more, that are working like always. And Luis still goes up the hillside and works. No problem. So I reckon Luis will be one of them.

L: Me, I've got to work. To feed the family, yes, but also because it's my nature. If I would stay in the house, I'd get sick. I wouldn't even be able to eat. It's happened to me a couple of times. No, hombre, I got no plans to stop working. What I am figuring to do, though, is change the *way* I'm working. Not right away. But what I'm planning out is to get a few more cows. I've got three now. With five more—say, eight or so in all—I'll be getting enough milk that I can sell that. Milk goes for a good price, and I can practically live on that income. That and, of course, growing some maíz and frijol. But not as many manzanas as I'm using now. Either one of my sons will use the rest, or I'll rent it out. You can make some income from that too. And then all that together with my pension—yes, I get a small pension—I'll be able to manage. There's even some talk that the government may be raising pensions for older people. With the FMLN in power, maybe that'll happen. It sure would be good for the poorer folks in this country.

Q: You see the FMLN making a big change here in the community and throughout the country in the future?

L: Well, like I told you before, it's going to take time. We in the FMLN got to stay with it. We can't just stop working for change. Not just talking but making sure that the party gets involved helping the people. The fight with ARENA isn't over, hell no. We've got them worried, on the run. But we can't just sit back and do nothing. [Luis pauses and glances over at Julia.] Like that one over there. I swear, I think she's gone Arenero.

J: Sure!

L: Well, where were you this last presidential campaign? Where were you when that bastard Saca and his police were trying to rob our water and firing tear gas at us? I'll tell you where: in the hammock!

J: [Slightly irritated.] A person's got to rest, no? Besides, you know what I've said before. Nine years in the monte was enough for me. After that, no more politics! And with all the bichos we've got now—no, no, I got my hands full, and I don't have any time for politics or any of that.

L: [Appeasingly.] Never mind, I'm the one in the family taking care of that. And these days we've got more and more young people from the community—like Chico, yes—and these young people are going to carry on the political work. They got their education, and they know how to go about things. I figure that in time the FMLN is going to get stronger and stronger. We no longer have so much ignorance like before. People can see what has to be done, and the FMLN is the political party to do it. Hell, we fought a long war to get to where we are today, and we're not about to give up now!

Q: We understand from all you've said, Luis, that you—you and Julia— are satisfied with what came out of the war, the arrangements of the peace accords.

J: Satisfied, yes, in many ways. Without the war, God knows where we would be. But no way I'd ever want to go through those years again. No, no!

L: Look, nobody can deny that we paid a heavy price to get where we are today. You know what happened to my family. I've told you. Two sisters disappeared. One sister raped, though she's doing all right today, got her six kids and a good husband—a guy who used to be in my platoon. But she's got her damage inside from all that. And my brother, he got all shot up in that "final offensive" of ours, the one I wouldn't take part in because I knew we were going to get beaten. Antonio—the one you saw over in Papaturro when you visited my mama. He's a mess. Doesn't talk. He had a good woman, Lucita's mama, but he was whacking her around, and she left him. Bad stuff! So what I'm saying is that my family alone—and you can talk to any family here in the community—we've all paid a price for what we have now. A heavy price! But if you ask me, of course it was worth it.

J: I agree. When I see how we are living today and compare that with how things were when I was a kid, I can hardly believe how good we have it. It's like, well, like before I got here I didn't have a life. Now I feel I've got a life.

L: We've had our problems here. Still do. We've got maras coming to this community like you've got all over the country. What was it, just two weeks ago that we had that incident?

J: The guy who got shot you're talking about, no?

L: Some gang boss who was coming up here to cause trouble. Lately, some of these maras have been coming to the community trying to extort money or rob folks. Well, this one didn't get out alive. Shot him dead! No, no, not me. Others. Some folks know who finished him off, but nobody is talking, and nobody is asking. And hopefully those guys will get the message. Anyway, like I'm saying, we've got problems—who the hell doesn't, everywhere?—but we're feeling real fine here in the community. We carved this place out of nothing. And now we've got so much. I feel like a king here, really! Look at all we've got. Our houses, electricity, good water, a health clinic, and we've got our school. When I was a kid I had nothing like this. I was walking around barefoot, hardly any clothes, and sometimes nothing to eat. My papa, he was the same. That poor guy never had anything. Just dirt-poor his whole life. And before him, the same. Poor and ignorant is how we grew up. I never imagined I'd ever have what we've got now.

J: That's the thing. Our kids have got a future. Them that want to take advantage of all this, they've got a future.

L: Yes, that's the thing. Me and Julia, we know what we had as kids—nada, nada! And there's a great satisfaction knowing that our kids are not going to have to live like we did. Me and Julia, we sit on our veranda sometimes, you know, in the evenings or Sunday, and get to talking about how lucky we are. And me, I'll tell you the truth, I feel like I got real lucky with this woman you see right here. I'm not going to hide it, I've known many women, but this one here is by far the best I've ever known. And even though I tease her sometimes—

J: Just *sometimes*?

L: Even though I talk my nonsense sometimes, she knows that all these years I've lived up to the oath I gave her. I don't drink—except for a beer now and then—I'm no bolo. And I've been absolutely one hundred percent loyal to her ever since I got together with her. I never gave her any cause to complain.

J: No, I'm not complaining.

L: And I'm no machista. I know what machismo is, I've seen it all around me. A man who's machista figures that if another woman catches his eye, he wants to start up with her, then why not? Or if he wants to have a few drinks, then he'll drink how much he likes. Or if he wants to gamble the household money, then he'll go gamble it. And to hell with anyone else! But I don't go for that stuff. I'm not like that. Never was and never will be. I don't act toward Julia the way some are treating their wives. And I won't permit any of the kids talking bad to her. I respect this woman. I listen to her. Why shouldn't I? Intelligent as she is, of course I listen to her. Don't I?

J: *I'm listening.* [Luis frowns.] No, you're no machista. I've got no complaints. I had my doubts in the beginning, I won't deny it. I wondered what I was getting into. But no regrets. Luis is a good man. He is.

L: And I'm still young enough to climb trees if I want. You get my meaning, right?

J: Now don't start with that again!

L: All right. Later. I'm just going to take advantage of this hammock now, if you don't mind.

J: Yes, you do that. You've talked enough today to fill the book, I reckon.

L: No, I already did that before we came here today, didn't I?

Epilogue

Having listened to the stories of Luis and others, we think it is worthwhile now to turn to an examination of some of the wider implications of these narratives. First, we would like to consider how the lives of our interviewees reflect some of the economic and political changes that have occurred in El Salvador as well as how the stories of the men and women point toward a shift in gender roles in a society that traditionally has been a bastion of machismo. Second, we would like to continue here the discussion that we began in the introduction, namely, some of the theoretical, practical, and ethical issues involved in the practice of gathering and writing oral histories.

Let us begin, then, with an area that Marta and I explored initially in our book *From Grandmother to Granddaughter: Salvadoran Women's Stories.* In that volume we noted the continuum of change in gender roles over three generations of Salvadoran women from all social classes. Twelve years later, I think it is clear that this trend has continued, even though significant vestiges of machismo remain part of the social fabric of El Salvador. Perhaps the most noticeable and important area of change has been in the area of education. Women are far better educated today than they were two generations or even one generation ago. This is reflected in statistical reports for the entire country, and it is evident in the stories of the women in this book.[1] We note, for example, that Margarita has just finished high school—the first woman in her family to do so. Her great-grandmother and grandmother did not go to school, and her mother managed to finish only the fourth grade. Margarita's sister Dorita is well on her way to finishing high school and intends to proceed to university. While it is true that a similar shift also has occurred for males (note that Luis had no formal schooling, while his son Chico is a university graduate), the principal change here is that many fathers, Luis included, are now encouraging their daughters to get an education and no longer consider such schooling to be solely the prerogative of their sons.

Furthermore, the increasing educational opportunities for women have led to the growing number and variety of occupational possibilities for women. Margarita was looking for employment outside of the community (when we last spoke to her), and her younger sister is hoping to follow in Chico's footsteps and become a lawyer—all this with the encouragement of not only Julia but also Luis. The story of Lucita, the school principal, is also instructive. Her husband and mother supported her educational aspirations, and today she holds a leadership position that was generally the province of men in past generations.

However, one can also observe in the stories here how machismo still has a rather firm grip within this family (and, in our experience, throughout Salvadoran society). Men work outside the house in this community, principally in their milpas. Thus, household tasks are still essentially left to women. They are the ones who still do the cooking, cleaning, washing of clothes, and rearing of children—with only an occasional assist from some men in the family. And as far as we could detect, there is little opposition in Luis's family or in Comunidad Guazapa to this traditional division of labor. For a woman to escape these household tasks, she literally has to leave the house and work outside the community, which, according to Lucita and Margarita, is why the girls of the community are even more determined than the boys to progress in their studies.

In addition, and perhaps more destructively (from our perspective), there continues to be a double standard in the area of sexual roles and expectations. Boys are permitted far more latitude in their sexual behavior. Girls are still expected to remain virgins until marriage. Margarita, for instance, has had to be cautious, while her brother Chico was allowed the liberties accorded to boys. And Luis himself experiences little shame from the fact that some, including his own son, regard him as a former mujerero; quite the opposite, he enjoys boasting to his sons of his skills in this area—much to their amusement. Even more disturbing (again, from our perspective) is the continued threat of physical or sexual abuse of girls and women. Margarita and her girlfriends have had to endure the harassment of male sugarcane workers as they walked home from school. And within the community—though not in Luis's household—men are known to physically mistreat their wives. What is changing, though, is the awareness on the part of women that they now have legal recourse if and when they are abused. Mari's story illustrates in dramatic fashion the changes that have taken place in her home and also (in her opinion) in other households. But when push comes to shove, it is still the women who bear the burden of abandonment. Despite the existence of laws requiring men to financially support their families in case of separation or divorce, it is common—especially in the campo and among the lower class in general—for men to leave their families without providing such support. Julia's first husband did so. Luis, too, apparently left his first wife, Flora, without financially supporting two of the children he had with her, though he did support his second wife, Meches, who continues to live in the community. In sum, then, there would seem to be a mixed picture regarding the changes in gender relations in this community and in the larger tapestry of the country: women in El Salvador have come a long way, but they still have a long way to go.

Part of what makes the future for women in El Salvador look bright—or at least brighter—is the economic growth and development of the country. There is a simple equation that has occurred here just as it has in other developing countries: as traditional economies based on agriculture give way to more industrial and service-oriented economies, women and men too have greater opportunities for employment and also to increase their standard of living. Again, there is statistical evidence of this change.[2]

As noted in the introduction and as can be seen in the stories of Julia and her mother, Mari, there has been a significant improvement in the standard of living in their households. The original houses made of laminated metal, wood, and plastic have been replaced by concrete structures of two or three rooms, and the floors are now made of concrete instead of packed earth. Within the houses there are also changes: more furniture— beds, in particular—and, in the case of Mari's home, a refrigerator and color television. These latter items, obviously, have been made possible by the connection of Comunidad Guazapa to the country's electricity grid, as has happened elsewhere in many rural areas of the country. Also, the installation of water pipes that now bring the plentiful underground springwater to the community's households has been a welcome improvement that has eliminated the burden of spending hours each day fetching water from a distant well or water source. Mari and Julia and Margarita, all of whom remember the days of water jugs lugged on their heads, are noticeably relieved by this change.

How have these changes been made possible? In part, the improved standard of living in this community is due to the improved farming methods and greater harvests of those, like Luis and Jorge and most others in the community, who continue to earn their living by farming their milpas. These men carry on farming in much the same way as did their fathers before them but with better seeds and with fertilizer and pesticides. Moreover, some of these campesinos, like Luis, are hopeful that with the FMLN's growing political power there will be inexpensive loans and financial assistance for the farmers. And while he is not optimistic about any immediate confiscation of the sugarcane land next to their community, neither Luis nor any of his fellow farmers would regret a governmental decision—an offer that the Morales family cannot afford to refuse—to make available those thirty-five manzanas to people in the community. If we take into account the rapid growth in the community's population, we can surely understand if this is a thought in their minds.

But let's return to the question of how Comunidad Guazapa has in fact been able to enjoy an improved standard of living. The answer would seem to lie principally in two factors.

First, an increasing number of the community's younger generation has been able to find employment in the towns and cities, and their salaries have benefited their families. Luis's son Chico, now that he is a lawyer, helps provide for his brothers and sisters. Chico has plans to buy an automobile, which he intends to use to help his father, including promising Luis that for the first time in his life he will be able to take a vacation: "My old man can finally have a chance to vacation at the ocean—which he has never done!" Along with these ever-increasing earnings from children who are now working in the urban areas, there has been a wave of children—almost all of them young men—who have gone as mojados to the United States and sent money home to El Salvador. Lucita estimates that many, if not most, of the young men in the community have done so. Three or four of Mari's sons are now living illegally in the United States and regularly sending back some money. Luis and Julia, actually, are one of the few families that do not have a son living abroad, and as a result they lack a refrigerator and TV, which many families have. "But I make no complaints," says Luis. "I want my kids to stay here. Get an education here and then maybe help us out in our old age."

Second, politics has contributed to the improvements in Comunidad Guazapa. Luis and others in the community point to the FMLN's victories in the local municipal elections, which have led to improvements in the community's infrastructure. But, to be completely fair, the rightist political party ARENA, which has held power on the national level until recently, has also made available funds throughout the country that have contributed to improvements for many campesinos living in the rural areas. Few residents of Comunidad Guazapa would deny that there is room for a good deal more governmental investment in the country's infrastructure as well as changes in the banking system that will make available loans and technical assistance to campesinos. For Luis and his former compas, this is a clearly expressed hope—and also, one senses, an equally clear expectation.[3]

The victory of the FMLN in the presidential election of 2009 was a moment of utter joy for Luis and his family and all those in the community. For weeks after the election a photo of the new president, Mauricio Funes, hung on the metal door of Luis's house, and a banner with his photo fluttered on a bamboo pole in the corner of Luis's yard. This was also true in many other yards and homes in the community, and even those who shied away from political involvement—like Luis's father-in-law, Jorge—could not hide their joy at this FMLN victory. Luis has eloquently expressed what this has meant to him personally, but he and others—Lucita and Chico, for example—make it abundantly evident that the country's future and political climate are far from secure. Despite a comment here and there from Luis and others, nobody actually expects that El Salvador will return to the violent political climate that antedated and culminated in the civil war. Yet neither do they think that there are likely to be rapid solutions to the political and social problems that continue to prevail in the country. The migration of Salvadorans to other countries, legally or illegally, does not seem likely to abate.[4] Nor does the problem of widespread delinquency and street crime appear to be on the wane. Chico and Lucita see these latter problems as rooted in the failure of the society to provide adequate employment for the country's population, including its youth, and, more insidiously, in the ongoing corruption among the relatively low paid police force, concomitantly with the growing spread of drug-related gangs that are now to be found throughout El Salvador. Thus, they feel (correctly, as we see it) that the rampant violence that one experiences in the country today is not primarily engendered by the clash of opposing political parties but rather is the outcome of a mix of factors: the proliferation of gangs that resulted in part from the deportation from the United States of many Salvadoran youths who had honed their criminal skills in American cities, the political corruption that has allowed the drug trade to flourish in El Salvador, and the continuation of broad economic inequality between the social classes.[5] There is also still a "culture of violence" that prevails in the family upbringing of many Salvadoran children.[6] In sum, nowhere in El Salvador today does one feel sufficiently safe, not even in remote places like Comunidad Guazapa, where violent crimes have increased and parents have had to worry that their children might become victims or, in one or two cases, perpetrators.[7]

In addition to the social, economic, and political changes noted above, there is an additional phenomenon that we, as psychologists, observed among some of those mentioned in the book, among other members of the community, and in general throughout Salvadoran society—namely, the enduring psychological impact of the civil war on the personal lives of those who lived through that period and on their children. Many of those who lived through the war period, whether or not they were combatants, still carry the psychological scars of that convulsion. Luis and Julia are remarkably free of such wounds (sometimes referred to as post-traumatic stress disorder, or PTSD), but a number of their family members are clearly still suffering from these internal scars. For example, Luis's sister who was raped, his brother who was badly wounded, and his mother who lost two daughters—all are, we believe, still psychologically damaged. So, too, is Julia's brother Marcos and, to a certain extent, both of her parents. It is our impression that the high incidence of alcoholism among many of their (male) neighbors, former guerrillas, is largely a result of the unresolved, and perhaps unresolvable, stress and trauma they experienced during the war.

Less obvious but nonetheless undeniable is the effect of the war on the second generation, that is, the children of those who lived through the war period. It is a well-documented phenomenon (e.g., among second-generation survivors of the Holocaust) that PTSD symptoms often persist in the children. It is beyond the scope of this book to discuss in depth how and why this occurs, but suffice it to say that the second generation comes to understand that their parents endured terrible experiences, and the shadow of these experiences, often unspeakable or simply unspoken, hangs perniciously over their heads. In fact, it would seem likely that the widespread reluctance of the children of Comunidad Guazapa to inquire about this period or even to take an interest in it is related to a type of anxious and depressive avoidance that is typical of second-generation children of survivors (again, this is well documented among Holocaust second-generation children). One of the results of this phenomenon is that children feel cut off in certain ways from their parents and even resentful toward them when they mention the past. The observations of the school principal, Lucita, who in some ways represents an exception, would seem to indicate that this shadow continues to exist throughout Comunidad Guazapa. And within Luis and Julia's family, Margarita's comments and reactions are also quite typical (while Francisco's response is atypical).[8]

What needs to happen from a sociopsychological perspective is that eventually El Salvador's civil war and its horrors will have to be openly discussed and examined—especially by subsequent generations. If the Holocaust provides any example, this process in El Salvador will take another generation or two to occur. And if the United States' experience both with slavery and the destruction of Native Americans is any indication, it might take longer. Ultimately, it will depend on the country's political climate in the years to come. But, in our judgment, coming to terms with what took place in the Salvadoran civil war is both psychologically necessary and inevitable.

At this point, we would like to turn from some of these social, psychological, economic, and political matters as reflected in the narratives of Luis and his family and direct our attention to various issues that are intrinsic to the process of collecting and writing up these very narratives. Much has been said and written about the theoretical and practical problems of the oral history genre. And frankly, we do not believe that our volume can add more than a minor point here and there to this ongoing discussion. But we do consider it imperative that we weigh in on some of these issues so that at the very least the reader will more clearly understand how we approached the story of Luis and his family.

One of the most serious concerns for us as well as for other practitioners of the oral history genre is the issue of "subjectivity" in the narratives of our interviewees. Simply stated, how do we know—and how can we know—that what we have been told by each of the interviewees is, in fact, true? Simply answered, the fact is that we cannot know with certainty. To some extent, all subjects have lapses in memory, and, at times, all deliberately choose to obfuscate or even deliberately distort what they do remember. Moreover, even when the interviewee describes an experience or event to the best of her or his ability, this recollection is influenced by personal sentiments and perspectives; hence, an element of subjectivity is unavoidable. However, we hasten to add, in agreement with the seminal work of oral historians Luisa Passerini and Alessandro Portelli, that often there is value in this very subjectivity.[9] As Portelli notes, this subjectivity on the part of the interviewee is a "fact" of interest and importance by itself. We agree, whether or not the interviewee is reporting an experience as he or she saw it or is actually deliberately distorting or obfuscating that experience. Take, for example, Luis's overall view of El Salvador's civil war. He sees it from the perspective of a poor campesino who sought social and economic justice for himself and his family and whose actions during and after the war were meritorious; similarly, he believes that the other side, the enemy, fought an unprincipled war and fully deserved the losses they incurred. Now even if one shares some of Luis's political perspective, it cannot be denied that this is a subjective point of view, one that many Salvadorans would heatedly contest. But from an oral historian's point of view, Luis's subjectivity is well worth reporting, and his perspective—shared by virtually everyone in Comunidad Guazapa—is an important historical "fact" in itself, even if some of his "factual" reporting is not supported by more traditional sources of historical evidence.

In addition to this subjectivity with regard to historical events, there is a subjectivity that adheres in many of the memories and accounts of Luis and others about their personal experiences. As writers with a psychological bent, we both acknowledge and delight in this "fact." We expect that different individuals will view the same experience in different ways: they will see the experience or event in keeping with their own psychological tendencies and needs. Indeed, in choosing a multivoiced set of narratives, we have deliberately sought to underscore the subjectivity of personal experience. Thus, we have purposefully edited the tales so as to include the different perceptions of various individuals about one or another experience. For instance, Luis's report about the witchcraft that beset Julia shortly after they became ajuntada is quite different from Julia's recollection of the experience (see chapters 7 and 8). We scrupulously avoided imposing on either of them our own subjective views of that witchcraft, though the reader can imagine that two psychologists might well question whether Julia's experience was not more likely the result of her own misgivings about her new relationship with Luis as well as her sense that she was then pregnant with their first child. Who can say for sure? What does seem interesting and self-revealing to us is precisely the subjectivity involved in the different reports, including our own.

Or take another example in which we can see the "Rashomon effect" played out in the narratives of our interviewees: the matter of Julia's being raised in the home of her paternal grandparents and not in the home of her own parents.[10] This experience has had a profound effect on the relationship of Julia and her parents and also on the relationship of Julia's parents to Julia's children. But if we listen to the various explanations of Julia, her mother, and her father, we get quite different points of view (and we might add that Luis's explanation and that of Julia's grandmother—both of which are not included in the text—are also somewhat different). By reporting these various points of view with regard to this experience and many others too, we have hoped to catch something of the personalities of the people involved, for it is evident that the different ways of viewing and reporting an event are often illuminative of an individual's character.

A further problem that occurred in reporting the narratives in this book is one that has troubled oral historians for years—and perhaps especially those of us who are translating the tales from the language in which they are told to a different language. There are two problems here. First, the transcription process has inherent flaws. When we take material that is presented in an aural form and convert it to a written form, we cannot avoid losing much of the style and manner of the presentation.[11] The gestures, the intonation—what we may call the "theater"—of the original narrative as told by the interviewee to the interviewer and also to the audience who will read the book are impossible to transcribe in any written form. The efforts we as writers make to compensate for this shortcoming unavoidably fail to capture the sound and fury of the original "performance." Up to a point we can try to paint the setting in which the interview occurs, and we can try to indicate through bracketed commentary or the written devices of punctuation some of the interviewee's speaking style. But our efforts ultimately are no better than the efforts of those who read Shakespeare's *Hamlet* to themselves compared to those who see and hear it performed onstage. We are left with the consolatory and perhaps self-justifying sense (to extend the previous metaphor) that, after all, if one cannot go to the theater, it is still worthwhile to read the play. We ask the reader to take our word for the fact that Luis, our main character, is a man who has a natural flair for the dramatic. That, indeed, is why we chose him—even if in the end we were unable to transmit his stories with the full punch and panache in which he recounted them.

Second, there is the problem that in transcribing and subsequently translating the language of Luis and others, we inevitably lose some of that unique verbal style that inheres in their stories. In El Salvador many campesinos use a grammar and vocabulary that are at times quite differ-ent from those of the educated urban middle and upper classes. Notably, they frequently employ incorrect grammatical constructions, and they also use many words that derive from the Nahuat language.[12] It is impos-sible, in the English language, to catch how these Nahuat words sound to a Spanish-speaking listener. Nor have we found a satisfactory way to incorporate in the English translation some of the grammatical mistakes or unconventional use of words that pepper the speech of Luis and others. It is no more possible to do this than it would be to catch the full meaning in Spanish of such English expressions as "okeydokey" and "you betcha" and "ain't" and "y'all." (And by the way, Spanish has three different forms of the singular pronoun "you"—*tu*, *usted*, and *vos*—each of which indi-cates a different type of relationship between the speaker and listener.) So again we find ourselves in the apologetic mode both to our reader and to Luis and his family, whose words have lost something in the translation.

Finally, we would like to mention some of the ethical concerns that are a necessary part of gathering and writing oral histories. We are aware of a sharp difference in what might be termed "journalistic ethics" and "oral history ethics." To take one example, when a source tells a journalist at the beginning of an interview that his or her comments are off the record, the journalist is obliged not to quote the source. The same is true for an oral historian. However, when no previous commitment is made, a journalist is not ethically bound to withhold any commentary that the interviewee has made. As a matter of fact, journalists—especially investigative reporters— often attempt to elicit and then report comments that the interviewee might prefer to have remained hidden. The relationship that an oral his-torian conscientiously constructs with a subject would seem to demand a different ethical standard. We must respect a subject's right *at any time* to request that a comment or piece of information be deleted from the story. Moreover, in light of the more profound relationship that oral histori-ans usually construct with their subjects, I believe that we must carefully evaluate whether reporting some anecdote or event might prove *unneces-sarily* embarrassing to the interviewee. I stress the word "unnecessarily" because we do at times knowingly report commentaries or accounts that the interviewee might find embarrassing when they appear in print. This is unavoidable if we want to retain some of the poignancy of the stories. Luis, for example, might indeed be uncomfortable if his mother were to hear Luis's version of his father's supposed dalliance with another woman. But we decided to leave that material in the book, aware that the story was common knowledge in Luis's family (and, frankly, Luis's mother was not likely to hear of his comments in the book). On the other hand, Luis made a string of remarks about individuals, including his in-laws, that we deleted from his accounts, since some of that material was sure to cause further problems in the family (and again, frankly, they *were* likely to hear of it). Similarly, we also did not report some of the piquant information that Luis gave us about his former comrade-in-arms, Joaquín, since the latter adamantly refused to give us these details about his role in the guerrillas; we simply felt it unnecessary to risk causing a dispute between the two of them (a consideration that I, in my former role as a journalist, would not have taken into account).

In addition to these concerns about what comments might be fairly and ethically included in the book, there is the issue of what other obligations we take on when we engage subjects in an oral history enterprise. Here I wish to shift hats and suggest what my training as a psychologist has made me realize about the process of doing oral history. On the positive side, I think there is little question that for our subjects the opportunity to have a sympathetic listener can be gratifying and self-affirming. Some interviewees, such as Luis, see the recounting of their life stories as an opportunity to leave something for posterity that otherwise would have gone unsaid and undone. Many times during our yearlong interviewing of Luis he indicated that this was the primary reason why he agreed to spend so much time with us. For some others whose stories appear in the book, this consideration likely played a lesser role. For them, the interviews were a kind of unexpected diversion, occasionally anxiety-provoking, but on the whole a pleasant and even meaningful experience. And then there were those whose stories we would have liked to include (and probably could have succeeded in gathering) but on ethical grounds it seemed best to avoid, for instance, Luis's sister who had been severely traumatized during the war. We approached her once but saw that she was trembling at the very thought of being interviewed; consequently, we chose not to ask Luis to intervene, since we dared not open up wounds that we in our role as oral historians—not psychologists—were in no position to sufficiently treat.

There is one final issue that I want to mention briefly here regarding the ethical approach to doing oral history projects: the question of what we might fairly give back to our subjects from the material gains that we, as authors, receive from doing our projects. Many practitioners have commented on this subject. None perhaps have done so more forcefully and critically than Daphne Patai, who argues that in light of the enormous disparity between the material advantages of interviewers from developed countries vis-à-vis subjects from developing countries, there is no possibility to do fair and ethical research; the authors necessarily are at an advantage and surely gain more.[13] I think her argument is compelling, even if I sense that she undervalues the psychological benefits for the subjects of such projects. But, over the years, in reflecting on her observations and my previous ventures in the area of oral history, I have come to the conclusion that we must, if possible, do something to lessen this disparity. Accordingly, we have decided to donate the bulk of whatever earnings come from this project to Luis and his family. Luis does not know that. He never asked for and never received a centavo from us, apart from an occasional box of Pollo Campero (the local equivalent of Kentucky Fried Chicken) that we brought with us when we visited him in the community and an occasional meal at Guazapa Café or at Marta's mother's house. Our plan, then, is to provide this money to help support the next child who manages to get accepted to university. We do not expect Daphne Patai to be fully satisfied with this arrangement—and neither are we, really—but, as the expression goes, it's the least we can do. Vaya, pues.

CHRONOLOGY

Significant Events in El Salvador's History

1524   The Spanish commander Pedro de Alvarado and his troops entered the territory of what today is El Salvador as part of Spain's conquests in the New World (starting in 1492). At the time its two major indigenous peoples were the Pipil tribe in western and central El Salvador and the Lenca tribe in the east. The Indians quickly fell victim to the superior weaponry of the Spanish and to the various diseases that the conquerors happened to be carrying.

1821   In the wave of independence movements that swept through the Spanish-controlled territories of the entire region, the territory of Guatemala, which included El Salvador, declared independence from Spain and within two years formed the Federal Republic of Central America.

1840   El Salvador began its existence as a separate political entity.

1876–85   Coffee became El Salvador's principal export, and an elite of coffee growers, producers, and exporters—sometimes called "the fourteen families"—effectively consolidated its control and rule in the country. Over the next half century this elite expanded its economic power into additional areas, including banking, industry, and other agricultural production (e.g., sugar and cotton).

1929–32   The Great Depression created an economic crisis in El Salvador that threatened the coffee elite's rule. A coup in 1931 overthrew the elected government, and Gen. Maximiliano Hernández Martínez assumed the presidency (military-led governments ruled El Salvador, with the support of the economic elite, until the 1980s).

1932   A planned peasant uprising led by the founder of the Communist Party of El Salvador, Farabundo Martí, was discovered and crushed. General Martínez carried out the killing of some thirty thousand people, primarily campesinos, who were suspected of being sympathetic to the uprising. As a result of this *matanza*, campesinos were politically quiescent until the 1970s, at which time many of them joined in the reformist and radical political movements that were forming in the towns and cities.

1950   The constitution granted women the right to vote.

1968   In the wake of the Second Vatican Council (1962–65) and the 1968 conference of Latin American bishops in Medellín, Colombia, a growing number of Catholic nuns and priests in El Salvador became involved in forming Christian-base communities in poor rural areas. These clergy members interpreted the Bible in a manner that encouraged campesinos to join in a struggle against their poverty. The political right wing in El Salvador deplored this new ecclesiastical approach, and many priests and nuns involved in these communities were subsequently attacked and killed.

1967–72   During this period there was a significant increase in strikes, street marches, and demonstrations led principally by labor unions, teacher and student organizations, and clergy. These protests were almost exclusively nonviolent, with participants petitioning for higher wages and better work conditions as well as political and educational reforms. Campesino groups also participated, demanding the right to form rural unions that would be able to improve conditions in the countryside; these demonstrations were almost entirely nonviolent. The military-led government of Col. Fidel Sánchez Hernández generally did not resort to violence in response to this wave of protests. However, there was some violence employed at times against protestors and their leaders, which did tend to radicalize some groups. (The FPL, or Fuerzas Populares de Liberación, was one such revolutionary group that formed during this period; it was this group, incidentally, that Luis joined in the mid-1970s.)

1972   During this year's "stolen election"—as it is sometimes called—in which the politically moderate engineer José Napoleón Duarte appeared to be leading in the vote count for the presidency, a military-led government halted the vote count, declared its candidate the winner, and forced Duarte into exile (he reemerged in 1980 as part of the civilian-military government and in 1984 as the country's president). Many observers cite this election as a watershed that made a revolution in El Salvador likely, if not inevitable, since from that point on the government became increasingly repressive in its response toward protesters and those suspected of sympathizing with reformist and radical organizations.

1979   The leftist Sandinistas assumed power in neighboring Nicaragua after the overthrow of Anastasio Somoza, thus providing a potent impetus to leftist groups in El Salvador.

1980   In an attempt to head off a revolution, the government instituted a land reform program. Due to rapid inflation and high rural rents, by 1980 as many as 65 percent of rural families were classified as landless. But despite the redistribution of 417,000 manzanas (approximately 15 percent of El Salvador's arable land), the slide into civil war had become unavoidable. Also during this year, five revolutionary organizations (including the FPL) joined to form the FMLN (Frente Farabundo Martí para la Liberación Nacional). And on March 24, 1980, assassins murdered the archbishop of El Salvador, Monseñor Oscar Romero, who in his sermons had supported the Christian-base communities and had spoken out against human rights abuses. By the end of the year, the FMLN and Fuerza Armada were fully engaged in a civil war that would last the next twelve years.

1981   The rightist political party, ARENA (Alianza Republicana Nacionalista), was formed under the leadership of Roberto d'Aubuisson, who formerly was head of an intelligence agency of the Fuerza Armada. It is widely believed, though not proved, that d'Aubuisson was involved in the murder of Monseñor Romero.

1989   The "final offensive" of the FMLN took place and—despite its forces' capture of some of the capital's suburbs—ended in a military stalemate. The ARENA Party won a victory in the country's parliamentary election this year, and its candidate, Alfredo Cristiani, a wealthy businessman, won the presidency.

1992   Under the auspices of the United Nations, on January 16, 1992, the Cristiani-led government and the FMLN signed a peace agreement in Chapultepec, Mexico, thus ending the civil war. As part of this agreement, the Fuerza Armada was vastly reduced in size and placed firmly under civilian control; the National Guard was disbanded; the discredited public security forces were replaced by a new civilian police force, the PNC (Policía Nacional Civil); and in exchange for demobilizing as an armed force, the FMLN was recognized as a legal political party.

1992–93   The Truth Commission for El Salvador, established by the United Nations as part of the 1992 peace accords, published the results of its investigation of war crimes and atrocities committed during El Salvador's civil war.

1993   The ARENA-controlled parliament decreed an amnesty such that nobody—from either the government's forces or the FMLN's forces—could be legally prosecuted for war crimes. As a result, those responsible for committing atrocities before, during, or in the immediate aftermath of the war have never been prosecuted. This decision and outcome has been condemned by a number of Salvadoran and international human rights groups.

1994   For the first time, the FMLN participated as a political party in El
         Salvador's presidential elections. The winner of that election was
         ARENA's candidate, the lawyer Armando Calderón Sol. The ARENA
         Party's candidates won the presidency again in 1999 and in 2004.
         However, the FMLN continued to gain popularity as a political party,
         winning municipal elections throughout the country during the next
         fifteen years as well as progressively increasing its number of legisla-
         tors in the eighty-four-member parliament (Asamblea Legislativa).

2001   The Salvadoran currency, the colón, was replaced by the U.S. dollar
         as the country's legal currency.

2004   With the ARENA Party's victory in the presidential elections, for the
         first time a woman, the economist Ana Wilma de Escobar, became the
         country's vice president. In an effort to privatize the delivery of water
         supply in the Suchitoto area, the government entered into a violent
         confrontation with members of the local communities—including
         Comunidad Guazapa—who were opposed to this measure.

2009   In March the FMLN's presidential candidate, journalist Mauri-
         cio Funes, won the presidential election; this was the first time an
         FMLN candidate had won the presidency. In addition, for the first
         time the FMLN won a larger number of seats in the parliament than
         did the ARENA Party (35 to 32); other small, centrist-oriented politi-
         cal parties won the remaining seventeen seats.

GLOSSARY

acompañarse. To live together in a common-law marriage.

agua ardiente. Literally, burning water; that is, hard liquor.

ajuntado/a. To be tied; the word is used to describe a common-law marriage; also used is the word *acompañada/o*.

ARENA. Alianza Republicana Nacionalista (Nationalist Republican Alliance). Its members are referred to as Areneros.

arroba. Twenty-five pounds.

Asamblea Legislativa. Legislative Assembly.

atol. A drink prepared with cornmeal.

Banco de Tierras. Land Bank.

bicho/a. Boy/girl.

bolo. Drunkard.

bueno. Good, well.

campesino/a. Peasant farmer or rural dweller.

campo. Countryside, field.

centavo. Cent.

chicha. Mild corn liquor.

cinco. Five centavos.

ciudadela. Small city. See note 1, chapter 3.

colón, colones. Former currency of El Salvador: 8.75 colones equals $1.00, and 100 centavos equals 1 colón.

comal. Clay or metal cooking hotplate on which tortillas are made.

comandante. Commanding officer.

combatiente. Combatant.

comedor. Communal dining hall.

compa. Comrade.

con qué. Food or spice that accompanies tortillas as part of the meal.

coyotes. Slang for men who sneak illegal immigrants across the U.S. border.

Cuerpo de Paz. Peace Corps.

curandero. Healer.

don/doña. Term of respect for a man or woman.

el de uno. Literally, "one's own," meaning one's personal bullet.

el que cura. One who cures.

finca. Farm or piece of property.

FMLN. Frente Farabundo Martí para la Liberación Nacional (Farabundo Martí National Liberation Front).

FPL. Fuerzas Populares de Liberación.

frijol(es). Dried beans. In El Salvador peasants usually refer to beans in the singular.

Fuerza Armada. Armed Forces.

gringo. North American (slightly pejorative).

Guardia. National Guard; rural police force (disbanded in 1992).

guaro. Hard liquor.

guerrillero. Guerrilla fighter.

hombre. Man.

igualito. Equal.

IMU. Instituto de Mujeres (Women's Institute).

jocote. Hog plum tree.

lempiras. Honduran currency.

llorón. Crybaby.

machismo. Male chauvinism.

machista. Male chauvinist.

maestro popular. Teacher from the people, that is, a nonacademically trained teacher.

maicillo. Sorghum.

maíz. Corn.

mandador. Work boss.

manzana. 1.7 acres.

mara. Delinquent, gang member.

masa. Lump of dough.

matanza. Massacre.

Médicos sin Fronteras. Doctors without Borders.

milpa. Small plot of land, usually for growing corn, sorghum, and beans.

mojado. An illegal immigrant to the United States.

molendera. Grinder; maker of tortillas, that is, a cook.

monseñor. Monsignor; a title for a Catholic prelate.

monte. Wilderness.

muchacha. Girl, maid.

mujerero. Womanizer, skirt-chaser; the word *mujeriego* is also sometimes used.

nada/nadita. Nothing.

niña. Young girl; the word is also used as a term of respect for a woman but is less formal than doña or señora.

novio/a. Boyfriend/girlfriend; fiancé/fiancée.

oreja. Ear; colloquially, it refers to a spy.

partera. Midwife.

petate. Sleeping mat made of straw or reeds.

platiada. Small silver-colored fish.

quesadilla. Cornmeal cake made with cheese.

radista. Radio operator.

rebelde. Rebel.

remesa. Remittance.

rico. Rich person.

sí. Yes.

sombrero. Brimmed hat.

tamal(es). Cornmeal filled with chicken or meat. The entire mixture is wrapped in a banana leaf and parboiled.

usted. The formal form of "you."

Vaya pues. Go on, then; used colloquially to mean "All right, then" or "So be it."

verdad. Truth, true.

vos. A familiar form of "you."

NOTES

Introduction

1. To ensure our subjects' anonymity, we have changed all their names as well as the name of their community. All other data and descriptions are, to the best of our knowledge, accurate.

2. Michael Gorkin, Marta Pineda, and Gloria Leal, *From Grandmother to Granddaughter: Salvadoran Women's Stories* (Berkeley: University of California Press, 2000).

3. For a detailed and rich historical discussion of Salvadoran history prior to the 1970s, Alastair White's volume *El Salvador* (London: Ernest Benn Limited, 1973) is an excellent source; and for a more recent account, see Christopher M. White, *The History of El Salvador*, Greenwood Histories of the Modern World (2009). For an interesting discussion of the psychological as well as the economic causes of the civil war from the campesinos' point of view, see Elizabeth Jean Wood, *Insurgent Collective Action and Civil War in El Salvador* (Cambridge: Cambridge University Press, 2003), which is both informative and compelling. In addition, some of the more gruesome abuses of power on the part of the government's forces are detailed in Leigh Binford's *The El Mozote Massacre: Anthropology and Human Rights* (Tucson: University of Arizona Press, 1996). And a well-researched, though in my opinion a somewhat overstated, view of postwar disenchantment in El Salvador can be found in Ellen Moodie, *El Salvador in the Aftermath of Peace: Crime, Uncertainty and the Transition to Democracy* (Philadelphia: University of Pennsylvania Press, 2010).

4. Five politico-military organizations joined forces in 1980 to form the FMLN (Frente Farabundo Martí para la Liberación Nacional). See the chronology for more information.

5. Between 1980 and 1992 the United States provided $4.2 billion in military and economic aid to El Salvador, thus making it the third largest recipient—after Israel and Egypt—of bilateral aid during that time period (U.S. Embassy in San Salvador).

6. As part of the peace accords signed on January 16, 1992, some 134,000 manzanas (1 manzana equals 1.7 acres) were redistributed to approximately 35,000 landless

and land-poor families, the vast majority of whom were combatants on both sides during the war (Ministerio de Agricultura y Ganadería, Tercer Censo agropecuario del Programa de Transferencia de Tierras, San Salvador, 1997).

7. It is estimated that in 2008 Salvadorans living abroad sent $3.79 billion annually in remittances to individuals residing in El Salvador; this figure equals approximately 18 percent of the country's GDP (report from "Business News Americas," http://www.bnamericas.com/news/banking).

8. See, for example, James Clifford and George E. Marcus, *Writing Culture: The Poetics and Politics of Ethnography* (Berkeley: University of California Press, 1986).

9. John G. Neihardt, *Black Elk Speaks: Being the Life Story of a Holy Man of the Oglala Sioux* (Lincoln: University of Nebraska Press, 1971); Studs Terkel, *Working: People Talk about What They Do All Day and How They Feel about What They Do* (New York: Random House, 1974).

10. Kevin Dwyer, *Moroccan Dialogues: Anthropology in Question* (Baltimore: Johns Hopkins University Press, 1982); Fatima Mernissi, *Doing Daily Battle: Interviews with Moroccan Women* (New Brunswick, N.J.: Rutgers University Press, 1989).

Chapter 3. Luis: The War Years

1. The ciudadela is the area where formerly the main housing of the land-owners was located and that subsequently became the site of the community's school and health clinic.

Chapter 4. Jorge: Julia's Father

1. The word *mojado* literally means "wet" and is employed by Salvadorans in referring to illegal emigrants from El Salvador to the United States. It does not, however, imply a pejorative connotation, as does the English term "wetback."

2. El Orden was a paramilitary group organized and financed by the government.

Chapter 10. Francisco: The Oldest Son

1. Areneros are supporters of the rightist political party ARENA.

Epilogue

1. Currently, the literacy rate for females between the ages of fifteen and twenty-four is approximately 83 percent; and of those receiving post-secondary school education, women outnumber men (UNESCO, World Development Indicators Database, 2008).

2. For example, between 1992 and 2007 the percentage of households in El Salvador that have electricity increased from 70 percent to 90 percent; refrigerators, from 32 percent to 52 percent; televisions, from 60 percent to 80 percent; and concrete walls, from 52 percent to 70 percent (Dirección de Estadísticas y Censos, *Censo de población y viviendas de 1992 y 2007*, San Salvador).

3. Comunidad Guazapa, like many rural communities, has benefited from assistance that has come not only from local and national governments but also from local, national, and international NGOs. The reader will note that the Lutheran Church, IMU, and some volunteers from Spain were crucial in providing funds and services right from the inception of Comunidad Guazapa and without which the community would not have been able to function. And still today, NGOs enable the community to operate its health clinic and to better equip its school and provide scholarships for students to attend university.

4. It is estimated that between 800,000 and 2.68 million Salvadorans currently live outside the country, the majority of whom are in the United States (Katherine Andrede-Eekhoff, "Migration and Development in El Salvador: Ideals versus Reality," *Migration Immigration Source*, 2006, http://www.migrationinformation.org). The actual figure, unknowable due to the number of undocumented immigrants in the United States, is probably closer to the higher figure indicated here.

5. The upper 20 percent of the country's population receive 56.5 percent of the country's annual income, while the bottom 20 percent receive 3.4 percent (UNESCO, World Development Indicators Database, 2000).

6. Personal communication from Dr. Mauricio Gaborit, director of the Psychology Department at Universidad Centroamericana, San Salvador.

7. Having read the narratives of Luis and others in this volume, the reader will note that, despite the crime and corruption that persists in El Salvador and that has disenchanted many Salvadorans (see Moodie, *El Salvador in the Aftermath of Peace*), there are also those campesinos who do feel that their lives and those of their children have improved substantially as a result of the war. I do not believe that Luis and his family are atypical but rather that they represent a sizeable number of formerly impoverished families who today, despite the persistent and horrendous happenings, are far from disenchanted but instead hopeful and even optimistic.

8. Having worked as a psychologist in several countries that have recently experienced wars (Israel, Palestine, Vietnam, and El Salvador), I have observed that the second generation usually avoids and even resents their parents' reminders of their personal war experiences. Some children do not want to hear the often repeated recollections of those hardships, which—from the children's perspectives—carry within them the psychological baggage of the parents' suffering. Some children, often unconsciously, feel guilt when their parents reproach them for not realizing how fortunate they are compared to their parents. As a result, the two generations often sense an unspoken, or barely spoken, degree of separation and even alienation with regard to the war, which has thrown its shadow over all their lives.

9. Luisa Passerini, *Fascism in Popular Memory: The Cultural Experience of the Turin Working Class* (Cambridge: Cambridge University Press, 1987); Alessandro Portelli, *The Death of Luigi Trastulli and Other Stories: Form and Meaning in Oral History* (Albany: State University of New York Press, 1991).

10. The concept of the "Rashomon effect" received its name from Japanese filmmaker Akira Kurosawa's film *Rashomon*, in which four observers of a crime give four different descriptions of the event. As employed in the literature on oral history, it thus refers to the influence of subjectivity on the perception and recollection of the same event by different observers and/or participants.

11. For an excellent discussion of this problem, see Francis Good, "Voice, Ear and Text," in *The Oral History Reader*, ed. Robert Perks and Alistair Thomson, 2nd ed. (New York: Routledge, 2006), 362–73.

12. Nahuat is a language of some of the indigenous population of Mexico and Central America, and while few of these indigenous people remain in El Salvador and speak Nahuat, many of their words have entered into the Salvadoran lexicon, particularly the everyday speech of many campesinos.

13. Daphne Patai, "U.S. Academics and Third World Women: Is Ethical Research Possible?," in *Women's Words: The Feminist Practice of Oral History*, ed. Sherna Berger Gluck and Daphne Patai (New York: Routledge, 1991), 137–53.

ABOUT THE AUTHORS

Michael Gorkin, PhD, is a psychologist and was twice a Fulbright scholar in El Salvador. He is the author of *Days of Honey, Days of Onion: The Story of a Palestinian Family in Israel* and *Three Mothers, Three Daughters: Palestinian Women's Stories*.

Marta Pineda is a Salvadoran-trained psychologist and co-author (with Michael Gorkin) of *From Grandmother to Granddaughter: Salvadoran Women's Stories*. She and Michael Gorkin are married, and they live in Florida.